Looking at Contemporary Dance

a guide for the internet age

Looking at Contemporary Dance

a guide for the internet age

Marc Raymond Strauss

with

Myron Howard Nadel

A Dance Horizons Book
Princeton Book Company, Publishers

copyright © 2012 by Marc Raymond Strauss

Cover photograph of Streb / The Company in *Gauntlet*. Photograph by Tom Caravaglia. Used by permission.

Text design and composition by Mulberry Tree Press

Cover design by Elizabeth Helmetsie

Princeton Book Company, Publishers
614 Route 130
Hightstown, NJ 08520
www.dancehorizons.com

ISBN: 978-0-87127-354-3

Publisher's Cataloging-In-Publication Data

Strauss, Marc.
  Looking at contemporary dance : a guide for the internet age / Marc Raymond Strauss with Myron Howard Nadel.

    p. ; cm.

  "A Dance Horizons book."
  Includes bibliographical references and index.
  ISBN: 978-0-87127-354-3

  1. Modern dance—History. 2. Dancers—Biography. 3. Modern dance—Video catalogs.
I. Nadel, Myron Howard. II. Title.

GV1619 .S77 2012
792.8/09

To Marc's beloved wife and fellow artist, Sarah A. Riley,

and the increasingly global Internet community.

Contents

Acknowledgements

The authors wish to thank all the heralded and unheralded dancers, choreographers, and artists throughout the world—we were able to highlight just a few in this book—who were and remain wholly committed to their art form in ways that keep rippling through our hearts, minds, and bodies.

Note

This book's decade-by-decade approach to the 20th and 21st centuries (starting after the entire 19th century) was chosen because birth dates and the founding dates of companies can immediately help pinpoint the beginnings of a person, organization, or event for the reader and serve as an overarching structure.

We consider the persons living within a particular decade to be generational cohorts, subject to shared influences whether artistic, political, social, or technological. It is these relationships that make history meaningful, and bring the past into present life.

Introduction

This is not a book! (Apologies to René Magritte)[1] Rather, think of it more like a gateway, a portal, a resource linking you to videos on Internet web sites that help you quickly jump around to all sorts of places and times. Don't read it straight through (unless you must)! Rather, have it near your iPad, iPhone or computer that is set on YouTube (www.youtube.com), flip to any page by chance, and type in the "search" address. Then... follow the images and ideas wherever they take you.

In addition to its reader-friendly text, there are over 220 search addresses sprinkled throughout this resource (most of them on the ubiquitous, above-mentioned YouTube) and more than 110 choreographers, companies, institutions and dancers discussed within these pages throughout the last 200 years and across the planet. Welcome to the 21st century!

The resource that you hold in your hands is about contemporary dance. How, then, might we define that word "contemporary" within the broader dance world context, and its predecessor, "modern" dance? Are they simply what the dictionary and thesaurus claim: new, fresh, up-to-the-minute, *avant garde*, cutting edge, novel, current, the latest, and state-of-the-art? Perhaps the phrases are tied irrevocably to the words embedded in the book title and content of *The Modern Dance* (1933), by *New York Times* dance critic John Martin (1893–1985) concerning the first-generation "moderns." Martin accurately noted at the time that from "this desire to externalize personal, authentic experience, it is evident that the scheme of modern dancing is all in the direction of individualism and away from standardization" (p. 299). Ironically, the individualism of that era required such intense focus *over time* that many of the choreographers Martin critiqued in the 1930s eventually became their own standard bearers for the postmoderns to rebel against. (Ironically, Martha Graham preferred the term "contemporary" over "modern.")

Perhaps, by the very definition of the terms, "modern" and "contemporary" are supposed to keep transforming themselves, continually evolving as we move further and further into the 21st century through endless experimentations, rejections and groundbreakings. Three examples:

- In Holland, Jiří Kylián (b. 1947) and the Nederlands Dans Theater (f. 1959) helped popularize the contemporary ballet world with his ultra-modern neoclassicism—watch, for example, a three-minute excerpt set to Part I of Steve Reich's (b. 1936) famous 1971 tune "Drumming," from Kylián's 1989 *tour de force* "Falling Angels," at www.youtube.com, search "Jiří Kylián's Falling Angels";

- In Japan, a post-postmodern "dance" by the Kyoto-based performance art-installation-multimedia group Dumb Type (f. 1984) embodies some of today's consumer society apocalyptic sensory assaults in the dance world—watch a 3-minute excerpt of their provocative 2007 piece "True," at www.youtube.com, search "Dumb Type True";

- From England, an underwater, prop-studded, polyrhythmic performance by the found-object percussion-movement ensemble Stomp (f. 1991) continues to fascinate and push the boundaries of "dance" performance—see Chapter 7, "Waterphonics," on their 1997 DVD *Stomp Out Loud* (www.hbo.com).

Today's dance world is more inclusive than ever, and often incorporates ballet, jazz, tap, hip hop, vernacular, a slew of ethnic/world dance influences, athleticism, multimedia works, and any number of other un-nameable "styles."

Thanks to the World Wide Web with YouTube and other avenues of visual and aural support, viewers can experience samples of professional dance from around the world at the press of a few keys. Although snippets of whole dances posted on the Internet are like seeing little blocks of a large painting or hearing a few musical phrases of a great symphony, they are a great choice for quickly sampling dance and seeing what is out there. And it's free.

This *Guide for the Internet Age* provides you with a loose yet logical chronological survey of contemporary dance. It is interspersed with references to Internet sources to satisfy readers who may not have access to live performances of the world's major dance centers. So rather than illustrating the book with photographs—Google, YouTube, Vimeo, and similar sites have become our illustrators!

Within each chapter there are historically important cross-references and, with subsequent chapters, reappearances of earlier details along with new events, new relationships, and new information. It is important to remember that choreographers and their company members, as well as other artists, especially in the 20th and 21st centuries, were and are well aware of the work of others (and with greater rapidity than ever before due to the Internet). This means that the people and companies discussed herein did not work in total isolation and that their creations were seen and analyzed by others who lived during their time, too. In short, influences can take the form of unconscious or conscious imitations, rejections (concerted efforts to make dances unlike others), or a building upon other successes from the same or past generations.

So: while the reader is provided a generally linear chronological organization to follow throughout the book, there are some liberties taken at times to help the narrative flow better by linking up like-minded or more closely affiliated figures (or companies).

For example, in Chapter 1, François Delsarte, Émile Jaques-Dalcroze, and Rudolf Laban, born in 1811, 1865, and 1879 respectively, are introduced as a trio of major influences on many subsequent modern dance pioneers; and they are discussed in that order. In the same chapter, Americans Ruth St. Denis and Ted Shawn were born in 1877 and 1891 respectively but, even though Russian-born Michel Fokine came into the world between their birth years, in 1880, St. Denis and Shawn are discussed back-to-back because their stories are so closely woven together. The book picks up with Fokine again after Shawn, and the reader should with relative ease recall the arc of Diaghilev's Ballets Russes from just a few sections earlier.

Again, while the authors believe a clear historical chronology to be most helpful in organizing the stories discussed in this book, individuals born within the strict order of marching time may very well be drawn to neighbors somewhat further afield in time or place.

Some of the truly knowledgeable dance critic/historian/archivists are quoted liberally in this book because they have been writing (and continue to write) the equivalent of a diary of their day's dance. Critics from major newspapers around the globe see more contemporary (current) dance works and companies in a month than many of us see in an entire decade—not only in their home cities, but also through travel to major dance centers and festivals that lie outside of their home region. In addition to the hundreds of Internet "search" addresses, the reader is invited to seek out those critics represented in this book and so many others who study the dance world with an intelligent, and so often incisive love.

Today's instantly accessible realm of dance is more worldwide and inclusive than ever before. It embodies diverse ideas, subject matter, choreographers, dancers, designers, movements, forms and styles, and movement techniques from right now—all the way back to 16th century Europe and even earlier. The categories that we are used to—"ballet," "modern dance," "contemporary dance," "folk," "ethnic," "experimental," "Broadway," "ballroom," and "tap"— can still be applied at times, but it is often fruitless to categorize our contemporary era because of the extraordinarily eclectic dance performance menu placed before us. In fact, believing you have found the perfect category name will, when scrutinized, become exasperating! Some have called our contemporary dance era "fusion"—which it is too, certainly—but "fusion" is itself a bewildering label unless you are familiar with all of the actual but elusive parts that are being fused.

So: when something is called "contemporary" when it was new at the time of its creation, how long does it remain contemporary?

Many still call the Diaghilev era, 1909 to 1929, the beginning of modern ballet—a valid contemporary phrase for its time. One could also say that "contemporary" dance means that which is or has been created recently. We could call it "experimental," but some "experiments" may actually be old hat if you do not know about the other hats. We could call it "avant-garde" if it is cutting or leading edge, but we would have to have a good idea of what combination of elements is considered "leading."

Choreographers, dancers, and designers of today are trying to make significant experiences for themselves first; then, for you, too. Ultimately, public concerts are about how you, the audience, enjoy those precious moments of kinetic and aural images that flow from the dancers outward. The authors hope that you find your way to more closely experience the evanescent instant of the dance for, with every new creation, the dance is wholly contemporary at that moment.

—Marc Raymond Strauss (with Myron Howard Nadel)
May 2012

Note

1   When asked about his 1928 oil painting of a pipe called *Ceci n'est pas une pipe* ("This is not a pipe" or "The Treachery of Images"), René Magritte (1898–1967) answered, "Just try to fill it with tobacco." The Belgian surrealist's obvious but forest-for-the-trees point was that any painting of an object is not the object itself but merely a representation of one. The applicable inference: when filled with hundreds of non-literary, cinematic references of dance, a book about dance may be so much more than just a book about dance.

Chapter One

Moving into the 20th Century: 1811–1900

François Delsarte, Émile Jaques-Dalcroze, Rudolf Laban, Loïe Fuller, Serge Diaghilev, Isadora Duncan, Ruth St. Denis and Ted Shawn, Michel Fokine, Mary Wigman, Vaslav Nijinsky, Asadata Dafora, Michio Ito, Hanya Holm, Martha Graham and Louis Horst, Doris Humphrey, Léonide Massine

As with folk dances and religious miracles, the inspirational origins of contemporary choreography cannot be easily identified. Still, while adding in the occasional sparkling idea or innovation, humanity has always built upon that which came before. For much 20th century modern dance, its theoretical substructures emanated from the teachings of 19th century European cognitive and movement theorists such as François Delsarte, Émile Jaques-Dalcroze, and Rudolf Laban.

François Delsarte

François Delsarte (November 11, 1811, Solesmes, France–July 20, 1871, Paris) was a music teacher and movement analyst who delved into the meaning of gesture. He may be considered a pioneer movement analyst who believed that the physical, emotional, and spiritual planes of the body coexist in time, co-penetrate space, and cooperate in motion. His concerns for concepts of tension-relaxation, form, force, design, and concentric (toward center) and eccentric (from center) movements provided a unique and still serviceable focus for creating and studying movement outside of the ballet vocabulary. Ted Shawn and other early modern dancers came to embrace these tenets.

Delsarte's ideas combining the physical and metaphysical worlds were also an inspiration to women, who felt that his holistic approach was the key to gracefulness and the finest forms of expression for the newly liberated female. During the early part of the 20th century, women were freeing themselves from binding corsets, their primary allegiance to motherhood, limited numbers of available careers, poor pay, and a ubiquitous sense of disenfranchisement. Delsarte and dance exhilaratingly offered the promise of a break, theoretical and then literal, from the Victorian handicaps of being a woman. These ideas manifested in part via women's clubs that featured dance tableaux, healthful dance exercises, and even a form of pseudo-Oriental dance called "Nautsch." In addition, although Ted Shawn was an ardent supporter of Delsartian ideas, his all-male dance company from 1933 to 1940 helped counteract America's perception that modern dance was only for women.

Émile Jaques-Dalcroze

Called "Eurhythmics," the work of Swiss composer, musician, and music educator Émile Jaques-Dalcroze (July 6, 1865, Vienna, Austria–July 1, 1950, Geneva, Switzerland) was a system of physical movements designed for the development of a synthesis of musical and rhythmic logic for musicians. Dalcroze teaching academies thrive all over the world to this day, such as the original Jaques-Dalcroze Institute, founded in 1915 in Geneva (http://www.dalcroze.ch/), and the Dalcroze Society of America (http://www.dalcrozeusa.org/).

The system was also found to have great application for training dancers and choreographers to form deeply felt relationships among the eye, ear, memory, and one's kinesthetic awareness. Dalcroze's philosophy was especially influential on Ruth St. Denis (1879–1968), who explored music visualization wherein melodic lines, harmonies, and forms of a piece of music were visually translated into corresponding dance movements. British ballet pioneer Marie Rambert (1888–1982) studied with Dalcroze and used his methods to come to the musical aid of Vaslav Nijinsky (1889–1950) as he puzzled over the irregular rhythms of Igor Stravinsky's *Rite of Spring* (1913; discussed in Chapter 3) while attempting the choreography of that work. "Through such pupils of Jaques-Dalcroze as Marie Rambert, Hanya Holm, and the mime Étienne Decroux, Eurythmics has also affected contemporary ballet and the dance of the theatre."[1]

The choreographic potential inherent in the great musical forms influenced the entire generation of American modern dancers after Isadora Duncan, St. Denis, and Shawn. Doris Humphrey and Martha Graham in particular were often able to use their intimate understanding of and training with music as inspiration for their quite sophisticated choreographic work. Dalcroze's influence was also felt through the application of his tenets in the modern ballets of the Russians Michel Fokine (1880–1942) and Nijinsky. "Symphonic" ballets (to stand-alone symphonic music) were one part of the legacy of 20ᵗʰ century Russian choreographers such as Léonide Massine

(1895–1979), Fyodor Lopukhov (1886–1973), and, later, George Balanchine (1904–1983). Complex and precise kinetic-rhythmic-musical correlations are frequent performance expectations to this day, and remain prudent choreographic devices for many dance compositions.

Rudolf Laban

Rudolf Laban (December 15, 1879, Bratislava, Austria-Hungary–July 1, 1958, Surrey, England) was a dancer-theoretician inspired in part by Delsarte's attempts to codify expressive gesture. His special genius lay in the conceptual analysis of movement in space and time with their characteristic energies. He first analyzed movement according to the speed, direction, and level of the body, and its parts within an imaginary twenty-sided combination sphere-cube called an "icosahedron." His scientific approach provided a clear language for movement in space[2] that gave the work of modern dancers, especially the Germans Mary Wigman and Kurt Jooss, an analytical basis from which to acquire greater sensitivity towards motion in relation to that surrounding space. These conceptual foundations still form an integral part of the characteristics of much modern dance (www.youtube.com, search "Rudolf Laban").

Several organizations carry on Laban's vision today. They include, in London, his own Laban Guild for Movement and Dance (f. 1946, http://www.labanguild.org.uk/) and, in New York City, two organizations: the Laban/Bartenieff Institute of Movement Studies (f. 1978, http://www.limsonline.org/) and the Dance Notation Bureau (f. 1940, http://dancenotation.org/), the latter of which archives on paper, via Labanotation, hundreds of dances available throughout the world (Trinity Laban Conservatoire of Music and Dance; http://www.trinitylaban.ac.uk/).

A naturalized German, Laban was initially cooperative with the pre-World War II socialist German government. However, his choreography for the 1936 Olympics opening ceremony was censored by Nazi authorities and he subsequently left Germany for England before the war. Laban's legacy is now attached to the United Kingdom.

Loïe Fuller

Loïe Fuller (January 15, 1862, Hinsdale, Illinois–January 1, 1928, Paris) was primarily an actress and singer who had studied a bit of ballet, and then began to perform solo movement pieces in the voluminous skirts she had worn in plays. Skirt dancing among women entertainers of the era was a popular pastime, but Fuller made its use an even hotter item in the performing world. When already a professional, she received a large piece of lovely cloth as a gift from a friend, and devised a theatrical movement piece that came to be known as *The Serpentine Dance* (1891). Add the developing art of stage lighting at the end of the 19th century to Fuller's skirt dances, place her on a glass plate lighted from below, and the scene was set for experiments based on the movement of body, fabric, shape, color, and light — without allegiance to the emotional motivation that was to influence many modern dancers to come in the 20th century. An 1896 49-second silent film excerpt of *The Serpentine Dance*, hand-painted frame-by-frame in color, is most likely of Fuller herself, and can be viewed at www.youtube.com, search "Serpentine Dance Loïe Fuller."

Serge Diaghilev

Serge Diaghilev (March 31, 1872 Novgorod, Russia–August 19, 1929, Venice) was never a dancer or a choreographer, but remains arguably one of the greatest impresarios the world has ever known in the visual and performing arts. Few people in the entertainment and arts fields—except, perhaps, Florenz Ziegfeld (1867–1932) in the United States, with his Ziegfeld Follies—were able to bring so many artists together for such single-minded purposes.

Diaghilev holds an essential place in the history and development of modern ballet, especially through his company, *Les Ballets Russes*, which began in 1909 and died with him twenty years later.[3] Among the extraordinary variety of artists, musicians, designers, dancers and choreographers that spent some time with him include many living in Europe during the early part of the 20th century: Henri Matisse, Pablo Picasso, Marc Chagall, Nicholas Roerich, Léon Bakst, Georges Braque, Maurice Utrillo, Maurice Ravel, Claude Debussy, Igor Stravinsky, Erik Satie, Anna Pavlova, Tamara Karsavina, Adolph Bolm, Anton Dolin, and five of the world's greatest choreographers: Michel Fokine (discussed below), Vaslav Nijinsky (discussed below and with *The Rite of Spring* in Chapter 3), Bronislava Nijinska, Léonide Massine (discussed below) and George Balanchine (discussed in Chapter 2). In fact, the list seems literally endless. The company

> was regarded as one of the most inspired and experimental troupes in the world. Its success was primarily due to Diaghilev's genius for spotting new talent and setting up collaborations between artists. He believed that ballet should be a complete theatrical art and that music, design, and choreography should equally break new ground. His ballets reflected, and were sometimes even catalysts for, new artistic trends.[4]

Dances created by the five choreographers mentioned above remain to this day—in memory, revival, and reconstruction—perfect examples of the move from a more purely classical ballet, as epitomized by Marius Petipa (1818–1910) and others in the 19ᵗʰ and early 20ᵗʰ centuries, to a radical reappraisal of what ballet—actually all dance—could do (www.youtube.com, search "Serge Diaghilev-A Portrait").

But first…Isadora beat them to it with her own style.

Isadora Duncan

Isadora Duncan (Angela Isadora Duncan; May 26, 1877 San Francisco–September 14, 1927, Nice, France), the most famous revolutionary outside of the male-dominated world of ballet, and those who followed in her footsteps, valued expression more than technique and form (which were valued by the pure romanticist or classicist in music and art). (www.youtube.com, search "Glimpses of Isadora Duncan"). Ironically, Duncan's was a classic art to the degree that she was inspired by forms of antiquity (primarily ancient Greece) and that she danced to musical masters like classical German composer Ludwig van Beethoven (1770–1827) and the romanticists, Polish-French Frédéric Chopin (1810–1869) and Austrian Franz Schubert (1797–1828). Duncan also insisted that her art was fundamentally American and influenced by nature, which led her to rediscover the glory of natural movements, made all the more expressive when untainted by balletic vocabulary and danced in bare feet and a tunic.

She performed in relatively unadorned dance recitals set in salons or humble theaters, accompanied only by a pianist playing, for example, Chopin's *Revolutionary Étude.* The very essence of the music provided Duncan with her sense of strength and flow. The recital form was both chic and avant-garde. Salons, mostly hosted and populated by the women intelligentsia, had a history dating all the way back to the French courts of the famous Louis XIII (1601–1643) and Louis XIV (1638–1715), so introducing novel ideas such as Isadora's was actually in keeping with the salon tradition. The 21ˢᵗ century still hails Duncan's groundbreaking work through literally dozens of companies across the world—France, Germany, Japan, Russia, and the United States—recreating works or honoring the artist with their own choreography "in the style of." Lori Belilove and The Isadora Duncan Dance Company (www.isadoraduncan.org) and the Isadora Duncan International Institute (www.isadoraduncan.net) are just two companies still dedicated to that dance visionary.

Ruth St. Denis and Ted Shawn

Modern forerunner Ruth St. Denis (Ruth Dennis; January 20, 1877 Newark, New Jersey–July 21, 1968, Los Angeles, California) promoted her art within established commercial theatrical (and cinematic) contexts in the early 20th century, such as plays, vaudeville, and revues. But in these venues, the search for new dance foundations depended ultimately on their audience appeal as seen by their employers. Producers in the world of commercial theater understood little of the spiritual fervor of dance's revolutionary energy, but both producers and audiences enjoyed new subjects, new movement arrangements, new personalities, and almost anything with exotic and especially pseudo-erotic, appeal [www.youtube.com, search "Ruth St Denis in the 'East Indian Nautch Dance' (1932)" and www.youtube.com, search "inciense Ruth St. Denis.wmv"].

Dancers, such as St. Denis, wary that their artistic attempts needed to satisfy large audiences, increased their need to self-produce concerts where their freedom to experiment could remain a primary concern. In addition, the freedom for women to express their own lives in artistic ways and then promote these expressions as salon or theatrical ventures—or even as a means for educational systems to nurture individuality, free of rote learning—derived power from the progeny of the transcendentalists, suffragettes such as Julia Ward Howe (1819–1910) and educator-thinkers such as Louisa May Alcott (1832–1888), Elizabeth Palmer Peabody (1804–1894), and John Dewey (1859–1952).

Excerpts from the long-standing repertoire of European ballet companies also fit well within the vaudeville milieu of family audiences, while shorter early works, such as St. Denis' *Radha* (1906; www.youtube.com, search "RSD Project Pt. 1 of 5") were often enjoyed in their entirety. Vaudeville performance meant being one of seven or more independent touring acts such as a dog and acrobatic number, tap dancer, singer, comedian, ventriloquist, contortionist and even opera and ballet performers, all on the same program. While many choreographers wanted to disregard the entertainment value of the dance, many of the pioneers of modern dance, such as Martha Graham, Doris Humphrey, and Charles Weidman, learned valuable lessons about salesmanship and the rules of commercial theater from St. Denis's company, called Denishawn (see below), and performed at times on these same vaudeville circuits.

Of course, audience appeal was a primary consideration for producers long before the early 20th century. The commercial theaters that sprang up in late 18th-century Paris and the music halls of 19th century England were under the same pressure to sell tickets, if not even earlier in the time of Shakespeare (1564–1616) or Molière (1622–1673).

Being a commercial draw was also a matter of survival, but the diverse personalities of modern dance cared more about expression, honesty, and creativity, as well as societal and even political issues. Its leaders wanted to be artists for a people's art—at times, even a socialist one (see New Dance Group, Chapter 5)—and express some very personal and valuable insights about themselves and the world through their work. To this day, and continuing into the future, similar thematic subjects remain integral driving forces for contemporary dancer and choreographer sensibilities. When Ted Shawn (Edwin Myers Shawn; October 21, 1891 Kansas City, Missouri–January 9, 1972, Orlando, Florida) joined the company of Ruth St. Denis and married her in 1914, he helped create dances within the given confines of commercial theater. Together, they also developed the school and independent company Denishawn (1915–1931), a confluence of their last names. Their concert tours gave them more leeway for artistic experimentation than works created solely for the vaudeville circuit [www.youtube.com, search "Ted Shawn Choer Dance (1926).m4v"].

Ted Shawn began studying dance as a young man to compensate for ill health. His father was a Methodist minister who was influenced by some of the same spiritual movements of the 19ᵗʰ century mentioned above, and he encouraged his son's combined interests in spirituality and physical movement. Miss Ruth tended to be more a seeker of spiritual truth. Her quest began well before the partnership, leading her into the field of ethnic dance, where she composed pieces of dual Oriental and spiritual origin. (The politically debatable term "Oriental," often associated with Western imperialism, was the conventional word for "Asian" at that time.)

St. Denis attempted to emulate the spiritual impetus and movements of East Indian dance through a sort of self-withdrawn trance state, assuming a committed (if imitative) "Oriental authenticity." Although Miss Ruth had an artist's mind, commercial audiences were not always capable of seeing and appreciating the artistic value embedded in her famous dances, such as the Hindu-inflected *Radha*, mentioned above, the Japanese-inspired *O-Mika* (1913), or the Babylonian ensemble choreography in American director D. W. Griffith's (1875–1948) epic silent film, "Intolerance" (1916; www.youtube.com, search "BOISTER: Music for Erotic Dance by Ruth St. Denis, D.W. Griffith's Intolerance"). Family audiences came to vaudeville to be entertained, and if images of "the Orient" worked, then that could help pay the bills for the producers and the salaries of the performers.

Shawn added opportunities for even greater commercial success by bringing more theatricalized versions of Oriental, Spanish, Aztec, American Indian, ballroom, and other dance forms to the Denishawn repertoire. He understood and followed a spiritual view of dance while adapting their works to more pragmatic theatrical needs. Dances choreographed by the prolific Shawn, who created nearly 200 pieces for Denishawn and his own company Ted Shawn and his Male Dancers (1933–1940), include the popular *Prometheus Bound* (1929) and the machismo *Kinetic Molpai* (1935). View a five-minute 2007 excerpt by composer David Borden (b. 1938) and his ensemble, Mother Mallard's Portable Masterpiece Company (f. 1969), with Shawn's Male Dancers showcased at www.youtube.com, search "David Borden Tribute to Ruth St. Denis & Ted Shawn.01."

Shawn's ideas may be the better guide to the realities of a dance art on commercial stages; St. Denis's were more the dreamer's art. His focused, hard-driving ebullience gave him the psychic ammunition to pioneer in a male art form that struggled against the grain of an audience used to liberated and graceful female art dancers in the homegrown ballet of the time.

Behind the scenes, the marriage between the younger Shawn and the more mature St. Denis may have been built more on respect, friendship, and convenience, especially after Shawn discovered his particular sexual proclivities. But there is no doubt that Shawn, who created the first and most unique group of male dancers—representing the strength, commitment, and artistry of the hard-working American dancing male—almost single-handedly paved the road that thousands of American male dancers have traveled in ballet, modern dance, and Broadway [www.youtube.com, search "Kinetic Molpai (1935) by Ted Shawn.mkv"].

Hundreds of dancers studied at the Denishawn schools, first in California and then in New York, where an inspired curriculum developed by Shawn included classes in Delsarte, Dalcroze Eurythmics, ballet, ballroom, and a variety of ethnic forms. This broad training formed the basis for much of the serious theatrical dance education study that was to come in America.

Michel Fokine

Seeing himself "as a reformer rather than a radical revolutionary à la Isadora Duncan,"[5] Michel Fokine (May 5, 1880 St. Petersburg–August 22, 1942, New

York) created some of the most innovative and—yes, radical—dance reforms the classical ballet ever saw.

> From the outset, Fokine sought to introduce fresh ideas into what he (and many young Russians) viewed as the stale, outmoded formulas left over from the lengthy regime of Marius Petipa. Fokine believed that dance had lost its soul by sacrificing veracity for virtuosity. He wanted each of his ballets to mirror its chosen subject as closely as possible, with both movement and design as authentic reflections of the chosen time and place.[6]

After leaving the Maryinsky Theatre (f. 1860, www.mariinsky.ru/en) to join Diaghilev's *Ballets Russes* in 1909, exotic fairy tales such as *The Firebird* (1910; www.youtube.com, search "Stravinsky-The Firebird") and *Petrushka* (1911; www.youtube.com, search "Stravinsky-Petrushka") helped transform classical ballet into condensed and fully unified one-act productions (still the norm for much 21st century dance) full of the grand artworks of the composers, designers and dancers Diaghilev had at his disposal. It is no coincidence that Fokine's atmospheric *Les Sylphides* (1909; www.youtube.com, search "Mikhail Baryshnikov Marianna Tcherkassky Les Sylphides Waltz"), is a mood piece only about dancing that many think of as an impressionistic interpretation of a classical ballet. *Les Sylphides* recalls Isadora Duncan's expressive naturalism (Fokine saw Duncan dance in Russia during her 1904 tour) while foretelling Balanchine's plotless masterpieces later in the century in the United States. Fokine was Diaghilev's first great choreographer, Balanchine his last; both eventually moved to the United States to continue their art.

But around the same time as the Ballets Russes, in Germany another choreographer was developing her own innovations that helped move dance toward a more modern sensibility:

Mary Wigman

A colleague and student of Rudolf Laban's, Mary Wigman (Marie Wiegmann, November 13, 1886, Hanover, Germany–September 18, 1973, West Berlin, Germany) saw space as a force to contend with, not just a necessary environment filled with air. She moved with an awareness of the conceivable qualities that stage space could have as a partner in motion by cutting through, piercing, pressing, and being enveloped by it, as in her famous 1914 solo *Witch Dance* (excerpt at www.youtube.com, search "Mary Wigman"). Wigman's interest in space, and her knowledge of the German Bauhaus group (1919–1933) of experimental dancers and designers who explored stage space in relation to masked figures, props, body extensions, and furniture, inspired her to create dances that were primarily concerned with the visual impact of the dancers' shapes.

The reader should also take a close look at excerpts of the 1922 *Triadic Ballet* created by one of the Bauhaus representatives, the polymath painter-sculptor-designer-choreographer Oskar Schlemmer (1888–1943), to get a sense of the way in which that group integrated dance into all the arts by breaking with artificial boundaries (historical reconstruction; www.youtube.com, search "Ballet triadico 1970 Parte 1: amarilla.m4v"). The Bauhaus represents another important step forward in the creation of a modern, inclusive performance art.

Wigman's dances are often considered to be part of a lineage of dance Expressionism—sometimes referred to as *Ausdruckstanz* and credited to Laban—a genre of art that reached its peak in 1920s Germany, and which finds sources for expression deeply embedded in the human psyche, often in relation to social conditions. Its depictions of subjective reality were not far from the Expressionistic dances of Wigman and Harald Kreutzberg (1902–1962), the latter of whom studied with Laban and Wigman as well as trained in ballet. Likewise, the young Mexican-American modern dancer and choreographer José Limón (1908–1972, discussed in Chapter 2) saw Kreutzberg perform and was inspired by his approach to movement.

Ultimately, the sparks that ignited the flames that became modern dance in the transitional period during the ending decades of the 19th century and the early ones of the 20th century were lighted by female revolutionaries who created dance recitals outside the sphere of, and dissimilar to, the conventional ballet of the time. These were groundbreakers in an exciting new experiment; their works might just as easily be considered "postromantic" or "postclassical" as "modern."

Vaslav Nijinsky

First renowned as an almost supernatural and charismatic performer[7] (some accounts have him performing *entrechats dix*, ten beats of the legs while in the air!), Nijinsky (March 12, 1889 Kiev–April 8, 1950, London) was also an extraordinary and sadly short-lived choreographer of controversy and a wholly fresh vocabulary—all in just four dances.

> [E]ach of these works presented a new aesthetic. Radical and unortho-
> dox, they turned their backs on the classical heritage and have since

garnered the accolade of being ballet's first 'modern' choreography. Each in its own specific way was a shock. *Jeux* (1913; www.youtube.com, search "Jeux Partes 1-2-3") the simplest of his works, used everyday movement; this trio for Nijinsky and two women was set on a tennis court with the game mirroring an emotionally tangled eternal triangle...

The only one of Nijinsky's ballets to survive intact, *L'Après-midi d'un faune* (1912; www.youtube.com, search "Rudolph Nureyev–'L'apres-midi d'un faune") is an essay in stylized eroticism...The final thrust of [the faune's] hips into the silken scarf sent scandalized shock waves through the first-night audience...but its lasting significance arises from Nijinsky's idiosyncratic movement motifs. Culled from Greek friezes, the choreography breaks every rule of classical ballet training. The dancers, in sandals, move in two-dimensional planes back and forth across the stage, as though compressed between two plates of glass. Arms and feet kept parallel to the audience, their sharply angled poses are an attempt to reproduce the flatness of vase painting and wall carvings.[8]

But his most infamous work, 1913's *The Rite of Spring* (discussed in Chapter 3), is the stuff of myth. Schizophrenia cut his career short before the age of forty, but as a choreographer "he is now considered one of the key voices in 20th-century modernism,"[9] and study of his work in the context of the Ballets Russes is essential to understanding many of the origins and still potent influences of much contemporary dance today.

Asadata Dafora

Far south of the European continent and the radical modernity of the Ballets Russes, Asadata Dafora came into the world (Austin Dafora Horton; August 4, 1890 Freetown, Sierra Leone–March 4, 1965, Harlem, New York City). Dafora predated and strongly influenced more familiar early African-American modern dancers and choreographers like Pearl Primus, Katherine Dunham, and Donald McKayle. Moving from Africa to the United States in 1929, Dafora is generally acknowledged as the first to present authentic African-based dance on the concert stage (he was also an accomplished drummer, folk opera and concert singer, composer, and writer). Dedicated to exposing people to African culture, his company, Shogolo Oloba (f. early 1930s), "strove to portray African culture in a complex and sophisticated light, not just an exotic array of mysterious spectacles."[10]

Being black and a groundbreaker in terms of movements and subjects set off some deep-seated, perhaps unconscious nerve in predominately white dance concert audiences. Nevertheless, Dafora's famous opera *Kykunkor* (Witch Woman), from 1934, was favorably reviewed by John Martin in *The New York Times*. His 1932 solo warrior's dance, *Awassa Astrige* (Ostrich), was reconstructed and performed in 2007 by the Dayton Contemporary Dance Company (f. 1968), a company "rooted in the African American experience" and dedicated to "deliver contemporary dance of the highest quality to the broadest possible audience" (http://www.dcdc.org/about/history/). A version of this solo performed by Charles Moore (1928–1986) can be seen at www.youtube.com, search "Dance Black America: Ostrich."

Dafora showed that African-based movement was (and still is) often organic and involves coordinated parts of the torso, hips and arms in a complex, polyrhythmic manner. But as modern dance was still in its early years, Dafora's dances, even further removed from those that people were used to seeing on the concert stage, was not immediately accepted as art.

Michio Ito

Another choreographer (and performer, teacher and costume designer) with Diaspora in his life—he put thousands of miles and several continents on his passport, some not by choice (he was interred in a concentration camp during World War II and deported back to his homeland)—was the Japanese-born Michio Ito (April 13, 1892 Tokyo–November 6, 1961, Tokyo). Inspired by watching both Nijinsky and Duncan perform in Paris in 1911, he studied at the Dalcroze Institute in Germany and, later, opened his own studios in New York and Los Angeles, counting Pauline Koner, Lester Horton, and Ruth St. Denis among his students. Graham and Shawn were also influenced by Ito.

"Duncan had asserted that each individual had a unique way of moving [but] Ito even more radically asserted that his personal style was not necessarily limited by his cultural heritage."[11] In many ways, his dances were true forerunners, a full century early, to our global contemporary world—and he called his own highly musical, impressionistic works "dance poems." One can get a good sense of his mellifluous and unadorned, Duncan-like choreography at www.vimeo.com "Michio Ito—Repertory Dance Theatre," with excerpts from *Étude #9* (1928), *Ladybug* (1929), *Pizzicati Shadow Dance* (1916), *Blue Wave* (1923), and others.

Hanya Holm

Mary Wigman's student Hanya Holm (Johanna Eckert, March 3, 1893, Worms, Germany–November 3, 1992, New York, New York) was contracted by her teacher to come to the United States in 1932 and open a Wigman school in New York. As a teacher herself, Holm brought a package of expressionistic/ *Ausdruckstanz* dance, technique, improvisation, Labanotation, dance composition, awareness of the dimension of space, and design in space that influenced such choreographers who attended her classes as Alwin Nikolais, Murray Louis, and Glen Tetley (see Chapters 3 and 4). Due to anti-German sentiment at the time, her New York school was named the Hanya Holm, not Wigman, School.

Holm's choreography was full of social criticism and spatial design effects, especially as seen in her early group work. Besides exploring Wigman's interest in design, Holm tried to find a more emotional truth, particularly in her solo work. Holm scholars point to her architectural work performed by a large group of women, *Trend* (1937), as her greatest contribution as a transplanted American pioneer, although there are no films of that dance left behind. But she will most likely be remembered more for her successful contributions to the Broadway stage in Cole Porter's *Kiss Me, Kate* (1948) and Lerner and Lowe's *My Fair Lady* (1956), as well as her work in Hollywood on *The Vagabond King* (1956) (www.youtube.com, search "Hanya Holm: A Retrospective").

Martha Graham and Louis Horst

Martha Graham's (May 11, 1894 Allegheny, Pennsylvania–April 1, 1991, New York City) dramatic dances required the perspective of acting as promoted by Stanislavsky. Founding the Martha Graham School of Contemporary Dance in 1926, out of which developed the Martha Graham Dance Company (www.marthagraham.org)—the oldest contemporary dance company in America—Graham created emotionally charged choreographic dramas through the 1940s and 1950s that were based on characters and situations from Greek plays and the literary canon. Her genius lay in an ability to preternaturally abstract archetypal psychological perspectives about a central female character that she herself embodied onstage. Her choreography for the vengeful Medea in *Cave of the Heart* (1946, excerpt from a 2008 rehearsal at www.youtube.com, search "Cave of the Heart/Medea Solo"), as well as Oedipus's mother, Jocasta (*Night Journey,* 1947), and Saint Joan in *Seraphic Dialogue* (1955, excerpt at www.youtube.com, search "Seraphic Dialogue"), are evocative examples.

Stanislavsky's ideas developed in the 1930s and 1940s at New York's Group Theater and the Actors Studio (sometimes called the "method acting" studio), and laid the foundation for the development of many of Graham's roles. Graham created movements from the perspective of a central character who experienced elements of a personal tragedy, and then presented these physicalized struggles onstage, not necessarily in chronological order, but envisioned as the character's partly fragmented dream. Her dances were unlike the old-fashioned, straightforward plots of classical ballet. Graham's chorus dancers never punctuated, enhanced, or provided diversion from the central action; instead, they added to the total visual and visceral theater of a dream state. Graham tenaciously dug into the physical basis of drama and found movements that ultimately became the kinesthetic essence of each moment.

Her more lyrical period, beginning towards the end of her life with, perhaps, *Acts of Light* in 1981 [www.youtube.com, search "'Acts of Light' (1984)–with Introduction by Martha Graham"], and continuing with later works in her company, softened and made more musical her sharp and formal structures in ways that allow more accessibility than her often harsh, troubling, difficult themes.

Patricia Birch (b. circa 1934), a soloist for Graham for a time but best known as a choreographer of Broadway musicals (notably 1972's *Grease,* for which she won a Tony Award), noted: "Nobody knew how to cut a stage better than Martha—diagonal, straight across, front to back. Nobody made spacing count for emotional content better than Martha or was more theatrical than Martha. No one lit a stage better or understood set design better. One of the most important lessons I learned from her is that the stage is a sacred place."[12]

Graham literally treated dance as her religion, and Birch's comment about the stage being a sacred place to Graham is wholly accurate. She found it difficult to retire because of that reason, performing into her seventies before arthritis forced her to only choreograph, which she did until her death at 96.

In 2010, 19 years after she died, her company revisited the world of Stanislavsky by collaborating with theater director Anne Bogart and the SITI Company (f. 1992; www.siti.org) with an intriguing integration of actors and dancers. The piece recapitulates parts of Graham's 1938 *American Document* with a new version called *American Document (2010)* that brings together filmed excerpts of the original with spoken text from the choreographer's original notes (www.youtube.com, search "American Document.mov"):

Graham's theatrical archetypes can seem dated to contemporary eyes. But here her movement is stripped to its muscular, angled attack, with lunging forward thrusts and arching leaps conjuring ideas of American space and speed (aided by Brian H. Scott's vibrant lighting design). How exciting to see the dancers arrow across the stage, or watch the burly Leon Ingulsrud swivel his pelvis and propel himself sideways as he recites a bit of Jack Kerouac's "cold dusk run to Santa Barbara."[13]

Musical accompaniment for dance can be composed for a specific dance, already exist as a (usually famous) composition, involve orchestras, chamber groups, or solo instruments, and include choruses or even silence and non-musical sounds. Musicians and choreographers have long held unique and potent relationships.

With his interest in dance accompaniment fostered while he was the music director for Denishawn, Louis Horst (January 12, 1884, Kansas City, Missouri–January 23, 1964, New York, New York) became a musician for and longtime mentor to Martha Graham. He recognized that choreographers needed to understand theories about materials, forms, and style in the same way composers and visual artists understood their own arts. Through his awareness of composition, theory, and style in music and the other arts, Horst became the foremost proponent of an original system for teaching dance composition, and was an important theorist for 20th century dance. Horst taught hundreds of dance students about composition, and later became the dance critic for his own journal *The Dance Observer*.

Prior to Horst's influence, the idea of learning about choreography in ways other than through an apprenticeship with a successful choreographer were unknown. As musical composers, visual artists, and writers learned theories about their art forms and then found their own voices, so with dance composition as taught by Horst. He created progressive, disciplined, compositional exercises for budding choreographers that provided invaluable experiences in a variety of forms and styles from the past, made relevant and contemporary by each student.

During the pioneering days of modern dance, a dancer's physical skills were not likely to be as fully honed as they are today. Instead, early modern dance choreographers possessed the courage, vision, intelligence, and will to make unique, meaningful statements about the human condition, sometimes for hostile audiences and critics who could not understand the dances onstage. Since dance-knowledgeable American audiences and dancers were used to seeing ballets containing relatively advanced classical technique—imported by Russian émigrés, for the most part—the efforts of the modern dance pioneers had to be explained. Hence, choreographers felt required to organize their vocabularies of movement and create methods for dissemination of these vocabularies.

For instance, Martha Graham's technique includes falls, suspensions, jumps, and lifts, but her signal gesture of the torso was the "contraction" followed by its immediate and inevitable tension-flexion "release" of the entire torso.

> In a technical sense, a contraction is the lengthening of the spine into a curve while the front of the body is shortened. The front of the hip bones move in such a way that their energy comes under the rib cage and out through the mouth like an incredible fountain. But you can have a contraction only if you have an awareness of the front and the back of the body. Dancers often think they're contracting when they're actually dropping all their weight into the pelvis and diminishing their height. The misconception is that you're shortening the body; in fact, it's rising ecstatically.[14]

This movement impulse became the trademark of her technique, and it was designed to support her dramatic dances. Each gesture—with varying degrees of tension/release, distance, and speed—joins a propulsive chain of movement. The insistent sequence could be a means to creating powerfully controlled movements such as falls to the floor, turns, and whole-body gestures that were often (rightly) interpreted in highly emotional, sensual, even sexual ways. The technical skills that Graham's dancers developed were different from, but no less rigorous than, the skills needed for classical ballet. Two decades after her death, Graham dancers can still be easily spotted in performance.

The Era's Influences: Philosophical, Psychological and Sociological

While choreographers in the ballet world seldom appeared in their own works, most all of the creators in modern dance were the lead if not the only performers in their dances. Since the subject matter in modern/contemporary dance was (and still often is) about the dancer-choreographer's self investigations, or in some relation to a larger group—Graham's 1930 solo *Lamentation* (www.youtube.com, search "Lamentation–Martha Graham") and Nijinsky's *Rite of Spring* (1913), for example—the works could be personal and expressionistic. In fact, the term "interpretive" was used quite often to characterize the early works of modern dance.

Analytical and philosophical outlooks of dancer/choreographers were changed to varying degrees through the prompting of late 19th and early 20th century philosophies of movement and social theorists. Even the philosophy of Karl Marx (1818–1883), who believed in a utopian socialist society, had some influence on perceptions of the hierarchy of stage roles representing class and gender. A common subject for modern dance was often seen in an arrangement of a soloist or duet appearing as the outsider against the group of insiders, as in Doris Humphrey's *With My Red Fires* (1936) or Martha Graham's *Heretic* (1929, excerpt at www.youtube.com, search "Martha Graham—Heretic"). The combination of these approaches with the self as subject and a kind of social-expressionistic genre of alienation became a take-off point for dozens of dances that followed, such as many works by Anna Sokolow (1910–2000, discussed in Chapter 3). But stage performance in both theater and dance became influenced by another, at first surprising, source.

The more superficial acting style of the 19th century (itself evolving out of pantomime) became a thing of the past, partly due to, as noted earlier, the great contributions of Constantin Stanislavsky (1863–1938), who created more genuine and realistic methods for training actors. Many dancers and choreographers were aware of the need to find a more honest performing style—one that could enter the emotional core of a character. Part of this search for psychological truth in acting, painting, literature, and music was also inspired by the scientific exploration of the psyche through the hypnosis and dream work of the 20th century Austrian psychiatrist Sigmund Freud (1856–1939). The Freud/Stanislavsky ideas that were folded into both dramatic modern dance and ballet were a far cry from the overacting common in the "romantic and classical" ballets inherited from the previous century.[15]

Another common subject for modern dance was the individual as a social creature cognizant of, responsible for, and at one with his fellow man, regardless of class—a kind of a classless society. These modern era notions evolved in part out of a socialist philosophy harkening back to Marx's *Communist Manifesto* (1848). While a hierarchy of characters marked by social status fills the dramas of romantic and classical ballet, abstract works in modern dance made it easier to display the notion of a more egalitarian society. For example, the more "architectural" dances of choreographers such as Mary Wigman, Hanya Holm, and Doris Humphrey were works of uniform groups of people, with sections of solos, duets, trios, and larger numbers all contributing to a group effect.

Doris Humphrey

Doris Humphrey's (October 17, 1895, Oak Park, Illinois–December 28, 1958, New York, New York) development of the concept of "fall-and-recovery" was but one of her major bequests. Humphrey's fall is a "letting go" from holding the weight of the arms, head, ribs, or torso in the standing position, while allowing the torso or a body part to drop towards the ground, dictated only by the speed and force of gravity, with the legs folding at the same speed. As the "bottom of the drop" is reached, the energy from the automatic contraction of the fully stretched muscles of the legs and/or torso provides the power for the following action—rebound. Fall-recovery could become a metaphor of biblical proportions, such as death and rebirth, but also as simple as the constant pull of and struggle against gravity on all matter (www.youtube.com, search "A New Dance for America: The Choreography, Teachings, and Legacy of Doris Humphrey").

While the movement sequences created for romantic and classical ballet seem to delight in the illusion of defying gravity, Humphrey took advantage of gravity's pull to compose shapes and movement patterns into phrases, sections, and whole dances. Equally facile with complex, even contrapuntal, designs (www.youtube.com, search "Day on Earth"), Humphrey was an architect of group movements that involved these regular displacements of weight and their subsequent rebounds. Her *Passacaglia and Fugue in C Minor* (1938; www.youtube.com, search "Passacaglia Goucher College") is instructive about that vocabulary and focus. Shapes were formed to specification regarding the height and position of the dancers' upper arms, flexion of elbows and wrists, rotation of the shoulders and lower arms, and the hands. Although the fall/rebound is demanded throughout most of the work, many movements of equal importance were directed by precisely isolated impulses in specific parts of the body.

The dance was constructed to match the number of variations in the music, as well as the optimistic outlook of this important organ composition (c. 1706–1713), composed by Johann Sebastian Bach (1685–1750). It is performed as a dance for a large group of women and five men, with one of the males and one of the females acting as leaders, and its division of labor provides opportunities for all dancers to be featured in large and small groupings. Not unlike the rigorously structured buildup in Bach's music, the dancers' movements on the stage floor as well as on a set constructed of simple rectangular blocks of varying sizes allow for a powerful impact of comparable architectural proportion in the audience's mind. Fall/rebound, shape, level, gestural development, symmetry versus asymmetry, and closeness to, but not slavish imitation of, the music are evident in this and many of Humphrey's dances. Her architectural devices (such as large blocks) remind one of Holm's *Trend* and some of the music visualizations of Ruth St. Denis.

Doris Humphrey was also a great teacher of composition and she articulated her theories in a book released in 1959, *The Art of Making Dances*. It was and remains a defining text for choreographers throughout the world. To hundreds of budding choreographers, including her student, José Limón, Humphrey imparted a strong sense of formally structured composition in order to solve the unique problems of choosing subject matter and developing movement for making dances.

The early and most frequently acknowledged modern dance "founders" remain Doris Humphrey, Charles Weidman, Martha Graham, and Graham's music director, composer, mentor, and accompanist Louis Horst, who all worked for Ruth St. Denis and Ted Shawn at various times.

In a summer session of 1934, at Bennington College in Bennington, Vermont, under the inspired directorship of pioneering dance educator Martha Hill,[16] these "founders" of modern dance gathered together (including Horst) and combined their expertise to further excellence in the training of modern dance techniques and composition. Shawn continued to influence the education of American dancers by augmenting his original ideas to include ballet training at Jacob's Pillow (begun around the same time and named after a huge boulder on the property roughly in a pillow's shape, http://www.jacobspillow.org/), his summer school in Lee, Massachusetts. "The Pillow" celebrated its seventy-fifth anniversary in 2009 and remains a modern dance Mecca to this day with dozens of companies in performance and residency from around the globe in a deliciously fulfilling array of styles throughout the summer months.

The rich and lasting ideas of Louis Horst, Hanya Holm, and Doris Humphrey became the 20th century foundation for dance composition learned by hundreds of modern dancers and choreographers and sometimes respectfully violated by the postmodern and alternative generations to come. Horst and Humphrey created a theoretical basis for choreographers in the same way as that learned by budding musical composers, visual artists, or playwrights in music, painting, or drama—much of which they then chose to break. Not surprisingly, this continuing iconoclastic and rebellious nature is one of the most important characteristics of modern and contemporary dance.

Léonide Massine

The still underrated Léonide Massine (Leonid Fyodorovich Myasin, August 9, 1896, Moscow, Russia–March 15, 1979, Cologne, Germany), who took over the Ballets Russes' primary choreographic responsibilities in 1915, after Nijinsky was unceremoniously dropped by Diaghilev for daring to marry a woman, likewise pushed against that envelope. Massine's audacious 1917 *Parade*, for example, is as unballetic as Nijinsky's work, interested more in exploring the effects of a truly avant-garde visual art form on everyday movement—a wholly modern endeavor:

> Choreographically, *Parade* is all fragments and splinters. But the fragmentation is intentional, for this ballet from 1917, with its score by Erik Satie [1866–1925] and decor by Pablo Picasso [1881–1973], is an early attempt to put Cubist [c. 1907–1919] principles to choreographic use. Just as Cubist still lifes show fragments of real objects, so *Parade's* depictions of acts given by strolling players derive from fragments of realistic gestures. Because many of the gestures are severely fragmented, their literal meanings may not always be clear.[17]

Many companies have performed Massine's masterpiece since the 1917 premiere. *Parade* must be seen because of the contributions to it (set, costumes, scenery and score) by of some of the greatest 20th century artists. You will get a sense of its quirky expressions in a short excerpt of a 2007 recreation by the Rome Opera Ballet (www.youtube.com, search "Riccardo Di Cosmo & Sara Loro in Massine's 'Parade'").

The last of the great modern ballet choreographers born in the 19th century, Massine's extraordinary energy is captured on film during his rightly famous work as both choreographer and performer as the crazed shoemaker in the "Red Shoes Ballet" centerpiece of the 1948 film *The Red Shoes,* directed by the British team of Michael Powell (1905–1990) and Emeric Pressburger (1902–1988). In the dance, Massine gives us more than "a glimmer of the febrile intensity of his personality"[18] within a hypnotically surrealistic modern ballet of his own creation (www.youtube.com, search "The Red Shoes Ballet").

Selected Videos/DVDs/Films

Ballets Russes

Ballets Russes (2006), Dance Horizons.

Picasso and the Dance: Le Train Bleu, Le Tricorne (2005), Dance Horizons.

Stravinsky and the Ballets Russes: The Rite of Spring, The Firebird (2008), Dance Horizons.

Asadata Dafora

The Ostrich, in Dancing in the Light (orig. 1932), Dance Horizons.

Isadora Duncan

Isadora (1968), Universal Pictures.

Isadora Duncan Dance: Technique and Repertory(1994), Dance Horizons.

Isadora Duncan Masterworks 1905-1923 (2008), Dance Horizons.

Isadora Duncan: Movement from the Soul (1994), Dance Horizons.

Katherine Dunham

Barrelhouse Blues, in Dancing in the Light (orig. 1943), Dance Horizons.

Shango, in Dance Black America (1990), Dance Horizons.

Loïe Fuller

Loïe Fuller: Dancing in the Light Fantastic (2010), Dance Horizons.

Martha Graham

3 by Martha Graham: Seraphic Dialogue (1965), *Cortege of Eagles (1967), Acrobats of God* (1969 and 2005), Dance Horizons.

Martha Graham: The Dancer Revealed (1994), Dance Horizons.

Martha Graham on Film: A Dancer's World (1957), *Appalachian Spring* (1958), *Night Journey* (1961 and 2007) (double disc set), Janus Films.

Hanya Holm

Hanya: Portrait of a Pioneer (1988), Dance Horizons.

See also German Lineage in Modern Dance, below.

Doris Humphrey

A New Dance for America: The Choreography, Teaching and Legacy of Doris Humphrey (2010), Dance Horizons.

Dance Works of Doris Humphrey: With My Red Fires and *New Dance* (1972), Dance Horizons.

Ritmo Jondo and Day on Earth (1999), Dance Horizons.

The Doris Humphrey Legacy: Air for the G-String, The Call/Breath of Fire, The Shakers, Two Ecstatic Themes, Water Study (1998), Dance Horizons.

The Doris Humphrey Technique (1992), Dance Horizons.

Rudolf Laban
The Makers of Modern Dance in Germany, Dance Horizons.

Vaslav Nijinsky
Stravinsky and the Ballets Russes, The Rite of Spring, The Firebird (2008), Dance Horizons.
Paris Dances Diaghilev (1990), Warner.

Ruth St. Denis and Ted Shawn
The Dancing Prophet (1980), Insight Media.
Denishawn Dances On! (2006), Dance Horizons.
Denishawn: The Birth of Modern Dance (2006), Dance Horizons.
The Men Who Danced (1990), Amazon.com.

Mary Wigman
Mary Wigman: 1886–1973 (1990), Dance Horizons,
German Lineage in Modern Dance: Solos by Mary Wigman, Dore Hoyer, Honya Holm, Alwin Nikolais (2012), Dance Horizons.

Notes

1   "Eurythmics," *Encyclopedia Britannica Online*, http://www.britannica.com/EBchecked/topic/196597/eurythmics.

2   On paper, that recorded language is generally called Labanotation; also in Europe and South America, Kinetography. Similarly, one popular process of using and understanding dance in practice is called Laban Movement Analysis, or LMA.

3   The dispersal after his death of his myriad dancers, choreographers, and visual artists still calls for dozens of books yet to be written.

4   Debra Craine and Judith Mackrell, eds., *The Oxford Dictionary of Dance* (Oxford, England: Oxford University Press, 2010, 2nd ed.), p. 133.

5   Allen Robertson and Donald Hutera, *The Dance Handbook* (Boston: G. K. Hall, 1988), p. 45.

6   Ibid.

7   The author's (Marc Strauss) grandmother marveled over her account of having actually seen Nijinsky leap from one end of the stage to the other during one of the company's last tours to New York City in 1916 (it could have been in *Till Eulenspiegel*, which Nijinsky choreographed himself that year). As a loving grandson, I will never question the veracity of her statement.

8   Robertson and Hutera, *The Dance Handbook*, pp. 56–57.

9   Craine and Mackrell, *Oxford Dictionary of Dance*, p. 325.

10 http://en.wikipedia.org/wiki/Asadata_Dafora.

11 Mary-Jean Cowell (2009). "Michio Ito Study Guide," http://www.rdtutah.org/artsedu/study%20guide%20michio%20ito.pdf.

12 Rose Eichenbaum, *Masters of movement: Portraits of America's great choreographers* (Washington, D. C.: Smithsonian Books, 2004), p. 94.

13 Claudia La Rocco, "Integrating Ensembles to Build a Hybrid Work," *The New York Times*, June 11, 2010, http://www.nytimes.com/2010/06/11/arts/dance/11graham.html?ref=dance.

14 Macel, Emily. (July 2009). Terese Capucilli. *Dance Magazine.* http://www.dancemagazine.com/issues/July-2009/Terese-Capucilli.

15 To be blunt, many of the dramatic dance works that came to the stage as modern ballet during more than sixty years in the Soviet Union tended to present delightful overacting rather than Stanislavsky honesty.

16 Martha Hill (December 1, 1900, East Palestine, Ohio–November 19, 1995, Brooklyn Heights, New York).

17 Jack Anderson, "Joffrey: Massine's 'Parade'," *The New York Times*, November 22, 1981, http://query.nytimes.com/gst/fullpage.html?res=9F02E3DD1638F931A15752C1A967948260.

18 Op. cit. Robertson and Hutera, *The Dance Handbook*, p. 50.

Chapter Two
The 20th Century: 1900 to 1910

George Balanchine, Frederick Ashton, Kurt Jooss,
Agnes de Mille and Antony Tudor, José Limón, Birgit Cullberg,
Erick Hawkins, Katherine Dunham

At the beginning of the new century, Michel Fokine, the first of
Diaghilev's major choreographers, was creating modern ballets of
lasting force. In the 20th century's first few years, one of the great
revolutionary ballet choreographers was born.

George Balanchine

George Balanchine (Georgi Balanchivadze, January 22, 1904, St. Petersburg,
Russia–April 30, 1983, New York, New York), initially affiliated with the
classical and modern ballet worlds via training in the Petipa and Diaghilev
realms respectively, was integral to the development of contemporary dance.
After the starburst that was Nijinsky in that most pivotal of 20th century
companies, Les Ballets Russes de Monte Carlo (1909–1929), Balanchine—
following Fokine, Bronislava Nijinska (1891–1972) and Massine—became
an equally essential contributor to that evolution by creating a new form of
dance: Neoclassicism.

To this day Balanchine's dances remain endlessly satisfying, ever new,
and fresh. In a 2009 review, Alastair Macaulay, senior dance critic for *The
New York Times*, touched on that very point when he wrote, "No ballets are
more rewatchable than Balanchine's: to return to them, even after decades of
acquaintance, is usually to recognize new points that you'd previously looked
at without really seeing."[1] Macaulay describes *The Four Temperaments* (1946)
as "radical modernist," noting that the "dancers repeatedly arch their torsos
backward while stretching a leg forward. (It's remarkably like my favorite step
in the [modernist] Alvin Ailey repertory.)"[2]

As the online repertory index of the New York City Ballet Company (f. 1948 by Balanchine and Lincoln Kirstein) states, *The Four Temperaments* (1946) was "one of [Balanchine's] earliest experimental works, fusing classical steps with a lean and angular style"[3]—very modern indeed. Balanchine's neoclassicism—classical ballet without (an obvious) story—was deemed abstract and stripped down, with simple sets and costumes, musical, fascinating patterns, and dance performed for no other reason than just to dance (see also Merce Cunningham, discussed in Chapter 3). Balanchine's style remains the prototype for similar creations by contemporary ballet choreographers such as Jiří Kylián, Nacho Duato, Jorma Elo, William Forsythe, Eliot Feld, and Lar Lubovitch (all discussed in later chapters)—as they are quite willing to admit. Even modern dance choreographer Paul Taylor (see Chapter 5) has rightly been called a neoclassicist, especially as seen in the luscious, myriad, and musical patterns of his setless and plotless *Esplanade* (1975) or *Aureole* (1962).

Balanchine also choreographed full-length story ballets created in the manner of Marius Petipa (1818–1910), such as the 1954 *Nutcracker*, the 1963 *Midsummer Night's Dream*, and 1965's *Don Quixote*; but there are dozens more neoclassical masterpieces such as *Serenade* (1934), *Concerto Barocco* (1941), *Theme and Variations* (1948), *Agon* (1957), *Jewels* (1967), and *Stravinsky Violin Concerto* (1972). Look for his facile use of modern turned-in legs, asymmetries, flexed hands, and jazz-style hips wedded to an impeccable classical ballet technique in excerpts of each of the six above-mentioned dances, as performed internationally, at www.youtube.com, search:

- "Companhia Nacional de Bailado Serenade" (Portugal)
- "Francia Russell rehearses Balanchine's Concerto Barocco" (Netherlands)
- "Theme and Variations—Dresden Semperoper Ballett" (Germany)
- "Day 4—Serenade and Agon" (England)
- "Balanchine, George: Jewels, Paris National Opera Ballet" (France)
- "In het spoor van Balanchine" (Dutch National Ballet).

Even in his 1929 one-act story ballet *The Prodigal Son*, Balanchine's last extant work for The Ballets Russes, the central and seductive *pas de deux* between the prodigal and siren has them intertwined all around the floor—not really traditional balletic motifs. The great work *Agon* could not be more angular at times, while still leaning on its purely classical roots—a rare skill repeated many, many times by this most avant-garde of ballet choreographers.

Balanchine was a consummate pianist and musically sensitive. Long after he died, *The New Yorker* critic Alex Ross noted that "what's striking about the N.Y.C.B. repertory is how much modern fare it contains. Balanchine trained audiences not to fear a post-Romantic sound."[4]

Not surprisingly, many of Balanchine's heirs—Suzanne Farrell and The Suzanne Farrell Ballet (f. 2000, www.suzannefarrell.org), Edward Villella and his Miami City Ballet (MCB, f. 1985, www.miamicityballet.org) (Villella retired in 2012 with noted Balanchine interpreter Lourdes Lopez his replacement), and Ib Andersen at Ballet Arizona (f. 1986, www.balletaz.org), to name only three—continue to carry on the living legacy of the great Russian émigré's extraordinary embrace of modernity.

Joan Acocella (b. 1945), dance critic at *The New Yorker* magazine, says as much in her review of Miami City Ballet's very first New York City Center season (2009) since its founding:

> Balanchine, his dancers say, never told them what his ballets were about, never gave them 'motivations.' He probably thought that he didn't need to. In his time, everyone knew what French stylishness was, not to speak of the Second World War. That is not the case with teenagers in Miami in 2009, and Villella, as he said in his *Times* interview, fills them in. 'Those three ladies who open "La Valse": who are they? You need to know about Dior's 1947 "new look."' As for "Square Dance" (1957), the opener of his second program, he must have told the cast that this American hoedown to the old Italian music of Vivaldi and Corelli was part of Balanchine's effort, in his company's insecure first decade, to convince Americans that they could be part of a classical tradition. Jeanette Delgado, leading the piece, encapsulated what I think Balanchine wanted: a marriage of barn-dance verve with European sophistication.[5]

Is this not a modern sensibility, to yearn so much to fit in with the times, not just the thirties, when Balanchine arrived in the United States, but through even the beginning of the eighties, sixty years later? He would choreograph square dances to the classics, patriotic themes to John Philip Sousa (*Stars and Stripes*, 1958), Broadway musical theater dance to Richard Rodgers's "Slaughter on Tenth Avenue" in *On Your Toes* (1936, reworked in 1968), extremely angular, abstract neoclassicism to composer Paul Hindemith's intellectual *The Four Temperaments* (1947), and a jazz-inflected classicism to Stravinsky's modernist *Agon* (1957). The American ethos of speed and jazz and musicals and Westerns and pure Americana was the Balanchine ethos, and was very modern indeed for its time—and still is today.

Journalist, fashion designer, and dancer Holly Brubach, in the popular 1984 DVD *Balanchine*, supports this characteristically American view of the choreographer:

> Balanchine's fondness for America ran deep, and the range of his ballets that draw on American material is broad and surprising. He used the music of an American composer, Charles Ives. In *Ivesiana* [1954], Balanchine choreographed a romantic adagio set to music romantic and peculiar enough to support the notion of a woman who never touches the ground… In [his] hands, classical ballet incorporated the past in the present, and nowhere was this more apparent than in *Agon* [1957], a ballet that reconciled the French dance forms of the 17th century with the anxieties of the 20th. In its nervous intensity, its nakedness of execution, *Agon* was unlike any ballet that had ever been made before.[6]

Clearly, Balanchine's work inhabits both the classical ballet and modern ballet worlds. Classically-trained star Aurélie Dupont says as much in the translated subtitles of the Paris Opera Ballet 2006 *Jewels* DVD:

> Balanchine is one of the choreographers who launched me at the Paris Opera. I was lucky enough to understudy for "Sanguinic", (part of) *The Four Temperaments* (1946)…and I have always enjoyed his choreography, which I still find very modern—you might almost think he is a modern choreographer of our own time, of today, because his choreography doesn't look dated. And the idea that he had of music, of choreography, of shifts, remains very current.[7]

Barbara Horgan's[8] assessment of Balanchine's work, as noted in that same 2006 DVD, confirms the choreographer's place in the contemporary world: "A repertory company can move into acquiring the modern ballets by modern choreographers who exist today, who are really fascinating, and they can mix with Balanchine on the same program… He was a genius of the 20th century, but he's moved into the 21st very easily."[9]

Frederick Ashton

Ecuador-born and Peru-raised (but ultimately British) Frederick Ashton (September 17, 1904, Guayaquil, Ecuador–August 19, 1988, Eye, England) was born just a few months after Balanchine. Like his peer, Ashton could create wonderful narrative ballets as well as anyone (*Cinderella*, 1948; *The Dream*,

1964) but what he brought to the classical lexicon was his own "distinctive sensual plastique" full of "fast, brilliant footwork…counterpointed by supple twists and curves in the body," a style that supported a number of equally contemporary nonnarrative dances.[10] Three of his plotless, yet evocative, ballets include: *A Wedding Bouquet*, from 1937, created alongside a Gertrude Stein text; the 1965 *Monotones*, set to Erik Satie's (1866–1925) melancholic and gently dissonant *Gymnopédies* (1888); and the Stravinsky-inspired *Scènes de Ballet* (1948, excerpt at www.youtube.com, search "Scenes de Ballet—Miyako Yoshida2.m4v"), a lovingly lilting, pure line tease of a dance "organized in a sculptural, balanced harmony."[11]

Kurt Jooss

Laban associate Kurt Jooss (January 12, 1901, Wasseralfingen, Germany–May 22, 1979, Heilbronn, Germany) developed dances that allowed the use of some ballet vocabulary but with little of its technical tricks (*pyrotechniques*). He was considered by the moderns to be too close in temperament to the ballet theater, while his ballet critics were offended by his use of movements considered to be "modern." Ignoring his critics, Jooss created a dance theater where his movement choices, like the traditional ballet, also included pantomimic gesture. His greatest work, *The Green Table* (1932), still performed today by ballet companies everywhere, is a biting satire on the futility of war and its associated political chicanery—a topic that sadly remains relevant. Photos from the ballet, set to live piano, can be seen at www.youtube.com, search "Cohen 'The Green Table' Scene 3 'The Battle.'" Also, look for the first seven minutes of The Joffrey Ballet's (f. 1956) 1967 reconstruction, through Jooss's own efforts, in the YouTube copy of a 1982 Dance in America TV production (www.youtube.com, search "Intro through Beginning of the Farewells").

More than anyone before him, Jooss bridged the ballet-modern divide and provided special inspiration to European choreographers and companies that fused these myriad styles and philosophies into an expressive art—especially people like his student Pina Bausch (1940–2009, discussed in Chapter 6)— most of whom were wholly unconcerned with labels.

Agnes de Mille and Antony Tudor

As noted earlier in the Chapter 1 discussion of Martha Graham, the search for honesty in acting was also the province of choreographers such as Agnes de Mille (September 18, 1905, New York, New York–October 7, 1993, New York, New York) and Antony Tudor (William John Cook, April 4,

1908, London, England–April 19, 1987, New York, New York), who func-
tioned within ballet organizations such as England's Ballet Rambert (f. 1926,
currently Rambert Dance Company) and, later, American Ballet Theatre
(ABT),[12] in New York City. Ballet contemporaries of Graham were leaders
in defining dramatic dance for the 20th century, creating ballets not radically
different from Graham's modern dance inventions, to the extent that their
works, while wed to a primarily balletic lexicon, tended to use sophisticated
nonpantomimic gestures in order to delve into a character's inner life.

Agnes de Mille is most remembered for her psychologically probing dance
contributions to Broadway musical theater in such groundbreaking works as
Oklahoma! [1943; www.youtube.com, search "Oklahoma dream ballet (Laurey
and Curly)"] and *Carousel* (1945; www.youtube.com, search "A Seaside Fantasy–
Susan Luckey, Jacques d'Amboise"), dances that can be readily referenced in
the film versions of those shows (1955 and 1956 respectively). Likewise, her
"Civil War Ballet" from the 1944 *Bloomer Girl* can be viewed in black and
white at www.youtube.com, search "Bloomer Girl–Civil War Ballet–Agnes de
Mille–Harold Arlen–James Mitchell."

However, the choreographer's concert dance *Fall River Legend* (1948;
excerpt from a 1989 Dance Theatre of Harlem (f. 1969) performance at
www.youtube.com, search "Fall River Legend"), a dance about the true story
of axe murderer Lizzie Borden, demonstrates the choreographer's ability
to bring together an incisive interpretation of a horrible tragedy, balletic
technical proficiency, and storytelling mime into one compelling piece.

Tudor, on the other hand, in such works as *Lilac Garden* (1936; excerpt by
the Alabama Ballet at www.youtube.com, search "Excerpt from 'Lilac Garden'–
Alabama Ballet"), *Echoing of Trumpets* (1963), and *The Leaves Are Fading* (1975;
pas de deux by American Ballet Theatre at www.youtube.com, search "The
Leaves Are Fading Ballet"), brought his own intensely personal psychological
insights to bear via the classical ballet.

Craine and Mackrell (2010) correctly noted that Tudor was

> an astute observer of human nature and behavior, and was able in his
> ballets to transmit a wealth of psychological detail—especially sorrow
> and yearning—with a single step or gesture. He was one of the first
> choreographers to concentrate on the emotional anguish of ordinary
> men and women, exploring the darkness of their interior lives with
> extraordinary grace and sympathy.[13]

Besides Tudor's insights, the acting of dancers such as Nora Kaye (1920–1987), Hugh Laing (1911–1988), and Sallie Wilson (b. 1932) must be given credit for bringing to fruition the characters he created.

Tudor's British background also included working with Ballet Rambert, where he presented exquisitely choreographed and challenging class combinations that inspired generations of dancers. His *Dark Elegies* (1937) for that company (www.youtube.com, search "Ballet Rambert Dark Elegies Tudor") is another example of his skill at revealing the inner psychological state of his characters.

José Limón

Another modern dance pioneer born near the beginning of the 20ᵗʰ century, and whose company, impressively, is still performing more than forty years after his passing, is José Limón (January 12, 1908, Culiacan, Mexico–December 2, 1972, Flemington, New Jersey). Limón infused his dances and technique with several important elements, *the least being* signature gestures (www.youtube.com, search "Danza Contemporanea–El Legado de José Limón"). His contribution to the currents of the dance world was in making his dancers see the glory and power of the human spirit on stage as well as in the classroom. Like his teacher, artistic director and mentor Doris Humphrey (discussed in Chapter 1), every gesture needed to have a clear motivation, whether it was based on a dramatic, emotional idea or an abstraction. "Abstract" movements in the art of dance—unlike abstract images in mathematics or music—are, in fact, concrete physical manifestations of the intellect, spirit, and body. Because Limón's powerful physique gave a rich weight and palpable energy to his movements, he repeatedly talked about the human body as a tangible instrument at least as complex as an orchestra's organization. The dancer needed to treat the shoulders, elbows, ribs, head, heels—all parts of the body—as individual instruments that, when "sounded" individually or in sequence, could simultaneously "play" a beautiful symphony of movement for an audience's senses.

Although he first trained as a painter, his dances were not necessarily painterly. Limón's dramatic talents as a choreographer and lead dancer in his own works, such as *The Moor's Pavane* (1949), based on Shakespeare's *Othello* (www.youtube.com, search "Jose Limon in 'The Moor's Pavane'") and the narrative *Emperor Jones* (1956, excerpt at www.youtube.com, search "Jose Limon bio"), and abstract pieces like *There is a Time* (1956, www.youtube.com, search "Jose Limon's 'There is a Time' Montage"), are about humanity and the gift of movement—the gift of life. No other artist of the modern era seemed to be on such a selfless mission to dignify the field of dance than Limón.

Birgit Cullberg

Like Limón, Birgit Cullberg (August 3, 1908, Nyköping, Sweden–September 8, 1999, Stockholm, Sweden) contributed in her own way to the unique power of the individual, but more by reaching out for a variety of nationalities to be represented among her dancers (only three of the original eight members of her company were Swedish), and treating all of them as equal-pay soloists, unheard of at the time in the conventional hierarchical structure of ballet companies. She had studied with Jooss for several years in England, so it was no surprise that she, too, pushed the boundaries of the dance world through "social-protest pieces." Also, like her contemporaries Graham, de Mille, and Tudor, the "psychological" ballet was an important breakthrough area of exploration for the choreographer. Founding the Cullberg Ballet in 1967 (www.cullbergballetten.se),

> Birgit Cullberg was a pioneering experimental choreographer in Sweden who earned an international reputation through her intense dramatic ballets and vigorous social-protest pieces [through which she] fused modern dance and ballet...
>
> Psychological insight was Miss Cullberg's strength...Never shy about exploring the neurotic and the erotic, Miss Cullberg was represented by a duet, "Adam and Eve," and an especially sensuous performance of "Miss Julie" [1950; her masterpiece], which nonetheless focused on the class differences between Julie and her servant. In "Adam and Eve," Daniela Malusardi and Niklas Ek, Miss Cullberg's elder son, moved seamlessly from innocent playfulness to adult passion, a couple expelled from Eden but rejecting God as well.[14]

Unlike Niklas, Mats Ek, another of Cullberg's sons, has become an internationally renowned contemporary ballet choreographer in his own right (see Chapter 5).

Erick Hawkins

Erick Hawkins (April 23, 1909, Trinidad, Colorado–November 23, 1994, New York, New York), another in the second generation of American modern dance pioneers, was a poet of motion deeply influenced by Eastern and Greek philosophies. Like Merce Cunningham, born ten years after him, Hawkins felt that dance needed to be what it is—dance and dance alone, not something else—and so he concentrated on the beauty of human motion in the moment, and the act of moving in the presence of an audience also in that moment. For Hawkins, dance was a transcendental Zen experience for both himself and his audience, which had the capacity to be equally "one" with the dancers as they danced.

Two of Erick Hawkins's most famous pieces are *Here and Now with Watchers* (1957) and *8 Clear Places* (1960), and their titles alone evoke that numinous sense of peaceful presence. Authors Robertson and Hutera note that he always performed with live music (his own Hawkins Theatre Orchestra), adding to the powerful sense of "now," as they speak of his "tender, virile virtuosity" wedded to an "ascetic aesthetic."[15] Founded in 1951, the Erick Hawkins Dance Company (www.erickhawkinsdance.org) continues to keep the choreographer's vision alive into the 21ˢᵗ century.

The choreographer collaborated closely with visual artists and composers alike, including Louise Bourgeois (1911–2010), Isamu Noguchi (1904–1988), and Robert Motherwell (1915–1991) in the first group and Virgil Thompson (1896–1989) and Lucia Dlugoszewski (1931–2000) in the second. In particular, Dlugoszewski created and played specially prepared instruments alongside Hawkins's dancers. Many of his costumes, masks, and headgear were reminiscent of Noguchi's semi-representational and evocative work for that company. Set to live music, a segment from *Plains Daybreak* (1979) can be studied at www.youtube.com, search "Plains Daybreak Erick Hawkins Dance."

It is possible for us to place in perspective those Hawkins dances and aspects of his technique with an authentic practice of Eastern philosophy that had been indicated years before by Ruth St. Denis. From 1948 to 1954, Hawkins, with some significant training in ballet under Balanchine, was married to Martha Graham (who was fifteen years his senior—not unlike the relationship between Ruth St. Denis and Ted Shawn). The techniques of ballet and Graham, however, came to seem antithetical to the kind of daily practice that could support Hawkins's Zen-like art or his body. Therefore, he developed a technique that put ease and efficiency to the service of his dance vision and movements.

After carefully and faithfully learning traditions, then breaking them—and creating their own technique that may then be subsequently appropriated or altered by a new generation of dancers—choreographers like Hawkins forged their own way in what can today be called contemporary dance—a world that we recognize is always in the making.

Katherine Dunham

The peripatetic Katherine Dunham (June 22, 1909, Glen Ellyn, Illinois–May 21, 2006, New York, New York) was trained in anthropology, modern dance, ballet, and Caribbean dances (particularly from Haiti, where she owned a home). She is perhaps the most famous of the early African American dancers and choreographers. "What Dunham gave…dance was a coherent lexicon of African and Caribbean styles of movement—a flexible torso and spine, articulated pelvis and isolation of the limbs [and] a polyrhythmic strategy of moving, which she integrated with techniques of ballet and modern dance."[16]

Dunham appeared in the Broadway musical *Cabin in the Sky* (1940, choreography by George Balanchine) and performed and choreographed for Hollywood musicals such as the 1942 *Star Spangled Rhythm* and the burlesque "Who's On First" comedy team of Bud Abbott and Lou Costello's *Pardon My Sarong* (1942). However, her work on film is best represented in the singular number "Stormy Weather," from the 1943 film of the same name, alongside many of the prominent African American performers of the day such as tap dancer extraordinaire Bill "Bojangles" Robinson (1878–1949) and the Nicholas Brothers (Fayard, 1914–2006, and Harold, 1921–2000).

In New York City in 1945, Dunham opened her own school, which attracted concert and Broadway dancers eager to learn movements from the African/Caribbean legacy that would eventually permeate concert and Broadway dance. At her school, professional and preprofessional dancers of many ethnicities learned together an historic and anthropologically relevant catalog of movement that enlarged the largely Eurocentric theater dance vocabulary for the discipline. The Katherine Dunham Technique carries on today, through dozens—even hundreds—of her former students and theirs. One can see the wonderful Dunham with her Katherine Dunham Dancers in the dance section of the song "Stormy Weather" at www.youtube.com, search "Katherine Dunham Stormy Weather," and a reconstruction of the steamy 1938 *Barrelhouse Blues* at www.youtube.com, search "Dancing in the Light: 'Ostrich,' 'Barrelhouse Blues.'"

Misinterpreted for too many years as, at best, unsophisticated dances—and, at worst, primitive—through the middle decades of the 20ᵗʰ century, dozens of unheralded and important African-American dance artists like Asadata Dafora (1890–1965; discussed in Chapter 1), Pearl Primus (1919–1994; discussed in Chapter 3), Dunham, and Donald McKayle (b. 1930; discussed in Chapter 5) have become increasingly recognized in the late 20ᵗʰ and early 21ˢᵗ century for their contributions to modern and contemporary dance, and our shared human heritage. Their works are finally being presented on the international concert stage more and more frequently.

Selected Videos/DVDs/Films

Frederick Ashton

Ashton—Tales of Beatrix Potter (2007), Naxos.
Cinderella: The Royal Ballet (1969), Kultur.
Dance in America: The Dream with American Ballet Theatre (2004), Kultur.
Frederick Ashton: Les Patineurs, Divertissements and Scenes de Ballet (2012), Dance Horizons.

George Balanchine

Balanchine (2004), Dance Horizons.
Bringing Balanchine Back: The Historic Return to Russia (2009), Kultur.
Choreography by Balanchine: Chaconne, Prodigal Son, Ballo Della Regina, The Steadfast Tin Soldier, Elegie, Tchaikovsky Pas de Deux (1977/1996), Dance Horizons and Amazon.com.
Choreography by Balanchine: Tzigane, Andante from Divertimento No. 15, The Four Temperaments, Selection from Jewels, Stravinsky Violin Concerto (1977/1996), Dance Horizons and Amazon.com.
George Balanchine's Jewels (2006), Dance Horizons.

Birgit Cullberg

Fröken Julie (1980/1959), TV movie (out of print).
Abbalett (1984), TV movie (out of print).

Agnes de Mille

Oklahoma! (1955), 20th Century Fox.
Fall River Legend (1989) in *Dance Theatre of Harlem*, Dance Horizons.

Katherine Dunham

Barrelhouse Blues, in *Dancing in the Light* (orig. 1938), Dance Horizons.
Shango, in *Dance Black America* (1990), Dance Horizons.

Erick Hawkins

Erick Hawkins' America (1994), Dance Horizons.
The Erick Hawkins Modern Dance Technique (2000), Dance Horizons.

Kurt Jooss

Kurt Jooss: A Commitment to Dance (2001), Insight Media.

José Limón

José Limón: A Life Beyond Words (2003), Dance Horizons.
José Limón Technique (1998), Dance Horizons.
José Limón: Three Modern Dance Classics: The Moor's Pavane, The Emperor Jones, The Traitor (2003), Dance Horizons.
The José Limón Company (1956), Insight Media.

Antony Tudor

Antony Tudor (2008), Dance Horizons.

Notes

1 Alastair Macaulay, "The Twirling Kaleidoscope That Is Balanchine," *The New York Times*, January 7, 2009, http://www.nytimes.com/2009/01/08/arts/dance/08temp.html?_r=1&ref=dance.

2 Ibid.

3 http://www.nycballet.com/company/rep.html?rep=79.

4 Alex Ross, "Music in Motion: New Scores at New York City Ballet," *The New Yorker*, June 28, 2010, p. 76.

5 Joan Acocella, "Local Hero," *The New Yorker*, February 9 & 16, 2009, p. 116.

6 Holly Brubach, in the popular *Balanchine*, PBS Dance in America (Los Angeles: Kultur Media, 1984), DVD. Transcription.

7 *Jewels Joyaux*, (London: Opus Arts, 2006), DVD.

8 Barbara Horgan is Chairman of the Board of Directors of the George Balanchine Trust (f. 1987), which licenses the choreographer's dances around the world (http://balanchine.com).

9 *Jewels Joyaux*, 2006.

10 Debra Craine and Judith Mackrell, eds., *Oxford Dictionary of Dance* (2nd ed.) (London: Oxford University Press, 2010), pp. 25–26.

11 Allen Robertson and Donald Hutera, *The Dance Handbook* (Boston: G. K. Hall, 1988), p. 92.

12 American Ballet Theatre was founded in 1937 as the Mordkin Ballet, became Ballet Theatre in 1940, and changed to its current name in 1956.

13 Craine and Mackrell, *Oxford Dictionary*, p. 458.

14   Anna Kisselgoff, "Birgit Cullberg, 91, Swedish Choreographer," *The New York Times*, September 13, 1999, http://www.nytimes.com/1999/09/13/arts/birgit-cullberg-91-swedish-choreographer.html.

15   Robertson and Hutera, *The Dance Handbook*, p. 71.

16   Sally Sommer, "Katherine Dunham," 2001, http://www.pbs.org/wnet/freetodance/biographies/dunham.html.

Chapter Three
1910 to 1920

**Anna Sokolow, Alwin Nikolais, Sophie Maslow,
Fresh Approaches to the Same Music, *The Rite of Spring*,
Jerome Robbins, Merce Cunningham, Pearl Primus**

Anna Sokolow

A child of immigrant Jews, Anna Sokolow (February 9, 1910, Hartford,
Connecticut–March 29, 2000, New York, New York) trained with Martha
Graham in the late 1920s and 1930s but soon focused her energies on
melding the burgeoning "new dance" techniques (the phrase "modern dance"
was not coined until 1933 by *New York Times* dance critic John Martin!) with
socially-conscious concerns, as in her work with the New Dance Group
(f. 1932) and dances such as the *Anti-War Trilogy* (1933) and *Dreams* (1961).
The latter was "inspired" by the horrors of the Holocaust. Globally extending
her interests into Israel and Mexico (where she founded that nation's
first modern dance company, La Paloma Azul, in 1940), Sokolow also
choreographed for Broadway, most notably Leonard Bernstein's opera *Candide*
(1956). From 1958 to 1993 she taught a dance-based version of "method
acting" at the Drama Division of New York City's Juilliard School (f. 1905).

Sokolow created "works full of dramatic contemporary imagery,
revealing the full spectrum of human experience and reflecting the tension
and alienation of her time."[1] Her 1955 *Rooms*, recreated by the Batsheva
Dance Company as seen in a 1973 rehearsal video (www.youtube.com, search
"Rooms—Escape Solo"), clearly embodies that constrained tautness.

> "Rooms" is a portrait of strangled emotions, desperate outbursts and
> all-too-brief respites. The dancers, often seated in straight-back chairs
> and largely isolated by squares of light, thrum with unspoken need in a
> series of vignettes with titles like "Alone" and "Escape."

> Sokolow's physical language is simple and stark [and the] dancers'
> coiled stillness is a counterpoint to [the] vibrantly (sometimes
> painfully) alive score. Rigid limbs scissor and stretch, bare feet slide
> rapidly back and forth, torsos spasm and curl.[2]

Sokolow was "uncompromising about her role as an artist with a social
conscience" and, "in her hope for a better world, slaps us in the face with
man's inhumanity to man."[3] In 2003, soon after the choreographer's death,
the Sokolow Dance Foundation (http://www.annasokolow.org/) was founded to
sustain her legacy.

While some modern choreographers lean toward political and social
activism (like Sokolow), athletic movement, lyrical pieces, dramatic themes,
or even dance as pure experience, others have tended to use the dance
to create and display forms that emerge from the technique itself and the
geometric shapes created by the human body. In modern dance, many of the
works of Hanya Holm and Doris Humphrey embody this emphasis on pure
shape, and much of Merce Cunningham's works can also be similarly viewed;
but none quite as much as Nikolais.

Alwin Nikolais

The 20th century master of pure design was Alwin Nikolais (November
25, 1910, Southington, Connecticut–May 8, 1993, New York, New York).
Trained as a puppeteer early in life, Nikolais was also influenced by some
of the ideas of the Bauhaus (1919–1933), the German school of design best
known for its aesthetic of simple functionalism: "form follows function."
These ideas were filtered through modern dance choreographer Mary
Wigman to Nikolais' early teacher, Hanya Holm. It was Nikolais, however,
who transformed the natural shapes of his dancers into depersonalized, often
intergalactic-appearing figures—and a wholly new dance theater aesthetic—
through his use of colorfully and dramatically lighted fabric and body
extensions. He also created his own electronic audiotapes containing musical
sound effects that accented the movements of these strange figures, which
seemed to gambol about the stage.

Some of Nikolais' memorable creations include the prop-filled *Kaleidoscope*
(1953), with its discs, poles and straps; the silhouette-suffused, alien-costumed,
full-length *Imago* (1963, excerpts at www.nikolaislouis.org, choose "Videos,"
then "Imago"); the black-light- and flash-pot-illuminated *Vaudeville of the Elements* (1965); *Pond* (1982), performed on "floating" platform rollers (excerpt

at www.nikolaislouis.org, choose "Videos," then "Pond"); and the shape-filled *Tensile Involvement* (1953, at www.youtube.com, search "Tensile Involvement").

A section of this last Nikolais favorite, *Tensile Involvement,* can be seen at the beginning of the film *The Company* (2003) by dancer-turned-actress Neve Campbell (b. 1973), loosely based on story of the Joffrey Ballet of Chicago (f. 1956; www.joffrey.org). Throughout the film, famed naturalistic film director Robert Altman (1925–2006) fortunately keeps many sections of all the dances performed intact, including Nikolais', respecting the works as a totality. All too often, directors of dance on film have chopped up choreography and bodies in their misguided effort to hold an audience's attention or to make an already-sufficient art form more artsy.[4]

Nikolais' world was a precursor to our own often-depersonalized age of technology, where the visual experience is made more facile through moving light instruments, video images, and new fabrics that can change their designs in an instant. His nonliteral dances were not to be explained but simply watched. "I…made dance a visual art rather than just a kinetic one," he says, as recounted by Alastair Macaulay in his *New York Times* review of the 2010 re-release of director Christian Blackwood's 1986 dance film *Nik and Murray,* celebrating the centenary of the choreographer's birth. "I invited the eye to see dance more as painting and sculpting rather than just motion."[5]

The Nikolais-Louis Foundation (http://www.nikolaislouis.org/), formed in 1968 by Nikolais and his life-long collaborator Murray Louis (b. 1926), housed both the Nikolais Dance Theater and Murray Louis Dance Company until 1999. In 2003, the Salt Lake City-based Ririe-Woodbury Dance Company (f. 1964, www.ririewoodbury.com) became the living repository of Nikolais' dances.

In an April 30, 2010, interview with *The New York Times* reporter Julie Bloom, Louis makes this compelling argument for the value of studying Nikolais long into the 21st century:

> We have to remind people that the giant is back in town. What was that title he had that I absolutely hated…? "The Magician." But these are the words used when his show goes on. It's thrilling. It's theater. It is what he pushed this otherwise dancing form into…. [It's] still ahead of its time. If you want to catch up to contemporary dance, you have to at least get through this…. He decided to take all the old things: the music became sound, the costumes became extensions, which opened a

huge range, and the libretto, if he used words, he used vocal sounds, he created a new vocabulary, a contemporary vocabulary for the dance.[6]

Although some companies like Pilobolus (f. 1971) and Momix (f. 1980), both discussed in Chapter 9, have highlighted spatial designs in their dances, many works of dramatic ballet and modern dance more deliberately evoke images through the design of movement, sets, costumes, and lights. These images were as crucial to Nikolais as those in Diaghilev's Ballets Russes decades earlier, a veritable living exhibit of dance and visual arts collaborations. It could be argued that contemporary companies that began in the seventies and eighties, like Pilobolus and Momix, owe a lot to Nikolais' groundbreaking work, even if they created much of their choreography without any conscious references.

Sophie Maslow

Fighter for justice Sophie Maslow (March 22, 1911, New York, New York– June 25, 2006 New York, New York), one of Anna Sokolow's fellow dancers in the early Graham troupe, was also a founding member in 1932 of the New Dance Group (NDG). This group of artists and dancers dedicated itself to social change. In 2006, NDG was named by the Library of Congress and the Dance Heritage Coalition to be "One of America's Irreplaceable First 100 Dance Treasures" (http://www.loc.gov/today/pr/2000/00-099.html).

Maslow was also an important member of the Bennington Festival and the American Dance Festival (ADF on Facebook). Original home to so many of the early modern dance pioneers, the Bennington Festival was established at Bennington College in 1934, moved to Connecticut College fourteen years later, and then to its current home at Duke University in 1978. Recently celebrating its seventy-fifth anniversary and its thirtieth at Duke, ADF still supports the modern dance heritage and mission forwarded by Maslow, her peers, and descendants (http://www.americandancefestival.org/).

In an interview near the end of her life, Maslow remembered being inspired to dance at the age of three by seeing Isadora Duncan dance:

> My mother took me to see [her] dance on the stage. I was very little, but it left a big imprint on me. She danced with a red shawl and spoke to the audience with a bouquet of flowers in her arms. I never forgot it.…When I was fourteen, I read Isadora's autobiography, *My Life*, and was very influenced by her ideas on movement, love and marriage.[7]

Maslow's fight against injustice drove much of her work. This is particularly true of the powerful *The Village I Knew*, which she developed throughout World War II but premiered in 1949:

> The (dances) I am most proud of were the ones that moved audiences and made them laugh or cry. *The Village I Knew* [www.youtube.com, search "Sophie Maslow Village Etude (excerpt)"] was a dance I did based on the stories of Sholem Aleichem. He was a Yiddish writer who romanticized Jewish life in Eastern Europe at the end of the nineteenth century. [The 1964 Broadway musical *Fiddler on the Roof* was based on Aleichem's stories.] I was very surprised at how the work impressed non-Jewish audiences, especially since it was being performed [not long after the] Nazis were killing Jews all over Europe. I wanted to help in some way, even though I personally felt that nothing I could do in dance could ever measure up to the horrors of the Holocaust.[8]

Excerpts from her 1942 *Folksay* (you can see a snippet at www.youtube.com, search "The New Dance Group Gala Historical Concert: Retrospective 1930s–1970s Screener") with music by political folksinger Woody Guthrie (1912–1967) and text by American poet, humorist, and civil rights supporter Carl Sandburg (1878–1967), is the grand finale of a 1993 concert on the 2008 DVD of the same name in the YouTube clip. *Folksay* was lovingly brought to life by the Alvin Ailey American Dance Theater dancers 44 years after its premier.

Fresh Approaches to the Same Music

In addition to its ability to address social issues in frank and challenging ways, contemporary choreographers sometimes choose to leave nothing sacred—at least at first glance. For every traditional Romantic ballet, Petipa classical ballet, or Fokine modern ballet—for example, *Giselle* (1841), *Swan Lake* (1895), and *Firebird* (1910)—contemporary versions can challenge conventions. Arthur Mitchell (b. 1934) of Dance Theatre of Harlem (f. 1969) set the 1984 full-length *Creole Giselle* in the free black society of the Louisiana swamps (excerpt at www.youtube.com, search "Virginia Johnson & Eddie J. Shellman in Giselle"), while John Neumeier choreographed a science fiction version of *Firebird* for the Frankfurt Ballet in 1970.

Keepers of the canon usually rate these "updates" as ghastly travesties rather than homage. And why shouldn't they? The timeless charm of reverently exact or slightly modified[9] performances *has* been justified. Audiences ask for and rightly receive the traditional *Giselle* and *Swan Lake* and *Firebird* so they can compare the technical virtuosity and narrative nuance of dozens of performers in the same roles over and over again, year after year.

Choreographers love to revisit the classics for a variety of reasons. Often it is the music that beckons. Would the famed *Nutcracker* (1892) with lesser music than Tchaikovsky's score have lasted as a ballet icon? Different people hear and see stories and images within music compositions that are generous enough to accommodate seemingly innumerable visions. American choreographer Mark Morris's *The Hard Nut* (1991) honors the original music while re-envisioning the story during the swinging era of the 1960s. (www.youtube. com, search "Mark Morris The Hard Nut by BAM.org") Today, both works remain staples of classical and contemporary ballet respectively. The British Matthew Bourne revisited *Swan Lake* (1895) exactly one hundred years after the original's premier. His contemporary version borrows liberally from moody noir Hitchcock films such as *Rebecca* (1940) and *Suspicion* (1941) while using an all-male cast for the swans. Again, the dance remains highly musical while offering a fresh take on the narrative (www.youtube.com, search "Mathew Bourne's Swan Lake – 3 minute preview").

Other timeless compositions have borne multiple fruits. Johann Sebastian Bach's elegiac *Concerto in D Minor for Two Violins* (c. 1730) has inspired luminaries like the neoclassical George Balanchine (*Concerto Barocco*, 1941, excerpt at www.youtube.com, search "Concerto Barocco") and the modern dance choreographer Paul Taylor (*Esplanade*, 1975, www.youtube.com, search "Paul Taylor's Esplanade"), among dozens of others. Each work is a masterpiece. Likewise, Claude Debussy's (1862–1918) dreamy and impressionistic *Prelude to the Afternoon of a Faun* (1894) has been tackled at least as often: Vaslav Nijinsky's 1912 version is foremost on the list, of course (excerpt at www.youtube.com, search "Afternoon of a Faun"), but Eliot Feld's (b. 1942) *Evoe* (1991), Jerome Robbins's *Afternoon of a Faun* (1953, excerpt at www. youtube.com, search "Jacques D'Amboise dances Afternoon of a Faun"), and Graeme Murphy's (b. 1950) *Late Afternoon of a Faun* (1987) offer up three more singular visions, well worth viewing.

In addition to the music as inspiration, sometimes it is the story or a theme, an idea or even an image, that moves choreographers. Ancient Greek tragedian Euripides's (c. 480–406 BC) *Medea* (431 BC), the story that embodies the phrase (from William Congreve, 1697) "hell hath no fury like a woman scorned," has spawned at least as many dance versions as theatrical interpretations. Perhaps the most famous one remains Martha Graham's choreography to a commission of *Medea's Meditation and Dance of Vengeance* from her friend, composer Samuel Barber. Graham created her harrowing, Jungian-inflected ballet *Cave of the Heart* (1946, excerpt at www.youtube.com, search "Cave of the Heart/Medea Solo"), illustrated by Japanese-American sculptor Isamu Noguchi's extraordinary set/dress of metal. But the versions of *Medea* by Jennifer Wood, (2005), for her Houston-based company Suchu Dance (f. 1998), José Granero (1936–2006) set on the Royal Spanish National Ballet (1988) or Michael Smuin (1938–2007) for the San Francisco Ballet (1977), are no less driven by that ancient tragedy's power.

The themes of war, murder, death, politics, evil vs. good, innocence lost, and horror have been frequently investigated in works of art. For every visual arts response to war such as the German Expressionist visual artist Otto Dix, with his grotesque yet heartbreaking *Wounded Soldier* (1916, http://cs.nga.gov.au/Detail.cfm?IRN=128588), or Pablo Picasso's masterpiece *Guernica* (1937, http://www.artchive.com/artchive/P/picasso/guernica.jpg.html), there are such noteworthy dance works as the seminal anti-war *The Green Table* (1932, excerpt at www.youtube.com, search "Intro thru beginning of The Farewells"), by the German expatriate Kurt Jooss (1901–1979), Antony Tudor's *Echoing of Trumpets* (1963), and Daniel Nagrin's two-hour solo, *The Peloponnesian War* (1968).

The Rite of Spring

Of all the versions of singular musical compositions and themes and narratives and ideas, Igor Stravinsky's heart-pounding *The Rite of Spring* (Le Sacre du Printemps) may be the epitome of choreographic inspiration. Commissioned by impresario Serge Diaghilev for his young dancer-choreographer Vaslav Nijinsky (1889–1950), the music and ballet premiered together on May 29, 1913, in Paris. Both artworks, the thirty-minute, one-act ballet and its score, hold pivotal places in the worlds of dance and music modernism—not least because that first performance ended in fistfights in the aisles, the choreographer's screaming counts from the wings, and the Paris police's attempt to restore order. Stravinsky's polyrhythmic, often dissonant, primitivism-inspired composition, accompanied by Nijinsky's shockingly turned-in legs, sharply angled elbows, and step-for-count phrasing in a dance set on a classical ballet company, literally tore the two art traditions asunder (www.youtube.com, search "Marie Rambert talks of assisting Vaslav Nijinsky with 'The Rite of Spring'").

A description of the composition from a purely musical perspective helps explain the fascination it has held for nearly 200 choreographers, at last count, by the year 2010:

> Stravinsky's music is harmonically adventurous, with an emphasis on dissonance for the purposes of color and musical energy. Rhythmically, it is similarly adventurous, with a number of sections having constantly changing time signatures and unpredictable off-beat accents. Stravinsky revitalizes rhythm in *The Rite of Spring* by using asymmetrical rhythm, percussive use of dissonance, polyrhythms, polytonality, layering of ostinati (repeated ideas) and melodic fragments to create complex webs of interactive lines, and is influenced by primitivism (specifically, West African tribal art).[10]

Another description of the work confirms Wikipedia's analysis, and is entitled "Stravinsky's *Le Sacre* at 90," from the online *Classical Net*:

> From when Stravinsky began writing, the initial fate of Le Sacre was determined. The ballet's subject—pagan rites—demanded music that was melodically simple, sporadic, and immodest. Stravinsky held nothing back in conveying a primitive atmosphere and revolutionized many facets of music all at once. Besides rhythmic modulation with great frequency, Le Sacre is based on melodic figures repeated many times. The string sections are often used like percussion instruments and the winds [are] used at extremely low and high registers. The percussion section, particularly the tympani, sounds more fit for a tribal meeting than a concert. What results is a work of unwavering tension, building to a final climax that leaves both performer and listener exhausted.[11]

With the year 2013 marking the original production's centennial, it remains clear that choreographers who have tackled this score would not have even tried had not the composer's music been so compelling:

> [T]he full physicality of this composer's sound [is astounding]—the airy resonance of his soft harmonies, the sucker punch of his nastier chords, the nonstop tremor of his rhythms. Looking around at the audience during the Miller festival, I noticed how many listeners were bopping gently in their seats. Meanwhile, the best of today's younger performers...find no difficulties in this music; whether they have studied Steve Reich's "Music for 18 Musicians" by day or danced to hip-hop by night, they are inheritors of Stravinsky's rhythmic DNA. In all, the composer emerged as...more visceral, more emotionally revealing.[12]

The approximate re-creation of Nijinsky's original ballet by choreographer and dance historian Millicent Hodson (b. 1945), which was set on the Joffrey Ballet (f. 1956) in 1987 [www.youtube.com, search "Vaslav Nijinsky–The Rite of Spring (reconstructed)–Parts 1, 2 and 3"] and revived on the company in 2009, was reviewed by Alastair Macaulay in *The New York Times* during its more recent production. The piece apparently still maintains a pivotal place in dance modernism:

> Dance historians should see it as Nijinsky's response to his choreographic predecessors Lev Ivanov [1834–1901] and Michel Fokine [1880–1942]. The frozen inward-facing rings, asymmetrically arranged, with which he first shows his tribe are surely his modernist answer to the more symmetrical and Romantic rings (also inward-facing) with which Ivanov in 1895 arranged the swan-maidens in Act IV of "Swan Lake." In 1909 Fokine staged for Diaghilev a famous scene of Romantic primitivism in the Polovtsian Dances of Borodin's opera "Prince Igor," with designs by (Nicholas) Roerich [1874–1947], who went on, in 1913, to design this "Sacre." The better you know the Russian ballets that preceded it, the more you sense how Nijinsky was taking other men's ideas and doing new things with them.[13]

The initial raging controversy over Nijinsky's performance ended quickly—or did it? For readers interested in comparing choreographic approaches to this powerful musical composition, a number of these singular visions are discussed throughout the remainder of this book at the times of their premieres.

Too often overlooked or merely not spoken of in the same light as her brother Vaslav is dancer-choreographer Bronislava Nijinska (1891–1972). Her best-known works were also created for Diaghilev's Ballets Russes and include *Les Noces* (The Wedding, 1923), *Le Train Bleu* (The Blue Train, 1924), and *Les Biches* (1925). They are regularly re-created for companies the world over. Rhythmically complex (like her brother's work), Nijinska's choreography was also architecturally crisp and structurally rigorous. Geometric, sharply angled movements and tableaux are systematically interlaced with typically precise ensemble work. (See an excerpt of *Les Noces* at www.youtube.com, search "Stravinsky's 'Les Noces'—The Royal Ballet, Part 1/3.") [Also see www.youtube.com, search "Le Train Bleu / The Blue Train / Diaghilev, Cocteau (1 part) T-portal.vu"]

Jerome Robbins

Born Jerome Rabinowitz (October 11, 1918 New York, New York–July 29, 1998, New York, New York), is one of the twentieth-century's most loved choreographers. He is best remembered for his first dance, *Fancy Free* (1944, www.youtube.com, search "Jerome Robbins Fancy Free.mp4"), about three sailors on 24-hour leave in Manhattan, originally set on (American) Ballet Theatre and expanded into the Broadway musical *On the Town* later that year, and his direction/choreography for the still resonating Broadway (1957) and Hollywood (1961) *West Side Story*, which was originally to have taken place on the East Side detailing the conflicts between Catholics and Jews, not Hispanics and Whites. (The film celebrated its 50th anniversary in 2011 with a 3 DVD/Blue-ray disk set loaded with extras.)

Robbins's training in acting, ballet, jazz, vernacular, Spanish, Oriental, and modern dance allowed him great latitude with his choreography. "This [mix] often gives his works a likeable and immediate sense of fraternal easiness and marks him out as the most accessible of modern ballet choreographers."[14] That passage was written in 1988, and it still holds true today.

In addition to the number of classical ballets that he created for New York City Ballet (he joined the NYCB at the age of 30 in 1948 as Assistant Artistic Director) and his many hit musicals (*The King and I, Gypsy*, and *Fiddler on the Roof*, to name just three), he choreographed an almost equal number of works that must rightly be called contemporary in both tone and content. *Glass Pieces* (1983; excerpts set on the Pacific Northwest Ballet at www.youtube.com, search "Jerome Robbins' Glass Pieces"), set to Philip Glass' mesmerizing music, is still fresh to first-time viewers, so full of the movements wed to the classical ballet lexicon; the plotless *Dances at a Gathering* (1969; www.youtube.com, search "New York City Ballet MOVES: Dances at a Gathering"), reminiscent of Balanchine's neoclassicism; the mimicry of insects of *The Cage* (1951; www.youtube.com, search "laetitia pujol the cage"), inspired by the oddly tempo-ed Stravinsky composition, *Basler*; and the transcendent *Antique Epigraphs* (1984; www.youtube.com, search "Balanchine/Robbins"), to Debussy. Robbins's work "became increasingly less reliant on narrative [and] embraced a wide range of styles and moods,"[15] making a place for himself beyond ballet and musicals in the contemporary dance world.

Merce Cunningham

Merce Cunningham (April 16, 1919, Centralia, Washington–July 26, 2009, New York, New York) is often considered the father of the postmoderns.

He completely redefined dance throughout his very full ninety years, right up to the end of the first decade of the 21st century. (The choreographer determined that the dancers he personally trained in his Merce Cunningham Dance Company, founded in 1953, could tour until the end of 2011 showcasing a total of 18 repertory pieces as part of the Legacy Plan, at which time the company officially disbanded; www.merce.org) Through hundreds of dance pieces such as *Minutiae* (1954), *Septet* (1964, excerpt of Cunningham himself performing with his company at www.youtube.com, search "Merce Cunningham Septet 1964"), *RainForest* (1968), and *Points in Space* (1986, excerpt at www.youtube.com, search "Merce Cunningham's Points in Space"), which was filmed in its entirety by his longtime collaborator, the filmmaker and video artist Charles Atlas (b. 1958), Cunningham constructed a wholly new approach to movement by deliberately incorporating the element of chance or randomness into his creations. More recently, as in the famed *Biped* (1999, www.youtube.com, search "Merce Cunningham Biped"), the choreographer developed movement phrases through his use of the computer program DanceForms.

Cunningham's dances never attempt to fulfill any preconceived poetic sense of natural beauty, but instead, express the ideas of ever-changing spatial centers, randomness, chaos, and multiple strands of activity occurring in what seem to be no particular order. Yet the connections between these elements exist due to physics, Eastern philosophies, and his audience's states of mind at the time, which usually involve a natural inclination to make sense out of whatever it is they are experiencing. Cunningham knew that no matter how his dances were structured, each would create a unique atmosphere, and audience members could interpret that atmosphere any way they chose to. He was most interested in that process for himself, too. Near the end of his life he stated, "In doing it, you find out something else about dance, something that you never thought of before. I always look forward to seeing what that will be in [the next] circumstance."[16]

Of course, Cunningham worked with exquisite dancers who received some or much of their technical skill through his classes. With such "ideal" bodies and flawless movements, audiences could accept or reject Cunning-ham's postmodern ideas while still believing they were seeing excellent dance. Cunningham's movement vocabulary—whether random, generated by a computer, or created in the studio—was not so different from what developed from the *danse d'école* (the historically rich academic style of classical ballet), although he used all levels, including work on the floor. His work also often used straight legs and the kind of balletic turn-out in the hips and legs that allowed for quick side-to-side movement, lending the dances a peculiar but often intriguing feeling of mixed genres.

Like Hawkins's association with Lucia Dlugoszewski (1931–2000), Cunningham was closely allied to a musician/composer: the avant-garde John Cage (1912–1992), who created sound and music accompaniment, giving an extraordinary atmospheric life to his collaborator's unique philosophy.

To this day, even after his death and the company's final performances, people—particularly frustrated first-timers—still walk out during Cunningham performances. The choreographer used the full range of spatial possibilities, including keeping dancers partially hidden, tucked away in corners, flitting here and there, or exiting offstage at the most unexpected of times; they rarely stayed front and center for long. To further challenge his audience (and dancers), Cunningham almost always commissioned composers to create the accompaniment—which included city street sounds and tree branch rustlings more often than any conventional sounds of music—*independently from the choreography*. Sometimes the score and commissioned sets all came together for the first time at the last dress rehearsal or on opening night. The dancers, audiences, choreographer, composer, and visual artists would all experience the piece together, pristine in its newness. The "only commonality between [the dance's elements] is that they happened at the same time."[17] This was a deliberate decision with all the artists willing accomplices, and it kept everyone quite on their toes and in the moment (or out the door).

Take a look at the www.youtube.com, search "Merce Cunningham—Beachbirds for Camera (1993) Part 2," a 1993 dance filmed in 2007 that is typical of the Merce Cunningham Dance Company style. See for yourself whether the sounds do or do not coincide with the movements of the camera and dancers—a dreamscape that huge fan Alastair Macaulay from *The New York Times* calls a wonder-filled layering of "simultaneous multiplicities"[18]— or how the costumes, in black and white during the first half and color for the second, work for this piece.

Influenced directly and obliquely by anthropology, nature studies (particularly of animals), the decentralized space of Abstract Expressionism (a primarily American post-World War II visual arts movement), Zen Buddhism (origins circa 7th century CE), and both ballet and modern dance, Cunningham is rightly placed equally alongside dance theater visionaries such as Duncan, Diaghilev, Graham, and Balanchine by Alastair Macaulay in his July 28, 2009 *New York Times* eulogy:

> He was American modern dance's equivalent of Nijinsky: the long neck, the animal intensity, the amazing leap…His animal-like qualities of grace and intensity were as remarkable as his jump. His dance vocabulary owed much to both Graham modern dance (especially its use of the back) and to ballet (especially its use of the legs and feet)…. Once, discovering that the company was booked to perform in a space without a proscenium arch, Mr. Cunningham decided to arrange a one-off anthology of separate sections of choreography, using costumes and music different from those of their original contexts. This became a new and important Cunningham genre, the Event. Events provoked questions about how choreography could look when decontextualized and recontextualized. How would a solo from a 2002 work look between a duet from a 1982 work and a 1997 quartet, all before a 1953 Rauschenberg [1925–2008] and in newly designed costumes?[19]

Ocean, a 90-minute Cage collaboration premiered two years after the composer's death in 1994, was re-presented in September 2008 in perhaps the choreographer's most unique venue—150 feet beneath the earth's surface within the granite Rainbow Quarry near St. Cloud, Minnesota. One hundred and fifty musicians propelled Cage's shore-bird-screeching, seal-barking, chance-determined electronic composition simultaneously upwards and around the thirteen dancers and fifteen hundred audience members. Late "in the dance, the surrounding quarry is suddenly illuminated, a startling shift in scale that transforms the concentric circles of *Ocean* into an archaeological dig."[20] Some insights into the piece can be gained from watching Cunningham himself talk about the work alongside Charles Atlas, with excerpts from the work, at www.youtube.com, search "Merce Cunningham Ocean, Minnesota 2008."

Many dance critics have admired, understood and carefully explained Cunningham to new and veteran audiences over the years. Alastair Macaulay's July 8, 2008, *New York Times* review of Cunningham's Dia:Beacon Event is worth reading in its entirety because it provides audiences with one of the clearest accounts of this extraordinary choreographer. The following is an excerpt from that article:

> To return to Merce Cunningham's choreography, no matter how good or bad any other dance you may have been watching of late, is to have the palate cleansed. At first you just see movement, much of which

is neither pretty nor obviously expressive, but it's always substantial, complex, arresting.

The dancers seem driven as they set about fulfilling its rigorous demands, and so you are drawn into its challenges. Soon you start to feel how the dance features you're watching add up to a style, even though the idioms before you keep changing. And as you sense a style, you recognize aspects of expression. Meanwhile, you're being led to attend to basic dance elements with a concentration that makes you feel them as if for the first time….

The virtues…in Mr. Cunningham's work have all been classical virtues, and the classicism of his work has been widely discussed for many years. Often, though, it seems as if nobody is keener to be anticlassical than Mr. Cunningham, who has said, "It's when movement starts to be awkward that it becomes interesting."[21]

What has happened to all of Cunningham's dancers after the last performance of the company on December 31, 2011? If the notion of dispersal in the dance world stays true to its nature, they will be as Diaghilev's "offspring" after his passing in 1929—newness will mix with homage in recognizable and subtle ways for decades. "We mourn the artist we scarcely had the chance to know, who kept moving on to the next idea before we had caught up with the last one,"[22] wrote Macaulay in his extended goodbye at year's end of 2011.

In late 2011, Darsie Alexander, chief curator at the Walker Art Center in Minneapolis, Minnesota, planned a symposium in spring 2013 that would "take an integrated look at all of Cunningham's work" in a way that would be an important "moment when we're going to be serious about writing him into a chapter of art history."[23]

Pearl Primus

As radical and challenging as his work could be, Cunningham's training with a myriad of techniques kept him within (or at least on the edge of) the Western formalist tradition. Born seven months after Cunningham and half a world away, the powerhouse dancer/choreographer Pearl Primus (November 29, 1919, Port of Spain, Trinidad–October 29, 1994, New Rochelle, New York) devoted herself "to research into West Indian, African, and other native dance forms, [believing] in dance as a means of fostering cultural understanding."[24] Although she also focused on issues of racial prejudice and oppression, training in modern dance with The New Dance Group in the early 1940s, it has been repeatedly reported that Primus could jump straight up a full five feet, and performed with tremendous dance energy and force (www.criticalpast.com/). Readers should see her 1943 solo *Strange Fruit* (referenced at www.youtube.com, search "AFRS 310 Pearl Primus") about the lynching of blacks in the Deep South, on the American Dance Festival's *Dancing in the Light: Six Dances by African-American Choreographers* 2007 DVD (www.kultur.com.) set on the Philadelphia Dance Company (affectionately called Philadanco; f. 1970, http://www.philadanco.org). The dance is "celebrated for its innovation, creativity and preservation of predominantly African-American traditions in dance" (www.philadanco.org), and provides the contemporary viewer with a glimpse into Primus's physical and philosophic energy.

Dance critic Anna Kisselgoff, in her June 19, 1988, *New York Times* article "Pearl Primus Rejoices in the Black Tradition," speaks to the potency of this particular dance, followed by a searing quote by the choreographer: "Miss Primus took the daring step of identifying herself with a white woman in a lynch mob. The solo is danced by this woman. 'The dance begins as the last person begins to leave the lynching ground,' Miss Primus said, 'and the horror of what she has seen grips her, and she has to do a smooth, fast roll away from that burning flesh.'"[25] Trying to channel the feelings onstage of an ethnic majority woman at the lynching (and subsequent burning) of a minority man in 1940s America was far from the conventional classical ballet repertory being developed at the time...but fits right in with many other provocative modern sensibilities being explored both then and now.

Selected Videos/DVDs/Films

Merce Cunningham
Cage/Cunningham (1991), Dance Horizons.
Cunningham Dance Technique: Elementary, Intermediate (1985/1987), Insight Media.
Merce Cunningham: A Lifetime of Dance (2000), Amazon.com.
Points in Space (1986), Dance Horizons.

Sophie Maslow
The New Dance Group Gala Historical Concert (2009), Dance Horizons.

Alwin Nikolais
German Lineage in Modern Dance: Mary Wigman, Dore Hoyer, Hanya Holm, Alwin Nikolais, Murray Louis (2012), Dance Horizons.
The World of Alwin Nikolais (1996), five volumes, Dance Horizons.

Pearl Primus

Dancing in the Light: Six Dances by African-American Choreographers (2007), Kultur.

The Rite of Spring

The Search for Nijinsky's "Rite of Spring" (2004), Classical Video Rarities.

Anna Sokolow

The New Dance Group Gala Historical Concert (2009), Dance Horizons.

Jerome Robbins

Jerome Robbins: Something to Dance About (2008), Dance Horizons.

Jerome Robbins's NY Export: Opus Jazz (2010), Factory 25.

Tribute to Jerome Robbins (En Sol, In the Night, The Concert by Robbins, *Triade* by Benjamin Millepied) (2012), Dance Horizons.

West Side Story (1961), Amazon.com.

Notes

1   Wikipedia, http://en.wikipedia.org/wiki/Anna Sokolow.

2   Claudia La Rocco, *The New York Times*, February 16, 2010, http://www.nytimes.com/2010/02/16/arts/dance/16limon.html?ref=dance.

3   Allen Robertson and Donald Hutera, *The Dance Handbook* (Boston: G. K. Hall, 1988), p. 82.

4   On the other hand, film director/choreographer Rob Marshall's handling of bits and pieces of movement in movies such as the 2002 Academy Award–winning *Chicago* and the 2009 *Nine*, or Baz Luhrmann's *Moulin Rouge!* (2001), may very well express our society's difficulty with extended attention spans—although such "visual bites" may tease more interest out of a viewer.

5   Alastair Macaulay, "A Kinetic Innovator, Plumbing the Surreal," *The New York Times*, January 28, 2010, http://www.nytimes.com/2010/01/29/arts/dance/29choreography.html?ref=dance.

6   Julie Bloom, "On Dance: Alwin Nikolais at 100," *The New York Times*, April 30, 2010, http://artsbeat.blogs.nytimes.com/2010/04/30/on-dance-alwin-nikolais-at-100/.

7   Rose Eichenbaum, *Masters of Movement: Portraits of America's Great Choreographers* (Washington, D. C.: Smithsonian Books, 2004), p. 101.

8   Ibid., p. 103.

9   Modifications to the scenery, costumes, sequences of steps, and more are quite common and acceptable even in interpretations that carry the "traditional" label.

10   Wikipedia, http://en.wikipedia.org/wiki/The_Rite_of_Spring.

11   Paul-John Ramos, 2003, http://www.classical.net/music/comp.lst/works/stravinsky/lesacre90.php.

12   Alex Ross, "Rite of Spring," *The New Yorker*, May 19, 2008, p. 83.

13   Alastair Macaulay, "Eternal Spring Rites, With the Look of 1913," *The New York Times*, February 19, 2009, http://www.nytimes.com/2009/02/20/arts/dance/20joff.html?pagewanted=1&ref=dance.

14   Robertson and Hutera, *The Dance Handbook*, p. 122.

15   Debra Craine and Judith Mackrell, eds., *The Oxford Dictionary of Dance* (Oxford, England: Oxford University Press, 2010; 2nd ed.), p. 375.

16   www.youtube.com, http://www.youtube.com/watch?v=1aBJdHnv5tM.

17   Craine and Mackrell, *The Oxford Dictionary of Dance,* p. 113.

18   Alastair Macaulay, "A Varied Dreamscape That's Also a Farewell," *The New York Times*, December 10, 2011, http://www.nytimes.com/2011/12/09/arts/dance/merce-cunningham-dance-company-in-roaratorio-review.html?pagewanted=all.

19   Alastair Macaulay, "Merce Cunningham, Dance Visionary, Dies," *The New York Times*, July 28, 2009, http://www.nytimes.com/2009/07/28/arts/dance/28cunningham.html?_r=1&ref=alastair_macaulay.

20   Linda Shapiro, "Merce Cunningham's *Ocean*," *Dance Magazine*, December 2008, 114.

21   Alastair Macaulay, "Walking To and Fro to Eye Dance, Sky and Sculpture," *The New York Times*, July 8, 2008, http://www.nytimes.com/2008/07/08/arts/dance/08cunn.html?_r=1.

22   Alastair Macaulay, "Space Travelers and Dragonflies, in Galaxies of Life and Death," *The New York Times*, December 10, 2011, http://www.nytimes.com/2011/12/10/arts/dance/merce-cunningham-troupe-in-biped-at-bam-review.html?pagewanted=all.

23   Hilarie M. Sheets, "Backdrops, Blobs, Pods, and Props," *ARTnews*, November 2011, p. 108.

24   Craine and Mackrell, *The Oxford Dictionary of Dance,* p. 358.

25   http://www.nytimes.com/1988/06/19/arts/dance-view-pearl-primus-rejoices-in-the-black-tradition.html?ref=anna_kisselgoff.

Chapter Four
1920 to 1930

**Anna Halprin, Gerald Arpino and Robert Joffrey,
Roland Petit, Glen Tetley, Maurice Béjart**

Anna Halprin

Unlike Cunningham, who chose chance over structure to help determine choreography—which often looked like improvisation (but was not)—Anna Halprin (Anna Schuman, b. July 13, 1920, Winnetka, Illinois), in her 10th decade, continues to rely frequently on improvisation in support of her collaborative dances. Responding to a diagnosis of cancer in 1971, Halprin used dance exploration (she called them "movement rituals") to develop healing and creative empathy techniques that addressed real life issues such as terminal illness and the need for community.

In a 2010 film called *Breath Made Visible* (theatrical trailer at www.youtube. com, search "Breath Made Visible—Final Theatrical Trailer"), director Ruedi Gerber splices events throughout the arc of Halprin's then-89 years with the choreographer's own words: "I danced for the fun of it. I danced to rebel. I danced with my children. I danced for social justice. If I was going to dance, I wanted to dance about real things that were real in my life. We broke as many barriers as we possibly could. I've always said, 'Dance is the breath made visible.' Anybody can do it. I don't care whether they've had any training at all."[1]

Halprin understood the relationship between psychology and dance—and the fact that "anybody can do it." That understanding foretold the postmodern movement's ideas, beginning in the 1960s, of performances in public spaces and the use of vernacular movement (see Chapter 8).

A 2009 site-specific work, *Spirit of Place*, gives the viewer a good sense of the choreographer's approach to movement and the "everyday": it is a performance with more than a dozen dancers harmonically singing, slowly walking, and proffering open and closed hand gestures in sensitive relation to the tiered, stone-laden topography, natural bird songs, and occasional dog barks of Stern Grove park in San Francisco (www.youtube.com, search "Anna Halprin—Spirit of Place").

Halprin's dances are gently but fiercely engaged with the world's concerns. *Planetary Dance*, which originated in 1981 but became a yearly event led by Halprin herself, had a particularly focused theme in 2008—climate change:

> [It] is a powerful springtime event of communities of people around the world who gather annually to bring concerns and contemporary issues into the context of spiritual life. Because of the global concerns regarding our planet's climatic condition, the theme of the 2008 Marin County Planetary Dance is *Make Peace with the Planet*. As is tradition, the Marin County Planetary Dance begins at dawn, with a ceremony on the top of Mt. Tamalpais. It continues to Santos Meadow, near Muir Woods, where the centerpiece of the daylong event, the Earth Run, takes place. A community feast follows. People of all ages, ethnicities, walks of life and physical abilities are invited to participate. (www.planetarydance.org)

The work came into existence because of a typical Halprin rejoinder to a serious problem: "Women hiking on Mt. Tamalpais and other trails were being stalked and murdered. In response to the terror, Anna Halprin led a group of people to the Mountain to reclaim it through a ritual of dance, music and prayer. Soon after the ceremony, the killer was captured."[2]

The borders between movement and real life become very blurry—or better, wholly permeable—in Halprin's art (www.annahalprin.org). Her story is that of a utilitarian art; local, beautiful, and warmly personal to those who participate.

Gerald Arpino and Robert Joffrey

Gerald Arpino (Gennaro Peter Arpino, January 14, 1923, Staten Island, New York–October 29, 2008, Chicago, Illinois) and Robert Joffrey (Abdulla Jaffa Anver Bey Khan, December 24, 1930, Seattle, Washington–March 25, 1988, New York, New York) are synonymous with The Joffrey Ballet (f. 1956). Arpino was always the primary choreographer of the company, which moved from New York City to Chicago in 1995 (www.joffrey.com). As with Béjart's work (discussed later in this chapter), ballets by Arpino and Joffrey could be "sleek and sensual, but are often thin and transparent."[3]

The rock ballet *Trinity*, from 1970 (excerpt at www.youtube.com, search "Gerald Arpino's ballet Trinity"), became their signature work, although Arpino's 1993 full-length *Billboards*, to music by Prince (Prince Rogers Nelson; b. 1958), remains a close second. The company's "commitment to taking world-class, artistically vibrant work to a broad and varied audience" while presenting "a unique repertoire encompassing masterpieces of the past and cutting-edge works" is a fair assessment of their mission (www.joffrey.org). Examples of fulfilling this mission are reviving Jooss's seminal *The Green Table* in 1967, the reconstruction of Nijinsky's *Rite of Spring* in 1987 and its 2011–2012 season presenting classics like Petipa's *Don Quixote* alongside contemporary works by choreographers with currency such as William Forsythe (see Chapter 6) and Christopher Wheeldon (see Chapter 9).

Roland Petit

Best known for his 1946 "*Le Jeune Homme et la Mort* (The Young Man and Death)," made famous by Mikhail Baryshnikov (b. 1948) over the opening credits of director Taylor Hackford's (b. 1944) dance film, *White Nights* (1985), French dancer/choreographer Roland Petit (January 13, 1924, Villemomble, France–July 10, 2011, Geneva, Switzerland) was not only a "product of the rigorous classical school [but] a consummate showman… just as happy working in revues, film [*Hans Christian Andersen*, 1952; *Daddy Long Legs*, 1955; *Anything Goes*, 1956], and television."[4] The entire psychological ballet from Hackford's film can be viewed at www.youtube.com, search "Baryshnikov—Le Jeune Homme et la Mort, Complete." It is typical Petit: "sexually brazen [and] explicit,"[5] and an "archetypal piece of postwar existentialism about a suicidal, lovelorn artist."[6]

Many of Petit's ballets qualify for the contemporary world's "cutting edge," especially *Le Jeune Homme* and his other ribald hit, *Carmen* (1949, watch a 2008 clip with Alessandra Ferri and Laurent Hilaire at www.youtube.com, search "Carmen—Roland Petit"), which deliberately grated against tradition's sometimes idealized sensibilities through its use of overt miming of lovemaking. Petit's theatrical predisposition to shock may be the primary reason so many of his works are not kept in the repertory of ballet companies beyond their commissioned premieres. Who can say? One shock might be enough!

Anna Kisselgoff's *New York Times* eulogy rightly noted that "American critics often called him chic [and even] French critics began to find him superficial. Yet after he turned to creating ballets based on opera and literature, he could surprise (www.youtube.com, search "Notre-Dame de Paris – Ballet by Roland Petit part 1")…Like Maurice Béjart, Mr. Petit sought to reach a wide audience. Yet he had a more solid choreographic foundation, and his early ballets work on an artistic level still valid today."[7]

Glen Tetley

Iconoclast Glen Tetley (February 3, 1926, Cleveland, Ohio–January 26, 2007, Palm Beach, Florida) successfully (for himself) and unsuccessfully (for many early separatist purists) merged his modern training from Hanya Holm and Martha Graham with his ballet study with Antony Tudor into his own fused style. Tetley always used 20th century compositions, a radical notion for ballet in his day. He is best known for his piece *Pierrot Lunaire* (1962), in which he took inspiration for his *commedia dell-arte* characters from the expressionist composer Arnold Schoenberg's (1874–1951) atonal song-cycle. The piece was performed on, around, and within an extraordinary scaffold built by famed Russian immigrant costume and set designer Rouben Ter-Arutunian (1920–1992).

> [*Pierrot Lunaire*]…epitomizes Tetley's style. Legs and feet [are] balletically elongated, torso arching with Graham fullness…the whole body now acknowledging tension, now soaring into release. Although today's choreographers are constantly breaking down the boundaries between genres, decades ago Tetley's pioneering fusion provoked disapproval from certain quarters. [He became more accepted in Europe than in the United States because of this early radicalism.] But he never doubted the rightness of his duality. "I have always existed in both worlds," he said, "and never felt them to be anything but one world."[8]

Mutations (1970), co-choreographed by Tetley and Hans Van Manen (b. 1932) at the Netherlands Dans Theater, was likewise scandalous due to its nudity, another radical departure for the ballet world. In 1974 Tetley created his own *Rite of Spring* for the Munich State Opera Ballet, transforming "the original woman's role as the Chosen One to a man's, sacrificing him midway through the dance rather than at the end, and then [having] him reincarnated to symbolize the rebirth of spring and the continuous cycle of life"[9] An excerpt from his evocative 1982 *The Firebird* (www.youtube.com, search "El Pájaro de Fuego.wmv") shows Tetley's mastery at mixing classical and contemporary movements. If one had to credit one choreographer with being the "Father of Fusion," it would have to be Tetley.

Maurice Béjart

Another European, Maurice Béjart (January 1, 1927, Marseilles, France–
November 22, 2007, Lausanne, Switzerland) was trained in ballet, but as
a choreographer he incorporated a populist theatricality and frequently
titillating eroticism, the latter either loved or hated by his audiences. Most
famous for his simplistic but frenzied *Bolero* [1960; www.youtube.com, search
"Maurice Béjart–Boléro (2002)"], set to French Impressionist composer
Maurice Ravel's (1875–1937) even more famous one-movement orchestral
piece of the same name (1928), Béjart came to the world's attention in
Belgium when he created his own *Rite of Spring* in 1959. This was a piece
"in which his dancers—clad in sleek, shiny tights—created an erotic aura with
impulsive, natural movements that became a standard of his interpretations."[10]

> Overtly sexual in the piece, Béjart…segregated the sexes into two acts,
> with the first featuring a male ensemble, replaced in the latter half
> of the ballet by an all-female cast. These large unified groups act as a
> prelude to the erotic unison that finalizes the rite with the dance of
> an intertwined male/female couple. In keeping with Béjart's quasi-
> philosophical approach, this sexual act is seen as the ultimate sacrifice.[11]

One can view the last five minutes of this ballet in a 2007 YouTube posting,
at www.youtube.com, search "Igor Stravinsky 'The Rite of Spring.'"

Selected Videos/DVDs/Films

Gerald Arpino and Robert Joffrey

Joffrey: Mavericks of American Dance (2012), Lakeview Films.

Maurice Béjart

L'amour–La Danse (2006), Amazon.com.
Béjart! Did You Say Béjart? (2012), Dance Horizons.

Anna Halprin

Breath Made Visible: Anna Halprin (2011), Projektor Film.

Roland Petit

Clavigo (2007), Dance Horizons.
La Dame de Pique & Passacaille (2005), Dance Horizons.
Le Jeune Homme at La Mort and Carmen (2005), Dance Horizons.

Glen Tetley

Stravinsky: The Firebird/Royal Danish Ballet (2002), Kultur.

Notes

1   http://www.youtube.com/watch?v=2KQnWkdgvsU.

2   www.youtube.com, search "Planetary Dance with Anna Halprin: Make Peace with the Planet."

3   Allen Robertson and Donald Hutera, *The Dance Handbook* (Boston: G. K. Hall, 1988), p. 164.

4   Debra Craine and Judith Mackrell, eds., *The Oxford Dictionary of Dance* (Oxford, England: Oxford University Press, 2010, 2nd ed.), p. 349.

5   Ibid, p. 349.

6   Ibid, p. 349.

7   Anna Kisselgoff, "Roland Petit, Choreographer, Dies at 87; Conquered Ballet Taboos and Hollywood," *The New York Times,* July 10, 2011, http://www.nytimes.com/2011/07/11/arts/dance/roland-petit-choreographer-is-dead-at-87.html.

8   Glen Tetley: Innovative Choreographer Who Fused Ballet and Modern Dance," *The Independent*, February 12, 2007, http://www.independent.co.uk/news/obituaries/glen-tetley-436066.html.

9   R. M. Campbell, "'Rite of Spring' is Fertile with Challenges for its Dancers," *Seattle Post-Intelligencer,* January 28, 2005, http://seattlepi.nwsource.com/classical/209664_clas28.html.

10 Robertson and Hutera, *The Dance Handbook*, p. 119.

11 Marisa C. Hayes, "Rites of Artistic Identity," *The Dance Insider,* http://www.danceinsider.com/f2008/f0627_2.html, 2008.

Chapter Five
1930 to 1940

Donald McKayle, Paul Taylor, Alvin Ailey,
New Dance Group, The 92nd Street Y, Trisha Brown

The dancer/choreographers born in the 1930s were deeply affected by the Great Depression. Living through that era gave many of them a perspective that helped nurture some of the most potent works still seen in their companies (and others) today. Of course, the artists who were already at work during that time were also greatly impacted. While the new decade brought a severe economic downturn, another of America's great contributions to world culture continued to flourish: jazz.

Donald McKayle

Donald McKayle (b. July 6, 1930, New York, New York) has worked on Broadway musicals (*Sophisticated Ladies*, 1981), in film (*The Jazz Singer*, 1980), and on television (*Good Times*, 1974), and he brought a bluesy and jazzy energy to much of his choreography. Nevertheless, he is best known for his starkly truthful concert dance about Southern chain gangs, *Rainbow 'Round My Shoulder* (1959, an excerpt of the piece performed in 2007 by the Dayton Contemporary Dance Company, can be seen at www.youtube.com, search "Donald McKayle's Rainbow 'Round My Shoulder").

McKayle has adroitly filtered many of his time period's struggles (and sassiness) into dances for over fifty years. Still, to view his work only in those contexts limits one's understanding of his richer interests. "McKayle's sensibilities were [also] formed by the theatrical dance of the 1950s.

A humanistic choreographer, he uses narratives and deals with potent emotion conveyed through dramatic characters. At times his stories are specific to the African–American experience, as in his protest dance *Rainbow 'Round My Shoulder*, but his choreography is universal in its implications."[1]

Inspired as a teen by a Pearl Primus performance (it "caused a chemical reaction in me"),[2] McKayle's influences are many, ranging from his early work with the New Dance Group and its training in ballet, jazz, tap, Afro-Caribbean, Hindu, and Haitian forms, to his study with Graham, Cunningham, Sokolow, Maslow, and many others. Besides *Sophisticated Ladies*, his other Broadway productions include the underappreciated musical *Golden Boy* (1964), which was adapted from the 1937 Clifford Odets play that focused on an interracial romance during the Civil Rights era and starred Sammy Davis, Jr.

In February 2010, almost 80, McKayle was in residence for three days at Montclair State University in New Jersey resetting his groundbreaking 1951 work about inner-city children, *Games*, on college students. His personal interactions with them recall Anna Halprin's similar connections with her community—a strong modern tenet that holds true to this day.

Distinguished Visiting Professor of History Neil Baldwin sat in on the residency and recounted much of the experience:

> "What's *happening* with you?" McKayle asked Josh. "Why did you *do* that?" he asked Tiana. "Try to remember everything I have just told you," he said to Carlos. "I never watched you but *now* I'm watching you," he warned Lisa. "What are you *thinking*? Let me see some *attitude!*" he demanded of Julian. "You can't riff it without getting it," he said to Nick. "Don't tell me it's hard—I know it!" he admonished Greg. "Scream like you're in terror," he told Arielle. "I have to hear *every word*," he told Sandy and Jackie, the singers.
>
> And on many occasions McKayle would turn to the cast who were not rehearsing, and sharply remind them to pay attention to those who were: "You are part of an *ensemble*," McKayle said. "You have to realize that you are a *group*! Everybody has an action that is concurrent. I have to *see this dance in your bodies* otherwise the audience will not understand…"
>
> Over and over and over again, McKayle asked the students to go through the motions with an extreme sense of the reality of it all…
>
> When the choreographer intervenes, he brings with him the historical record built up since youth in East Harlem and the Bronx, and memories of those brownstone-lined streets. He observes the new generation portraying his remembered language and then—despite so-called "notations" and "interpretations" of bygone years, begins anew.

That's the theater of it all with McKayle's work, and I see it, now that I have literally *seen* it: He is most at home emotionally when he is out there, quite literally in action.

The theatricality of theater—the element that requires an audience for it to come alive—that's what Donald McKayle thrives upon. In this respect he himself is ageless and this work possesses a timeless quality, propelled forward into the future, not only by momentum of the accretions of the past, but also by the sheer fact that our dancers are the same age as McKayle was when he made *Games*.[3]

McKayle's importance to the dance world was cemented in 1999 when he was named by the Dance Heritage Coalition and the Library of Congress as one of thirty-plus modern dance choreographers, companies, and sponsors on the list of "America's Irreplaceable Dance Treasures: the First 100" (www.danceheritage.org).

Paul Taylor

A third generation modern dancer also marching to his own tune more than 80 years on (who is also on the above-mentioned Irreplaceable Dance Treasures list), Paul Taylor (b. July 29, 1930, Wilkinsburg, Pennsylvania) has a style of movement that employs a large vocabulary, and his dancers are capable of virtuoso feats. Taylor, however, has not pushed for quite as clearly marked a technique as many of his contemporaries, concentrating instead on "just making dances," as he often says. Taylor started his career as a true avant-garde upstart, with some dances done in total silence with minimal movement. One version, the 12-minute, wholly immobile *Epic*, received composer-author Louis Horst's infamous "blank review" on October 20, 1957, in the magazine *Dance Observer*: a word-free, two-column "empty" spot where the review should have been! Absurdly funny creatures, such as the dancers in the quirky *Three Epitaphs* from the previous year, were equally startling in their audacity during Taylor's early years.

Many of Taylor's later works from the 1960s through the present have become classics. Using music ranging from Handel, Beethoven, and Bach to The Andrews Sisters, a large number of his dances—musically sensitive, athletic, lyrical, and engaging—are more and more frequently requested for contemporary and classical ballet companies the world over.

Readers may want to take a look at an excerpt (or the entire dance) of the Paul Taylor Dance Company (f. 1954) performing in the powerful 2002

Promethean Fire (at www.youtube.com, search "Promethean Fire"). It has grandeur, majesty and a spiritual dimension—and is also quite simply one of his best dance works:

> Commissioned by the American Dance Festival to open its annual summer season at Duke University…*Promethean Fire*, as this premiere is called with unabashed cosmic flair, is set to Bach. It seems initially still another inspired Taylor work to Baroque music.
>
> On another level it may be Mr. Taylor's response to the September 11 attacks. The occasional images of despair, rage and physical collapse are direct, but to reduce the choreography to any literal interpretation is to lose the breadth of its formal beauty.
>
> Just the sheer architectonics of the complex and contrapuntal patterns overwhelm the eye. *Promethean Fire* is a big piece, spreading 16 dancers in black velvet with glistening trim into constantly reconfigured structures. They are building blocks in the human cathedral that Mr. Taylor constructs uncannily and perfectly with such powerful emotional resonance. To say *Promethean Fire* lifted the audience out of its seats on Saturday night at the Page Auditorium at Duke would not be an exaggeration…
>
> To appreciate the work mainly for its formal composition would be right. It is a plotless dance that pays tribute to Bach's architectonics. Yet Mr. Taylor has always argued that gesture and spatial composition are never devoid of dramatic meaning, and here he operates on several levels.
>
> The dancers are introduced as vertical forms facing the audience, hands at their sides. Santo Loquasto's [b. 1944] costumes are marvelously apt: black velvet tank suits with winding ribbons rendered brown and silvery under Jennifer Tipton's [b. 1937] superbly dramatic and half-dark lighting. The beginning of Bach's *Toccata and Fugue in D minor* breaks up the symmetry of this initial formation and spreads the dancers into horizontal lines that dominate the work. Waves of movement travel from one line to another, dancers crisscross or one line plays against the other…
>
> There are an unusual number of lifts for Mr. Taylor. But one interesting aspect is that with few exceptions, the movement is not new. The

Taylor idiom, with its curved arms, slides across the floor and images of women carried on a man's hips, is in full view...”[4]

Elsewhere, Taylor's wry sense of humor and ability to symbolize the troubled aspects of our society are evident in works such as *Big Bertha* (1970, about incest and dysfunctional families) and *Company B* (1991 about World War II; www.youtube.com, search "Backstage Pass–Company B").

> Like *Promethean Fire, Company B* is a masterpiece. Taylor reminds you that the fluffy old Andrews Sisters recordings accompanying *Company B* and the popular dances of the 1940s that still delight audiences were born out of the desperation of World War II. Behind these party people you see the silhouettes of men dying in battle and daring to love each other, and they complicate our responses. *Company B* is anything but a wallow in nostalgia.[5]

One can easily see the bouncy, graceful musicality in many of Taylor's signature works such as *Aureole* (1962) (www.youtube.com, search "Excerpts from Aureole"), *Esplanade* (1975) (www.youtube.com, search "Paul Taylor's Esplanade"), *Arden Court* (1981) (www.youtube.com, search "Paul Taylor Arden Court"), and *Roses* (1985), as well as his clear-sighted gaze at the harshness of life in *Last Look* (1985) and the elegiac *Promethean Fire*, noted above. Dance critic Alastair Macaulay addresses other characteristic elements of this extraordinary choreographer that bespeak personal and stylistic essentials—musicality, topicality, and poignancy—areas both consonant with and dissonant to conventional notions of modern dance:

> It is fair to say, though few have done so, that Mr. Taylor's work became the mainstream of American modern dance more than 35 years ago. For decades, Martha Graham, queen of psychological dance-drama, was the central figure of the genre. (Mr. Taylor had been a leading dancer with her company.) But starting with "Aureole" (1962, to Handel) and climaxing in "Esplanade" (1975, to Bach—Taylor's most perennially beloved work), he took much of Graham's modern dance vocabulary and linked it powerfully to the beat, the impulse and the current of music.
>
> The results had the force of revelation: *he rediscovered the danciness of modern dance.* [Italics added] In "Esplanade" his movements weren't from the Graham lexicon: they were just (just!) walks, runs, jumps,

slides, skids. Modern and postmodern dance folk had been talking about "democratic" dance, composed of movements anyone could do. Much earlier Isadora Duncan had composed dances largely of walks, runs, hops and skips. Mr. Taylor connected himself to both democrats and Duncan...

[But] much of his great talent is dark [and] disquieting... Running deliberately against composers' intentions, again and again over the decades, Mr. Taylor has repeatedly run the risk of being called unmusical. Instead, he has often revealed music anew. There are implications here that the musical world has not yet absorbed adequately: they have to do with musical expression, which, as nobody shows better than Mr. Taylor, so often turns out to be conveying much more than what the composer said he had in mind...

What other artist today makes poetic drama of such variety and eloquence? A Taylor season is a journey through one of the most singular and searching imaginations of our time.[6]

Taylor's delicate and democratic sensibility belies his size—he is a tall man (6' 4" in his prime) and he was an equally expansive performer, as are so many of his dancers. In Macaulay's understanding, the moderns can help the classicists learn more about their own musical powers than they themselves might be consciously aware of:[7] "Mr. Taylor takes music that its composers never intended for dancing and reveals, marvelously, its dance qualities."[8]

Life lessons are really what good dance can support, modern or otherwise, and Taylor is full of them. Even though the quote below has been taken down since this writer retrieved it, Taylor's company's 2010 website deftly defined his currency:

More than a half-century ago, Paul Taylor became the youngest member of the pantheon that created American modern dance. Now in his 80th year—an age when most artists' best work is behind them—Mr. Taylor is acclaimed for the vibrancy, relevance and power of his dances. As prolific as ever, he continues to offer cogent observations on life's complexities while tackling some of society's thorniest issues. He may propel his dancers through space for the sheer beauty of it, or use them to wordlessly illuminate war, spirituality, sexuality, morality and mortality. If, as Balanchine said, there are no mothers-in-law in ballet, there certainly are dysfunctional families, ex-lovers, fallen preachers, rapists, angels and insects in Taylor dance. (www.ptdc.org)

Brief Encounters, from 2009, is about those momentary chance meetings we all experience from time to time—and what hints of intimacy or fleeting sensory insights brush up against us when they occur. Set to Claude Debussy's playful, fast, and typically impressionistic 1908 composition *Children's Corner,* the men and women flit about in their countless serendipitous rendezvous clad only in tight black underwear, pulling us into their world in the way that good art always does:

> The more I watch "Brief Encounters," especially in the context of older dances, the more I see its derivations, and its use of "Children's Corner" is by no means Mr. Taylor's first use of Debussy. Yet not a jot of this work feels stale: it's a mysterious, highly sensuous piece that has its audience puzzling. I'm not alone: others find that after more than one viewing it has gotten deep under their skin. Its dancers seldom address the audience; we watch most of it as if from a great distance; and yet what occurs in it—brief encounters and casual exclusions that happen to young adults apparently for the first time—is often as real, as encompassing, as if it were happening to us, as if we were in its world.[9]

It has been said that Taylor wants to keep choreographing at least as long as one of his most influential teachers lived—the nonagenarian Martha Graham; if so, we shall be seeing his work until at least the year 2026.

Alvin Ailey

Born a year after Taylor was Alvin Ailey (January 5, 1931, Rogers, Texas– December 1, 1989, New York, New York), whose work combines elements of modern, jazz, and African dance with his own flamboyant and accessible aesthetic. He was well trained in the broad, physically powerful technique of Californian Lester Horton (1906–1953), whose "undiluted...approach... makes dizzyingly full use of the whole body, sending it in one single move from a spiraling torso sinking into the ground to a sudden rise again."[10] Ailey also danced on Broadway and studied the techniques of Graham, Humphrey, Holm, and others.

The dancer-choreographer established the Alvin Ailey American Dance Theater (AAADT, www.alvinailey.org) in 1958. This New York-based company brought the electricity of Broadway dance to the concert stage, and it remains an important part of the serious modern dance repertoire. Often accompanied by energizing music such as spiritual, blues, and jazz, Ailey and his successors have brought popular recognition to a company that continues to be in great demand worldwide. Ironically, his dances are so accessible that they have often been criticized as too "commercial."

Ailey's most famous piece, perhaps the most celebrated and infectious of all works of modern dance, is *Revelations* (1960), a large, many-segmented group testimony to Negro spirituals (excerpt at www.youtube.com, search "Alvin Ailey Revelations Sinnerman"). It remains as fresh today as when it premiered due in no small part to the living investment of the current Ailey dancers, several dance generations after the choreographer's death.

Ailey taught us that theatrical excitement can be generated in serious dance, and that we can demand the highest level of technique from modern dance. At The Ailey School, students perpetuate this vital choreographer's vision through the study of Horton- and Graham-based modern techniques, ballet, and jazz.

The company's 2008 50th anniversary milestone celebration involved some of the Ailey-Duke Ellington (1899–1974) jazz-modern-classicism collaborations, this time set to live music coordinated onstage by the virtuoso trumpeter Wynton Marsalis (b. 1961):

> It's a thrill to hear the big-band sound projecting through the theater. At some moments the brass section comes in like a massive wall of sound; at others its long chords hang in the air like clouds. Dan Nimmer (on piano) and Carlos Henriquez (on bass) are marvelous sources of rhythm. Ellington called his work "American music" rather than jazz, and throughout these two programs you hear how he took the American jazz roots of his style and pushed them into aspects of classicism, European modernism and more.
>
> This American-based diversity is one reason that Ellington was so often the composer to whose scores Ailey chose to choreograph. Both of these current Ailey-Ellington programs show the range of styles that Ailey could use. The hip-tilting jazz dance that is the main idiom of "Night Creature" (1974) is far from the controlled, modern-dance adagio of "Reflections in D" (1962), even though some of the same steps occur in both. In "Night Creature" you feel Ailey's dancers surfing the wave of the music; in "Reflections" you feel the male soloist rigorously, soberly countering it.[11]

In July 2011, the company's Artistic Director baton changed hands from Ailey legend Judith Jamison (b. 1943), who had taken over after the founder's

death in 1989, to Robert Battle (b. 1973; discussed in Chapter 9). The 2011–
2012 season augured well: among other pieces, Ohad Naharin's (discussed in
Chapter 7) stylized *Minus 16* (1999), Joyce Trisler's (1934–1979) eloquent
Journey (1958),[12] Paul Taylor's elegiac *Arden Court* (1981), and Battle's own
breakneck *Takademe* (1999), influenced by India's kathak style, all infused the
company, and the critics, with new enthusiasm.

New Dance Group

The year after Ailey was born, during perhaps the darkest period of The
Great Depression, a new group of dancers, began, largely in response to the
challenges the country was facing at that time, to move its collective voices—
and bodies—to a more hopeful and energizing beat. This New Dance Group
(NDG) was comprised of "…a group of artists and choreographers dedicated
to social change through dance and movement.…For just a dime, students
received an hour-long dance class, an hour of improvisation based on a social
theme, and an hour of discussion on social issues. Those members wishing to
choreograph followed two rules: dance about something important to you,
and create work so that the audience could understand the dance's thrust."[13]

In part because NDG's first three decades—by far the group's most
vibrant—live in the now distant past (especially in relation to so many other
current dance organizations that continue their tradition), NDG received little
recognition of its contributions until 1993. At that time, the American Dance
Guild held a retrospective gala concert showcasing over a dozen of the group's
choreographers with pieces restaged for the occasion—some for the first time
in decades (www.youtube.com, search "The New Dance Group Gala Historical
Concert: Retrospective 1930s–1970s").

The 92ⁿᵈ Street Y

Begun in 1874 as a Young Men's Hebrew Association on 92ⁿᵈ Street in
Manhattan (and, beginning in 2001, a satellite Y in the downtown Tribeca
area, too)—the 92Y (www.92y.org) remains one of the city's most active
cultural institutions. Its dance center opened in 1936 and, even more than the
NDG, it became a portal for the leaders of the modern dance movement to
pass through; and, to this day, generations of their heirs as well. Those taking
part in Y programs are recognized by their first names alone—Doris, Martha,
Sophie, Alvin, Lester, Hanya, both Pearls, Paul, Anna, Agnes, Erick, Jerome,
Katherine, José, Ohad, Bill T., the list goes on—and for contemporary dance,
the 92Y remains the heart of Manhattan. The Y offers performances, classes

and workshops in dance, from "Isadora for Children" to Pilates, yoga and much more for seniors.

Trisha Brown

One choreographer associated with the pioneering of postmodern dance (further discussed in Chapter 8) is Trisha Brown (b. November 25, 1936, Aberdeen, Washington). With mathematically-driven, often site-specific, and at times maddeningly hypnotic works, Brown was a founding member of the Judson Dance Theater (see Chapter 8) in 1962 and Grand Union, an experimental dance collective begun in 1970. She remains most famous for three pieces: the 1971 *Walking on the Wall* (reconceived in 2008 on the outside of the Walker Art Center in Minneapolis; www.youtube.com, search "Trisha Brown's Man Walking Down the Side of a Building") with her dancers in harnesses doing what the title says; 1973's *Roof Piece*, occurring simultaneously on twelve separate roofs in New York City; and *Primary Group Accumulation*, also from 1973, re-presented during the 2008 Paris *Quartier d'Été* festival with the dancers lying on their backs on rafts floating in the formal pond of the Tuileries Garden outside the Louvre Museum.

By 2008, climbing up and down and on the sides of buildings was nothing new anymore. For example, in the dance work *311,* as part of the River to River Festival 2008 performance series Sitelines, the contemporary group Risa Jaroslow (b. 1948) & Dancers (f. 1985, www.hightidedance.com) "trod the sides of the pillars [and represented] an impeccable sampler of New York modern or postmodern dance of the post-1970 era"[14] outside the Municipal Building at One Centre Street. But Brown did it first.

By the late '70s and early '80s, Brown had transformed her repetitive yet captivating pedestrian movements into a "fluid virtuosity" in works such as *Glacial Decoy* (1979) and *Set and Reset* (1983), restaged in 2010 on the Budapest (Hungary) Dance School (Budapest Tánc Iskola; www.tanc.org.hu/; www.youtube.com, search "SET&RESET/RESET I. rész").

In reviewing the above-mentioned *Primary Group Accumulation* in 2008 Paris, Denise Luccioni succinctly captures Brown's still provocative aesthetic: "Trisha Brown's early works have kept the power to change one's vision—of dance, of art, of the world. Beyond their intact matter-of-factness, humor, and inventiveness, they simply redefine the form once again. And today, they appear like the tabula rasa regularly needed to refresh a medium."[15]

From the influences of the Great Depression, which Ailey drew on to create *Revelations,* to the constant redefinition of what dance can be as embodied
by other 1930s-born choreographers still working today like Paul Taylor and
Trisha Brown, many of these venerable creators' works remain rich in currency.

Selected Videos/DVDs/Films

Alvin Ailey
Four by Ailey (1986), Dance Horizons.
A Tribute to Alvin Ailey (1992), Dance Horizons.

Trisha Brown
Trisha Brown (1996), Insight Media.

Donald McKayle
Donald McKayle: Early Work (1960), Insight Media.
Donald McKayle: Heartbeats of a Dancemaker (2005), Dance Horizons.

New Dance Group
New Dance Group Gala Historical Concert (2008), Dance Horizons.

Paul Taylor
Paul Taylor Dance Company (1978), Amazon.com.
*Paul Taylor: Dancemaker (*1999), Paul Taylor Dance Company.

Notes

1   Kimberly Pittman, "Free to Dance Biographies: Donald McKayle,"
    http://www.pbs.org/wnet/freetodance/biographies/mckayle.html.

2   Rose Eichenbaum, *Masters of Movement: Portraits of America's Great
    Choreographers* (Washington, D. C.: Smithsonian Books, 2004), p. 1.

3   Neil Baldwin; "Notes from a Danceaturg—February 15, 2010,"
    http://www.montclair.edu/news/article.php?ArticleID=5022.

4   Anna Kisselgoff, "Promethean Light Illuminates Hope," *The New York
    Times,* June 10, 2002, http://www.nytimes.com/2002/06/10/arts/
    dance-review-promethean-light-illuminates-hope.html?pagewanted=1.

5   Allan Ulrich, "What's So Funny? The Lighter Side of Paul Taylor,"
    Dance Magazine, March 2010, Vol. 84, p. 38.

6   Alastair Macaulay, "Paul Taylor: Return of the Beloved Ren-
    egade," *The New York Times,* February 21, 2010, http://www.nytimes.
    com/2010/02/21/arts/dance/21taylor.html?ref=dance.

7   In contrast to Taylor's illuminating musicality, as it will be argued elsewhere, the "austere, demanding and riveting" Anne Teresa de Keersmaeker (b. 1960, see Chapter 8) can bring to light new ideas in iconoclastic composers like Steve Reich who, in 1999, upon finally viewing her signature 1982 work *Fase*, exclaimed, "Of all the choreography done to my music…this was by far the best thing I'd seen… it was all analogous to the music. On an emotional and psychological level I felt I'd learned something about my own work" (Sanjoy Roy, "Step-By-Step Guide to Dance: Anne Teresa de Keersmaeker and Rosas," *The Guardian*, September 8, 2009, http://www.guardian.co.uk/stage/2009/sep/08/dance-anne-teresa-de-keersmaeker-rosas).

8   Alastair Macaulay, "A Choreographer Recycling and Reusing, but Always Reinventing," *The New York Times*, March 4, 2010, http://www.nytimes.com/2010/03/04/arts/dance/04gala.html?adxnnl=1&ref=dance&adxnnlx=1268013339-QCk83RNJpRqS2smETIlaoA.

9   Alastair Macaulay, "A Choreographer Recycling and Reusing, but Always Reinventing," *The New York Times*, March 4, 2010, http://www.nytimes.com/2010/03/04/arts/dance/04gala.html?adxnnl=1&ref=dance&adxnnlx=1268013339-QCk83RNJpRqS2smETIlaoA.

10   Jennifer Dunning, "A Belated Farewell to a Free-Thinking Choreographer," *The New York Times*, November 14, 1993, p. 58; http://www.nytimes.com/1993/11/14/movies/dance-a-belated-farewell-to-a-free-thinking-choreographer.html.

11   Alastair Macaulay, "Experiencing America, With Foot and Instrument"; *The New York Times*, December 19, 2008, http://www.nytimes.com/2008/12/20/arts/dance/20jazz.html?_r=1&ref=dance.

12   Alastair Macaulay, "Destination Unknown, but a Quest Pushes Gentle Motion to the Fore," *The New York Times*, December 7, 2011, http://www.nytimes.com/2011/12/08/arts/dance/alvin-ailey-american-dance-theater-at-city-center-review.html.

13   http://en.wikipedia.org/wiki/New_Dance_Group.

14   Alastair Macaulay, "Stepping Out in Public to the Beat of a Chat on Civics," *The New York Times*, July 10, 2008, http://www.nytimes.com/2008/07/10/arts/dance/10risa.html.

15   Denise Luccioni, "C'est Trisha Brown," *Dance Magazine*, December 2008, pp. 20, 22.

Chapter Six

1940 to 1950

Garth Fagan, Pina Bausch, Twyla Tharp, Meredith Monk, Carolyn Carlson, Lar Lubovitch, Mats Ek, Laura Dean, Butoh, Ulysses Dove, Jiří Kylián, Richard Alston, William Forsythe

Garth Fagan

Garth Fagan (Gawain Garth Fagan, b. May 3, 1940, Kingston, Jamaica) is the Artistic Director of Garth Fagan Dance, founded in the upstate New York city of Rochester in 1970 as "The Bottom of the Bucket BUT...Dance Theatre"—his original dancers consisted of inner-city youth and students who came late to the discipline.[1] His company, now in its fifh decade, is internationally acclaimed. In watching his work, one finds in his company a potpourri of virtuoso modern, ballet, vernacular, and jazz, the dancers all charming, unmannered, and accessible—"the sense of weight in modern dance, the torso-centered movement and energy of Afro-Caribbean, the speed and precision of ballet, and the rule-breaking experimentation of the postmoderns."[2]

Garth Fagan is most famous for his Tony, Drama Desk, Outer Critics, Astaire, Ovation, Olivier, and Helpmann Award-winning choreography for Broadway's *The Lion King* (1997) (www.youtube.com, search "The Lion King on Broadway 1998 Tony Award preview clips"). Like Robbins's *West Side Story* (1957), Hanya Holm's *My Fair Lady* (1956) and Agnes de Mille's *Oklahoma!* (1943) before him, Fagan found a way to be both artistic *and* popular. He is well represented in the concert dance idiom as well. Readers should find a way to see any revival of *Griot New York,* his live onstage 1991 collaboration with trumpeter-composer Wynton Marsalis (b. 1961), the Wynton Marsalis Septet, and sculptor Martin Puryear. The performers reach across the footlights through their rhythmic commitment, and the piece's interplay and counterpoint remain daring and unmatched in contemporary dance (excerpt at www.youtube.com, search "Garth Fagan Dance at Jacob's Pillow").

Pina Bausch

Dancer-choreographer provocateur Pina Bausch (July 27, 1940, Solingen, Germany–June 30, 2009, Wuppertal, Germany), through her Wuppertal Tanztheater (f. 1973; www.pina-bausch.de, following Kurt Jooss), was one "of the most influential dance artists of the late 20th century."[3] Studying with the socially conscious, forward-thinking modern ballet choreographer Kurt Jooss and the complex and dramatic ballet choreographer Antony Tudor, Bausch became the

> natural heir to the German expressionist dance tradition called *Ausdruckstanz*, [with] her productions stress[ing] ideas and emotions… [they are] masterpieces of theatrical invention…[—in] *Arien* [1979] the stage was covered with water; in *Viktor* [1986] the action took place inside a huge earthwork grave; in *Nelken* [1982] the stage was covered with thousands of carnations…[In] her landmark staging of Stravinsky's *Rite of Spring* (1975), [she created] a work of primal power in which the dancers, divided tribally between the two sexes, performed on a stage covered with bare earth.[4]

Her final piece, *Bamboo Blues* (2008), continued her envelope-pushing with often surprising sets; the piece was created "after [she visited] five cities in India [and included] a deconstructed Bharata Natyam solo, costumes for the men that extend their sleeves into what looks like a ribbon dance, and a wall of billowing red silk—all to contemporary Indian music."[5]

Bausch's most famous creation, *Rite of Spring* (1975), remains the most notorious version after Nijinsky's. Its final primal eight minutes can be seen at www.youtube.com, search "Le Sacre Du Printemps by Pina Bausch Wuppertal Dance Theater." Typical of her work, the dance is full of

> …brutal representations of modern man's isolation—not only from other human beings, but even from his own inner self. Desolate, funny, violent, grand and messy…her international company of twenty-six performers seems to use the innermost secrets of their lives as the springboard into these performances. They spew out their guts both physically and emotionally with an honesty that has become a byword for all of the Bausch imitators.[6]

The final two paragraphs of Alastair Macaulay's eulogy to Bausch sum up her uncompromising, modernist visions:

> She was a theater poet. Whether the images added up to successful poetry became part of the debate. I have used the word incoherent about her: it applied most obviously to the structure of most of her works. Yet that incoherence wasn't quite a flaw. To me, most of her pieces expressed the inner landscape of the depressed mind, here obsessed and there rambling, often compelling. But she was at pains to elude definition.
>
> In thinking of the Bausch works that might have been, you imagine aspects of beauty, humor, big-scale visual imagination, as well as darkness, sarcasm and intensity. And the simplest way to feel her loss is to reflect that now there will be no more Bausch pieces for us to argue about. The scene is smaller without her.[7]

Fortunately, famed German film director Wim Wenders (b. 1945; *Until the End of the World*, 1991 and *Buena Vista Social Club*, 1999), created the posthumous *Pina* in 2011, a 3-D homage that brings the viewer, as Bausch herself said, into the feelings of "what moves" the dancers, not how they move.[8] [www.youtube.com, search "Pina (2011)—official trailer (HD)"]

Twyla Tharp

One of the most eccentric individualists in the modern dance world, Twyla Tharp (b. July 1, 1941, Portland, Indiana) has quite outdone her contemporaries in having an eclectic background. Early in life she studied piano, violin, viola, acrobatics, ballet, tap, modern, jazz, drums, baton-twirling, and even gypsy dancing, and with Graham, Cunningham, and Taylor in her twenties. Aptly called the "virtuoso choreographer of crossover,"[9] her work embraces a wide range of experimental approaches, including dances performed in silence; dances heard but not seen; dances done to jazz, rock 'n' roll, popular songs, and classical music; dances for video; and dances with extreme minimalism.

Joan Acocella (b. 1945), dance critic for *The New Yorker* magazine since 1992, concisely captures the essence of Tharp's relentless ability to meld so many ideas and styles into coherent works: "Her fixation [is] on the idea of miscellany (of steps, of groups, of musical elements) as opposed to unity—because this is not really a gambit but the very center of her art, her permanent subject…[Tharp's work is a] serious, long-meditated thought, which I believe is about America (individualism vs. concord)."[10]

One of her most celebrated dances, set originally on the Joffrey Ballet while the company was centered in New York City, is *Deuce Coupe* (1973), a hilarious, yet rigorously choreographed, construction on a suite of Beach Boys tunes. *In the Upper Room* (1986, excerpt at www.youtube.com, search "Twyla Tharp's In the Upper Room"), set to the hypnotic music of Philip Glass (b. 1937), is likewise typical of the choreographer's eclectic mix of styles, while "The Golden Section," from the full-length 1981 *The Catherine Wheel*, is a compilation of her signature mélange of modern, ballet, and vernacular. Years ahead of her time, a greater and greater number of companies and dancers around the world have come to the same conclusion as Tharp: borrow, mix-and-match, overlap, and use whatever works.

Tharp is at ease with ballet companies and dancers such as Mikhail Baryshnikov (b. 1948) and those in American Ballet Theatre (with whom she has had a close relationship for more than thirty years), Paris Opera Ballet; modern dance companies such as the current Martha Graham Dance Company and her own Twyla Tharp Dance (f. 1965). She has choreographed for film as in *Hair* (1979) (www.youtube.com, search "Hair – Aquarius") and *White Nights* (1985), among others, and for television, including the Emmy-winning *Baryshnikov by Tharp* (1984)—which includes the incomparable 1976 concert dance *Push Comes to Shove*—with Baryshnikov who introduces all three dances in his charming English [excerpt at www.youtube.com, search "Baryshnikov Dances Sinatra and More (Broadway show, Tharp, American Ballet (start at 12:38)"]. Her work has been on Broadway—*Movin' Out* (2002, www.youtube.com, search "Twyla Tharp Movin' Out"), set to Billy Joel songs, *The Times They Are a Changin'* (2005, based on Bob Dylan music) and *Come Fly Away* (2010, set to one of her old favorites, Frank Sinatra).

Tharp is a writer, too. Her 1992 autobiography, *Push Comes to Shove*, is named after the 1976 dance noted above. Her 2010 book, *The Collaborative Habit*, continues her story. Twyla Tharp's many well-recorded dances are in company repertories the world over.

Meredith Monk

Tharp's ballet, Broadway, and concert dance is in sharp contrast to Meredith Monk's (b. November 20, 1942, New York, New York). "More interested in choreographing time than in devising steps for dancers,"[11] Monk is often an acquired taste. Her *Education of the Girlchild* (1971) included a dance solo for the choreographer herself: "she begins seated on a dais draped in white, an ancient Sybil imparting deep knowledge in a foreign tongue. Gradually, as she moves down from her perch to travel a winding white fabric path, she disposes of her grey wig and glasses and trips back through time to childhood and a state of innocence. Her choreography, with its little steps, hops and spins, has the intentional naïveté of folk dance."[12]

What authors Robertson and Hutera interpret above as an "ancient Sybil imparting deep knowledge in a foreign tongue" could just as easily be seen as a bunch of gibberish as an intriguing, mysterious monologue. Likewise, the movements that prompted the description "tripping back through time to childhood...with little steps, hops, and spins" could, to an audience member, feel pointless and absurd, signifying nothing beyond juvenile displays of facile movement...*or* bring a another viewer back to that childhood in all its blessed simplicity. The wide variety of interpretations and evaluations remain essential notions embraced by postmodernists such as Monk.

Famed British director Peter Greenaway made a 1983 film about Monk as part of the "Four American Composers" series. In it, Monk engagingly explains the process of her work and a hypnotic section of *Education* that she was working on at the time. Monk's combination of movement, visual images, singing, and sound has also been called "opera," which places her in a musical as well as dance environment. While we may be reminded that narrative, dance, music, singing, and other components of opera were inseparable from the development of theatrical dance prior to the French Revolution (1789), Monk's all-inclusive combinations are more like avant-garde chamber opera. See what you think–(www.youtube.com, search "Meredith Monk, Four American Composers").

Carolyn Carlson

Carolyn Carlson (b. March 7, 1943, Oakland, California), as with many other modern-contemporary choreographers, remains difficult to define exactly but has been called a "new age, post-Woodstock, version of Isadora Duncan."[13] Her lanky, expressive arms and love of the "mystical...world composed of sensations, dreams, traces of memory"[14] belie her training with the formalist Alwin Nikolais (even though Carlson draws on his sense of structure for coherence in her works). Her dances reference the "feel" of improvisation, like Duncan's, as well as her own 1960s upbringing.

French multiinstrumentalist composer-musician René Aubry (b. 1956) remains a favorite collaborator of hers; the two can be seen in the live

2004 presentation of Carlson's famous solo *Blue Lady* (1985) available at www.youtube.com, search "Rene Aubry-Carolyn Carlson/Blue Lady at Bataclan." And a lovely section of her 1997 fully-staged *Signes* reveals more of her organic, symphonious work with ensembles (again, with Aubry's music) available at www.youtube.com, search "Victoires des Signes." Here is a dance, with its formidable designs in both costumes and décor, not so radically different from the approach that Massine and Nijinska used in Diaghilev's Ballets Russes seventy years earlier!

Lar Lubovitch

Audiences sometimes confuse (understandably) the more grounded lyrical qualities of choreographers such as Paul Taylor and Lar Lubovitch (b. April 9, 1943 Chicago, Illinois) with the mellifluousness of romantic ballet. Lubovitch studied with Tudor, Sokolow, Limón, and Graham, but his own work is "renowned for its musicality, rhapsodic style…sophisticated formal structures [and] highly technical choreography."[15]

Lubovitch's contemporary lyricism and at times unconventional partnering can be seen in the four-minute teaser (available at www.youtube.com, search "Lar Lubovitch Dance Company at Jacob's Pillow") for the Lar Lubovitch Dance Company's (f. 1968, www.lubovitch.org) Fortieth Anniversary season presented by the University of Arizona in October 2008. In a revealing cameo, Lubo-vitch played himself in the 2003 dance film *The Company*, Neve Campbell and Robert Altman's loving homage to The Joffrey Ballet (in Chicago; f. 1995), in which he is shown at work rehearsing a typically "amiable" duet "full of sculp-tured lifts, swooping torsos and outstretched limbs,"[16] set to the tender Rodg-ers and Hart ballad *My Funny Valentine*. (In fact, since Tharp's appropriation of popular music like The Beach Boys and Frank Sinatra in the 1970s, pop music took on a much more prominent role as accompaniment for dance.)

Because Lubovitch's dances (like those of Richard Alston, discussed later in this chapter) are easy on the eyes and ears (Lubovitch loves jazz and classi-cal music), it is easy to overlook his prodigious skill in making pure and simple dances. Perhaps this straightforward manner with composition and clarity comes from his formal training as a visual artist early in life. Former Lubovitch dancer Peggy Baker said as much in a wide-ranging "Coffee and Conversa-tion" preshow talk series for Dance Theatre Workshop on October 7, 2008:

> Because he did come from painting, he's always treated the stage like a canvas. I think he sees groups moving on the stage like big, big gestures the same way that you'd see paint on a canvas and not as individual

steps in space. And very often, still, he sketches out his work by sending dancers purely through spatial patterns and slowly layering choreographic ideas to build phrases through the spatial configurations he's already made.[17]

Joining fellow Chicago companies River North Chicago Dance Company and Hubbard Street Dance Company in similar pursuits, Lubovitch founded the Chicago Dancing Company (CDC) in 2007.

Mats Ek

Sweden's Mats Ek (b. April 18, 1945, Malmö, Sweden), the youngest son of famed modern and ballet choreographer Birgit Cullberg (1908–1999), has created works for major ballet companies. His choreography illuminates contemporary social, emotional, and psychological dilemmas to his audiences— usually leavened with a subtle humor—while remaining rooted in classical ballet technique. In reworked versions of classics for the Cullberg Ballet (f. 1967) such as *Giselle* (1982), *Swan Lake* (1987) and *Carmen* (1992), and *The Sleeping Beauty* (1996) for The Hamburg Ballet, Ek

> …ripped (them) out of their traditional dramatic, choreographic and stylistic molds in order to examine them under the spotlight of sociologically oriented modern psychology so that the characters take on the appearance of our own contemporaries…He did this… to discover the motives for the way these people behave. As with Pina Bausch, central questions about human existence lie at the heart of Mats Ek's psychological probing…(In revealing a recurrent, easily recognizable conceit of his choreography, Ek has said,) "The prolongation, the extension of movements is very important to me. For instance, sometimes the foot or the head stays in a position while the body is already going into the next movement."[18]

Viewers can gain insight into Ek's choreographic concerns and character in the intense two-and-a-half minute solo, *Wet Woman* (1996), set on the equally intense, extraordinarily flexible virtuoso ballerina Sylvie Guillem (b. 1965) (www.youtube.com, search "Sylvie Guillem–Wet Woman–Mats Ek"). Ek's sustained "extension of movements" is quite evident in this popular, video-gone-viral dance.

A discussion of the choreographer's full-length *Giselle*, set on the Paris Opera Ballet, reveals Ek's cutting edge approach to the classics:

The setting has been up-dated to a claustrophobic rural community on some distant island, and his Giselle is a solitary young girl who longs for true love and children of her own. Extremely vulnerable, she breaks down when the man of her dreams betrays her… "Of course there are no pointe shoes, and I had to almost forget about my classical training, going further forward with different gestures and staccato, angular, almost brutal movements," [said Marie-Agnès Gillot, the Paris Opera Ballet dancer who played Giselle in 2004]…

Act two takes place in the surrealistic setting of a mental hospital, where pieces of the human body decorate the walls. Myrtha, the Queen of the Wilis…has become the forbidding sister of the ward Giselle is led to after a lobotomy. The nurse serves as a defense against sexual attraction in this self-contained world where the inmates are condemned to frustration.[19] (www.youtube.com, search "Mats Ek Giselle Ana Laguna")

Laura Dean

Many contemporary dance concoctions push the envelope, becoming one person's poison and another's delight. There are those who found Laura Dean's (b. December 3, 1945, Staten Island, New York) early whirling dervish dances, such as *Drumming* (1975) and *Song* (1976), set to the hypnotic droning of Steve Reich's (b. 1936) minimalist sounds, fascinating in their geometric, repetitive designs; others felt physically ill. If anything, Dean will get a mention in just about any dance history book because of her choreographic response to the minimalist movement (often set to the scores of composers Reich and Philip Glass) and her interest in world dance influences. The repetitive music and the embodiment of those sounds in dance can be viewed as reaching some transcendent end—or can be agonizingly annoying. You may decide for yourself by watching an excerpt of the 2008 Scripps Award Ceremony tribute to Dean's work by the American Dance Festival in Durham, North Carolina, on www.youtube.com, search "ADF: Laura Dean Tribute."

Butoh

The Japanese dance theater known as Butoh (translated as "dance of utter darkness") compels audience reevaluation of performance by confronting it with the devastating tragedy of atomic bomb fallout. Developed after World War II primarily by Kazuo Ohno (1906–2010) and Tatsumi Hijikata (1928–1986), the movement utilizes an extremely slow pace, seemingly interminable length, and difficult subject matter.

For example, "[o]ne of Mr. Ohno's earliest works, *Jellyfish Dance*, created in the 1950s, grew out of seeing jellyfish swimming in water where combatants, dead from hunger and disease, had been buried at sea."[20] Often naked, sporting shaved heads painted white, the dancers can move at a glacial pace with limbs akimbo, horror-stricken expressions on their faces. See a short three-minute excerpt from a piece by one of the more popular Butoh companies, Sankai Juku (f. 1975,) at www.youtube.com, search "Sankai Juku Butoh Dance."

Ulysses Dove

On a more upbeat note, aptly-named choreographer of flight, Ulysses Dove (January 17, 1947, Columbia, South Carolina–June 11, 1996, New York, New York), who danced with both Cunningham and Ailey in the 1970s, created work "characterized by an urgent athleticism and…vigorous if abstract emotion."[21] His high energy, often erotic dances are great fun for performers and audiences alike and many companies have Dove in their repertory, most notably the Ailey company, American Ballet Theatre, the Royal Swedish Ballet, Dayton Contemporary Ballet Company, and New York City Ballet.

Episodes (1987) is a typical work, poignantly introduced by the choreographer himself (www.youtube.com, search "A Tribute to Alvin Ailey, Episodes Part I"). Dying at too early an age, Dove remains a sentimental favorite of the Ailey company.

Jiří Kylián

Jiří Kylián (b. March 21, 1947, Prague, The Czech Republic), whose best work *New York Times* dance critic Claudia La Rocco smartly defines as a "voluptuous, surging theatrical language, a stylized marriage of balletic clarity and precision with an earthier modern weight and freedom,"[22] is primarily associated with the Nederlands Dans Theater (NDT; www.ndt.nl), centered in The Hague in Holland where he was Artistic Director. At NDT he has choreographed since 1973 and remains, even after his official "retirement" from the company, as Resident Choreographer and Artistic Advisor. As one of the company's premier guiding lights, he is credited with bringing international recognition to the company. In one of his more notable pieces, the 1989 *Falling Angels* (excerpt at www.youtube.com, search "Jiří Kylián's Falling Angels"), set to the typically hypnotic drumming of a Steve Reich score, we see the hands on a group of eight women

> slap, caress, cover, flick, move body parts [and] splay. Flat-footed jumps with bent knees recall Nijinsky's faun [1912]. In spirit it is primitive,

ritualistic; they look rather like displaying insects totally in command of their prey. Dancers break free, duets break out, but the group always reclaims them. Contrasting moments of dramatic stillness create a surreal sense of space, even in the midst of this frenzied drumming. They are pious one minute, military another, but can then subvert it all with a fey lean to the side, hands draping diagonally across their bodies, or by flirtatiously pulling their swimsuits away from their flesh as if to taunt the audience.[23]

NDT had three companies—NDT1, NDT2, and NDT3—the primary performing group, students under 21, and dancers aged "between 40 and death," respectively, all hotbeds of choreographic intensity. As of 2005, however, NDT3 has been on temporary hiatus. All three companies house works by a host of veterans such as Hans van Manen (b. 1932), who cofounded the company in 1959, William Forsythe (discussed later in this chapter), Mats Ek, and Ohad Naharin (b. 1952) as well as up-and-comers like Crystal Pite (b. 1970) and over a dozen others from around the globe. NDT is, like so many other contemporary companies today, wholly international with both its dancers and choreographers.

London *Guardian's* dance critic Sanjoy Roy, in his monthly "Step-by-Step Guide to Dance" byline, accurately encapsulated NDT's mission in July 2010: "NDT stays true to its founding vision of merging modern dance with classical ballet. Ballet technique is the basis of both the dancers' training and the choreography, but it is alloyed with other ingredients—the curves and falls of modern dance, everyday gestures, folk steps. Van Manen's work is plotless, but nevertheless it's highly charged with emotional, social or sexual symbolism."[24]

A 2007 excerpt of a work entitled *27' 52"*, set by Kylián on the youngest troupe, gives the viewer a good idea of the intensity, skill, and training that goes on right from the start at NDT (www.youtube.com, search "NDT II Jiří Kylián 27' 52'"). *No Brazil* (2009, www.youtube.com, search "NDT II no Brasil") shows Kylián's propensity for androgyny, using skirts or buskets for both men and women and his frequent use of moving sets, such as slowly dropping curtain wings. A one-minute excerpt from *Tar and Feathers* (www.youtube.com, search "Tar and Feathers, Jiří Kylián Nederlands Dans Theater I") demonstrates his use of women partnering men just as often as men partner women.[25]

Perhaps Kylián's signature early work, *Sinfonietta* (1980), set to the ravishing 1926 orchestral work by Czech compatriot Leoš Janáček (1854–1928), captures the choreographer's essence—fleetness of foot, successive vignettes (especially the two charming, elaborate, parallel *pas de deux* that turn into a trio near the middle of the piece), surprise foot flexions, and recurring double *pirouettes* or *chaîné* turns that move immediately into a jazzy *contretemps* motif (www.youtube.com, search "Nederlands Dans Theatre—Sinfonietta Part 1, Part 2").

Conscious homage or not, Kylián's *Sinfonietta* seems like a fifteen-minute reference to Balanchine's neoclassical *Stravinsky Violin Concerto* (1972). The evocative backdrop is universally seen as an ode to Janáček's and Kylián's Czech backgrounds.

Richard Alston

Although primarily associated with ballet companies as a choreographer in the '70s and '80s, the gentle Englishman Richard Alston (b. October 30, 1948, Stoughton, Sussex, England) is equally at home in the contemporary world, having trained at the London Contemporary Dance School (LCDS; f. 1966, but expanded into The Place three years later, www.theplace.org.uk). LCDS was originally closely linked with Martha Graham's company and Robert Cohan (b. 1925) (a Graham disciple and striking choreographer in his own right, training students in Graham's style). In 1994 Alston became the Artistic Director of The Place, when he also founded its resident company Richard Alston Dance Company (www.richardalstondance.com).

In terms of the complexity of his patterns, Alston is favorably compared to both Cunningham (with whom he trained for two years) and Balanchine. He has stated that he also loves Ashton, whom he knew, and Fred Astaire (1899–1987) and August Bournonville (1805–1879), for all their fast steps. South African-bred dance writer Roslyn Sulcas, however, considers Alston's work to perhaps have more of an affinity to Lubovitch's in that it is pleasantly accessible and "easy on the eye."[26]

Alston's 2009 *Shuffle It Right*, danced to the jazz-inflected pop music of composer Hoagy Carmichael (1899–1981), is fluid, musically sensitive, and grounded in ballet, yet gently quirky (excerpt at www.youtube.com, search "Richard Alston Dance Company"). Likewise, the choreographer's 2003 *Overdrive* liltingly propels his dancers via duets and trios in his open, straight-ahead style, set to the urgent rhythms of American minimalist Terry Riley's *Keyboard Studies* (excerpt at www.youtube.com, search "Richard Alston Dance Company—Overdrive").

Roslyn Sulcas quotes the choreographer as saying, "I still believe in steps and articulate performers…Sometimes I feel that people are straining and distorting in order to be inventive. I don't feel that need. I find the activity of dancing a very harmonious and joyful one."[27] He likes "rhythmically exact" details, "demanding, rigorous and fiercely purist" movements, and "great attack and innate musicality" in his dancers,[28] but his work is eminently approachable and not striving to make forcible statements. Alston's work goes about exploring the possibilities between strong technicians and the ballet-contemporary world.

Consistent with the lyricism in most of his choreography, Alston created his own version of *The Rite of Spring*—much softer in tone than Nijinsky's or Bausch's more famous and controversial sensory attacks:

> Wearing peasant costumes by Anne Guyon, Mr. Alston's tribe honored the earth. Women bent low to it, men rose from it and girls stepped shyly on it as if newborn. At the entrance of a Sage (Yair Vardi), everyone rolled in obeisance before him and the girls were placed at his feet. The ballet's most complex character, the Sage was both tender as he blessed the girls and imposing as he readied them for a human sacrifice.
>
> The victim (Diane Walker) was chosen in what resembled a children's game and the scene's very sweetness made it macabre. After cradling her gently, Mr. Vardi sent her forth to dance herself to death. Thrashing until she collapsed in exhaustion, she grew ever more automaton-like, as if she had relinquished her will to become an agent of the gods.[29]

As a member of the "older guard" of contemporary ballet choreographers, Alston is perhaps better able to sense the arc of history than many of his younger colleagues. In a "Q & A" article for *London Dance* magazine (www.londondance.com) on his sixtieth birthday, he stated succinctly, "the link between contemporary dance choreographers and established successful dance companies has made dance as a whole far more broadly accessible."[30]

In 1987, the year after he was named artistic director to the famed Ballet Rambert (f. 1935; but with earlier origins), Alston suggested the company change its name to Rambert Dance Company, a more style-inclusive title. Alston has been doing his best to carry out this plan. *The Guardian* dance reviewer Sanjoy Roy ably captures some of Alston's essence in this 2009 article:

Alston has a distinctive style, and his dancers are top-notch exponents of it. Partly his choreography looks like Merce Cunningham, with lots of curves and tilts in the body, and detailed steps; it's also balletic in its combination of fleet footwork, harmonious lines and proportioned phrases. But Alston uses more weight, breath and flow than either, resulting in a lilting, fluid quality enlivened by clear shapes and rhythms. His love of music is evident; less well-known is his interest in new architecture. In fact, it's possible to see his work in architectural terms, with its space and light, paths and portals, flows of people.[31]

William Forsythe

Classicist but contemporary choreographer William Forsythe (b. December 30, 1949, New York), while born in the United States, is mostly known, like Ek, by his international credentials. Resident choreographer for Germany's Stuttgart Ballet from 1976 to 1984, he followed this tenure by holding a similar role at the Frankfurt Ballet for the next twenty years.[32] He remains centered in Germany, having launched The Forsythe Company (www.theforsythecompany.com) in 2004.

Forsythe's multimedia installation-performance artworks in traditional venues as well as public spaces invariably include spoken text, song, dance, video projections, and large-scale props that all compete for an audience's attention. His choreography is characterized by extreme speed (the dancers often claim exhaustion after performing in one of his dances) and highly expressive and enunciated arms, hands, and hips.

A short example of many of these qualities can be seen in the solo studio rehearsal of Paris Opera Ballet's *étoile* Hervé Moreau as he dances an excerpt from one of Forsythe's most popular works, *In the Middle, Somewhat Elevated* (1987), at the same title on www.youtube.com. Forsythe can be seen rehearsing the dance for ten minutes (while he eats a hot dog!) at www.youtube.com, search "Sylvie Guillem–In the Middle, Somewhat Elevated."

The evening-length work *Kammer/Kammer* (`Room/Room, 2000) has Forsythe swamping his audience with multiple simultaneous perspectives of onstage action via several large video projections and TVs of different sizes, self-conscious actors singing and reciting narratives directly at the audience (breaking the fourth wall), and onstage performers, movable walls, tables, and a grand piano being dragged about—all while a person with a video camera trailing its wiring records the goings-on. Two solid ten-minute sections of this challenging, but fascinating, extravaganza can be seen at www.youtube.com, search "Kammer/Kammer (part 2)–Frankfurt Ballet."

Further insight into the choreographer's process—which includes improvisation, frequent and even last-minute changes, and order reordering (reminiscent of Cunningham)—can be gleaned from the following excerpt of a review of *Woundwork V* (1999), another Forsythe piece set on the Paris Opera Ballet:

> [José] Martinez remembered the first night clearly. Just before going on stage, the order of the steps of his solo was reversed, the steps themselves were altered, and the music was changed. "Everything was different; it was virtually another ballet! The music, which had already been changed three times, was shortened again by several seconds, possibly to make the end [livelier]," he said. "I think Forsythe finally wanted me to do all the same steps, but in another order, but fortunately he allows us to improvise as long as it is in the style of his ballet. Make all the mistakes you want, he said, it's unimportant as long as you move in the proper way. Obviously," the étoile added cautiously, "he didn't tell us to go wrong on purpose!"
>
> "And improvisations," added [Agnes] Letestu, "were limited by the presence of a 'timer,' a sort of television screen in the wings to tell us when we had to go on stage: at 12m 8sec, for example, because so much was happening on stage at the same time, and we couldn't be guided by the repetitious sequences of the music."…Letestu believes that Forsythe's constant changes are not the fruit of hazard, but are premeditated to keep the dancer in a state of perpetual tension. "He deliberately puts the dancer in danger to avoid routine and keep an element of stress. He's a past master of the nonpermanent, and can't stand keeping the same choreography. Were he to return tomorrow, I'm sure he'd start changing everything again. He's in perpetual evolution because what interests him is to create."[33]

Forsythe remains a pivotal, adventurous figure whose work embodies the dissolution of categories, an attitude that continues to shape the contemporary dance world.

Selected Videos/DVDs/Films

Richard Alston

Essential Alston (2008), The Place.

Gypsy Mixture and Nigredo (2005), The Place.
Overdrive (2007), The Place.

Pina Bausch
Orpheus and Eurydice (2008), Dance Horizons.
Understanding Pina: The Legacy of Pina Bausch (2010), Insight Media.

Butoh
Butoh: Piercing the Mask (1991), Ronin Films.

Carolyn Carlson
Signes, in Paris Opera Ballet Boxed Set (2010), Dance Horizons.

Ulysses Dove
A Tribute to Alvin Ailey (2003), Dance Horizons.

Mats Ek
Appartement (2003), Dance Horizons.
Mats Ek's Carmen (1994), Dance Horizons.

Garth Fagan
Griot New York (2001), Amazon.com.
From Before, in Dance Black America (1990), Dance Horizons.

William Forsythe
From a Classical Position (2007), Dance Horizons.

Jiří Kylián
Jiří Kylián's Black and White Ballets (1997), Image Entertainment.
Jiří Kylián: Nederlands Dance Theater (2003), Dance Horizons.
Kaguyahime (The Moon Princess) (2010), Dance Horizons.
Nederlands Dans Theater Celebrates Jiří Kylián (2007), Dance Horizons.
Nederlands Dans Theater 3: Coming and Going (1992), Insight Media.

Lar Lubovitch
Lar Lubovitch Othello: San Francisco Ballet (2003), Kultur.

Meredith Monk
Meredith Monk: Inner Voice (2009), First Run Features.

Twyla Tharp
Baryshnikov Dances Sinatra (1984/2005), Dance Horizons.
The Catherine Wheel (1983), Kultur.
Twyla Tharp: Making Television Dance (1980), Insight Media.

Notes

1   Julinda Lewis-Ferguson, "Free to Dance Biographies: Garth Fagan," http://www.pbs.org/wnet/freetodance/biographies/fagan.html).

2   http://garthfagandance.org/about-us/garth-fagan.

3   Debra Craine and Judith Mackrell, eds., *The Oxford Dictionary of Dance* (Oxford, England: Oxford University Press, 2010, 2nd ed.), p. 49.

4   Ibid., p. 50.

5   Wendy Perron, "New York Notebook," *Dance Magazine*, December 2008, p. 24.

6   Allen Robertson and Donald Hutera, *The Dance Handbook* (Boston: G. K. Hall, 1988), p. 228.

7   Alastair Macaulay, "A Stage for Social Ego to Battle Anguished Id," *The New York Times*, June 30, 2009, http://www.nytimes.com/2009/07/01/arts/dance/01assess.html?_r=1&ref=arts.

8   Julie Bloom, "A Vision of Dance, Preserved in 3-D," *The New York Times*, December 11, 2011, http://www.nytimes.com/2011/12/11/movies/wim-wenders-on-pina-his-film-on-pina-bauschs-dances.html.

9   Alastair Macaulay, "Three Choreographers, Bound by Their Way with a Ballet Twist," *The New York Times*, January 28, 2010, http://www.nytimes.com/2010/01/28/arts/dance/28triple.html?ref=dance.

10 Joan Acocella, "Guy Stuff: Twyla Tharp at American Ballet Theatre," *The New Yorker*, June 30, 2008; p. 85, http://www.newyorker.com/arts/critics/dancing/2008/06/30/080630crda_dancing_acocella?currentPage=all.

11 Robertson and Hutera, *The Dance Handbook*, p. 249.

12 Ibid.

13 Ibid., p. 198.

14 Ann Veronica Turnbull, "Carolyn Carlson." In Martha Bremser, ed. *Fifty Contemporary Choreographers* (London, UK: Routledge, 1999), p. 55.

15 Wikipedia, http://en.wikipedia.org/wiki/Lar_Lubovitch.

16 Ibid.

17 www.youtube.com, search "Coffee and Conversation with Lar Lubovitch," http://www.youtube.com/watch?v=Z7U5UypuRWo.

18   Claudia La Rocco, "Movements in Jazz, With Pollock and Col-
      trane," *The New York Times*, March 1, 2010, http://www.nytimes.
      com/2010/03/02/arts/dance/02lubovitch.html.

19   Patricia Boccadoro, "Giselle: Choreography Mats Ek, Paris Opéra Ballet,"
      Culture Kiosque Dance: Reviews July 13, 2004, http://www.culturekiosque.
      com/dance/reviews/mats_ek.html.

20   Jennifer Dunning, "Kazuo Ohno, a Founder of Japanese Butoh,
      Dies at 103," *The New York Times*, June 1, 2010, http://www.nytimes.
      com/2010/06/02/arts/dance/02ohno.html?ref=dance.

21   Craine and Mackrell, *The Oxford Dictionary*, p. 138.

22   Claudia La Rocco, "The Fires of Youth on a Restless Night," *The New
      York Times*, April 10, 2009, http://www.nytimes.com/2009/04/11/arts/
      dance/11neder.html?ref=dance.

23   Lesley-Anne Sayers, "Jiří Kylián," in Bremser, 1999, pp. 135–136.

24   Sanjoy Roy, "Step-by-Step Guide to Dance: Nederlands Dans The-
      ater," *The Guardian*, July 1, 2010, http://www.guardian.co.uk/stage/2010/
      jun/30/nederlands-dans-theater/.

25   From the 1960s on the Post-Modernists, too, had been experimenting
      with supports, lifts and tosses without gender bias.

26   Roslyn Sulcas, "The Light Alston Touch: 40 Years of Casual
      Grace," *The New York Times*, January 10, 2010, http://www.nytimes.
      com/2010/01/10/arts/dance/10alston.html.

27   Ibid.

28   London Dance Interview (author unknown), "Happy Birthday Richard
      Alston," *LondonDance.com,* October 2-3, 2008, http://www.londondance.
      com/content.asp?CategoryID=3086.

29   Jack Anderson, "Richard Alston's Varied 'Rite of Spring,'" *The New
      York Times*, October 19, 1982, http://query.nytimes.com/gst/fullpage.html
      ?res=950DE5D6143BF93AA25753C1A964948260&sec=&spon.

30   London Dance Interview (author unknown), "Happy Birthday Richard
      Alston," *LondonDance.com,* October 2-3, 2008, http://www.londondance.
      com/content.asp?CategoryID=3086.

31   Sanjoy Roy, "Step-by-Step Guide to Dance: Richard Alston," *The
      Guardian*, November 2, 2009, http://www.guardian.co.uk/stage/2009/
      nov/02/richard-alston-choreography-dance.

32 Forsythe's professional arc is similar to Milwaukee-born choreographer John Neumeier's (b. February 24, 1942) pattern via the Frankfurt and then Hamburg Ballet companies.

33 Patricia Boccadoro, "William Forsythe's Recent Paris Saga," *Culture Kiosk Dance: Reviews*, May 31, 1999, http://www.culturekiosque.com/dance/reviews/rheforsythe.html.

Chapter Seven
1950 to 1960

**Elizabeth Streb, Siobhan Davies, Bill T. Jones, Ohad Naharin,
Karole Armitage, Meryl Tankard, James Kudelka,
Stephen Petronio, Mark Morris, Nacho Duato, Angelin Preljocaj,
Claude Brumachon, David Parsons, Dance Funding**

Elizabeth Streb

Like Alwin Nikolais earlier in the century, Elizabeth Streb (b. February 23,
1950, Rochester, New York) makes works that are not purely dance but a
mix of movement styles, illusions, and acrobatics. By the first decade of our
century, Streb had added unique mechanical contraptions for those actions
to be performed on human-sized rat wheels, giant pendulums with attached
concrete slabs (that is her company midflight on this book's cover, performing
in *Gauntlet*, from 2004) and a variety of trampolines and scaffolds, some with
flying harnesses. These "set pieces" include a real sense of danger for both
her performers and audience members; like an intimate theater in the round,
everyone feels up close to the flying bodies just avoiding being hit by the slabs
or pendulums, hears the loud splats as they crash, usually safely, onto thick
floor (or wall) mats.

> Yes, there are endless conversations about where I fit in. Is what I do
> dance or isn't it? But it's really not my job to define what dance is.
> I'm interested in a vigorous investigation of movement in its relation
> to time, space, and human body potential…I passed through athletics
> and was trained in dance. In high school I played varsity basketball and
> baseball and was an obsessive downhill skier and motorcycle rider. I
> started dancing at the age of seventeen when I majored in dance at the
> State University of New York at Brockport. My modern dance train-
> ing was along the lines of Doris Humphrey, Charles Weidman, and José
> Limón. Through this and my history of extreme sports, I developed

an interest in action. Action is what makes movement possible. This quickly became my passion, and dance was the only place in the arts that accepted what I was doing.[1]

Having danced for several years with Molissa Fenley (b. 1954) and Margaret Jenkins (b. ca.1940), she founded a company in 1979, now called just Streb (www.streb.org). Promotional excerpts of tours such as "Wild Blue Yonder" (2005, www.youtube.com, search "Streb Wild Blue Yonder") and "Streb vs. Gravity" (2008, www.youtube.com, search "Streb vs. Gravity") reveal the intensity, dynamism, and genuine fear that infuse her work. She calls her choreography "PopAction" and established a laboratory workshop entitled SLAM in 2003 in Brooklyn, New York, which stands for Streb Lab for Action Mechanics. By 2010, her vision had evolved into a hopeful community forum with real economic and social consequences—contemporary art made functional!

> The doors of SLAM are never closed. Performances at SLAM are not stiff, class-coded, regimented affairs; they are neighborhood happenings where the company's longtime fans from the high-art crowd mingle with the at-risk kids from the local public schools and their parents. At the heart of this machine is the driving force of art and action, and the belief that art can provide a service to a community such that voters, taxpayers, and consumers will consider it indispensable.[2]

An articulate artist who speaks knowledgeably about her work (Streb holds an M.A. from New York University), her website includes an academically rigorous and engaging 20-minute PowerPoint presentation by Streb herself that deconstructs the pieces into the physics of her space, time and form investigations. In it she quotes one of her great heroes, Evel Knievel (early on, Streb was fittingly called the Evel Knievel of the dance world): "I never had any trouble with the take-off…it's the landing that's a problem."

Intensely concerned with a visceral response from her audience, the dangers that her performers take are often powerfully felt across the stage lights. Earlier in her life Streb had studied skydiving and bull riding, and her quest is still to bring onto a stage and into our minds the feeling of those eight seconds of hell required for scoring points to survive riding a bull. Excerpts of *Moon* (2006), *Ricochet* (2006), *Air* (2003), and *Fly* (1997, commissioned by Wolf Trap to celebrate the Wright Brothers anniversary of flight) are on the PowerPoint presentation, as are numerous insightful videos on her website. One of her imperatives strikingly rings true for dance's mission, too: "If *action* is a verb, can it be the subject?" She states. "What I attempt to do in almost every piece I make is to twist time and space to an anti-gravity place so that the temporality and the spatial-ness of it will be not earth-like…[I like to] question the frozen real-estate of audience seating…Basic Research: Shoot an arrow into the air and where it lands, paint a bulls-eye."[3]

Not far from this vein is the immensely popular Cirque du Soleil (f. 1984). (Streb was honored when invited to celebrate their 20th anniversary with them, so the companies are mutually supportive.) Here the performers are acrobats twirling, juggling, dancing, clowning, etc., and their show is a combination of thematic, pseudo-abstract subjects such as water, burlesque, the sun, various animals, and other phenomena [for example: 2007, www.youtube, search "Cirque du Soleil O (Terre Aride)"]. The viewer may embrace this showmanship as "circus" or as dance theater; regardless, audiences nightly pay more than $100 per seat for admission and are hardly disappointed at the breathtaking spectacle of human will, daring, and theatrical excitement. Cirque dancers earn decent union salaries and work steadily for years in the same production. Such arrangements run counter to the often pick-up nature of work for the majority of dancers in the contemporary dance world or even the seasonal (rarely yearly) contracted salaries of dancers in continuing ballet companies.

Streb's company was commissioned by the London Olympics organizing committee to "bungee jump off the Millennium Bridge and perform on the spokes of the London Eye, the 443-foot-tall Ferris wheel,"[4] in Summer 2012. It was no surprise to learn that for many years, she didn't want any comfortable couches in her SoHo (New York) loft apartment.

Siobhan Davies

Alongside Ian Spink (b. 1947) and Robert North (b. 1945), dancer and choreographer Siobhan Davies (b. September 18, 1950, London, England) apprenticed at London Contemporary Dance School (under Richard Alston and Robert Cohan), eventually developing her own mellifluous mix of implied narrative and abstraction. Her work often feels warm and intimate, in large part due to the personal involvement of the dancers themselves in the choreographic process and the contributions of her lighting and musical composition collaborators.

There is a "fluid, sensuous and rippling dynamic" that "luxuriates in its physical substance and presence" in Davies's work.[5] Her *13 Different Keys* (1999, excerpts at www.youtube.com, search "13 Different Keys—Siobhan Davies") reveals the enjoyable tensions Davies sets up between the coolness of the steps and the congeniality of the movements felt through her dancers. Set to the live music (another preference of Davies) of harpsichord and viola da gamba, the piece was a

> collaboration with Artangel [f. 1992; London-based contemporary arts organization], The Royal Ballet and dancers from her own Company [and] was made as a site specific work for the Atlantis Gallery in Brick Lane, London. The work was set on three dance platforms; a main one stretching diagonally across the space between the building's pillars and two shorter platforms, set slightly away from the main one, which the dancers criss-cross. The audience viewed the work both in close proximity to the dancing and further away.[6]

The website for Siobhan Davies Dance (f. 1988; http://www.siobhandavies.com) is a real treat: state-of-the-art, packed with insightful information, full-length videos of her work, numerous dance links, and multiple helpful categories of organization. One can spend hours happily exploring Davies's interests. Especially fascinating is the section "Siobhan Davies Replay," named after an early dance and an archive project begun in 2007 "with the aim of bringing together all of the materials and documentation associated with Davies's choreographies into a single collection. It is the first online dance archive in the UK and contains thousands of fully searchable digital records including moving image, still image, audio and text."[7]

Bill T. Jones

Bill T. Jones (b. February 15, 1952, Bunnell, Florida), a dancer-choreographer trained in modern dance, Afro-Caribbean, and contact improvisation, incorporates multimedia and spoken text into his gracefully athletic, emotionally provocative (and sometimes downright uncomfortable) dances. His works deal with challenging issues such as homosexuality, gender bias, racism, unfashionable body types, and AIDS. The full-length *Still/Here* (1994) "generated a heated debate in the dance world" through its in-depth, arresting investigation of "people dealing with terminal illness.[8] Nondancers "of all ages, classes, races, sexual preferences, and states of health"[9] shared their painful lives through excerpted large-screen projection video footage of direct-to-audience narratives, while onstage dancers performed technically demanding dancing and gesture.

How does one label such a work? Certainly, Jones's interests lie somewhere within the postmodern realms of confrontation, experimentalism, intellectualism, and a mixture of trained and untrained dancers, but they also draw on traditional modern dance and modern ballet conventions like the choreographer's frequent use of concert stages, strong technique (his choreography is in the repertory of some ballet companies), and a sophisticated musical sensibility. Take a look at an excerpt from a typical multimedia, thought-provoking piece called *Blind Date* (2005, available at www.youtube.com, search "Bill T. Jones 'Blind Date'"). Elsewhere, his more pure dance pieces can be "sporty, joyous display[s] of ensemble virtuosity,"[10] like *D-Man in the Waters* (1989; www.youtube.com, search "D-MAN in the Waters–Bill.T.Jones.mp4."

Jones's breadth extends as well to Broadway as the Tony Award-winning choreographer of *Spring Awakening* (2007) and as director/choreographer of *Fela!* (2009) about the radical Nigerian singer Fela Anikulapo Kuti (1938–1997), where Jones's efforts at combining African dance with his brand of contemporary movement also won him a Tony. Jones is an acquired taste, albeit with solid technical dancing.

Ohad Naharin

Another of the many peripatetic dancer/choreographers mentioned throughout this book (true sponges, dancers do love to travel, for fun, research, and support), Israeli-born Ohad Naharin (b. June 22, 1952) trained in New York at The Juilliard School and with Graham, apprenticed with the Batsheva Dance Company (f. 1964, www.batsheva.co.il), where he has been Artistic Director since 1990. He danced for Graham, Béjart's Ballet of the 20th Century in Brussels, and Bat-Dor (1968–2006), another homeland (Israeli) company. His choreography has traveled the world, too, through dozens of commissions, and

> is distinguished by the primal physicality of its movement style, usually in tension with a rigorous formal structure, the eclectic choice of its musical repertory, and by its occasionally surreal staging.[11]

Naharin also created a dance form named Gaga a full decade before Stefanie Joanne Angelina Germanotta (b. 1986), had renamed herself Lady Gaga in 2006 after the 1984 Queen song *Radio Ga Ga*.[12]

> The technique strives to establish a flow throughout the body that allows complete fluidity."[13] Gaga allows the user to discover agility, flexibility, strength, speed, efficiency, stamina, explosive power, groove, delicacy, the connection between pleasure and effort, and isolation and articulation of the joints. Gaga also fosters the awareness of

weakness and atrophy and encourages the development of new movement habits.[14]

Three, from 2005 (www.youtube.com, search "Three by Ohad Naharin, Batsheva Dance Company"), is typical of his work. Multiple dancers move in duets, trios, solos, and a variety of groupings that feel chaotic, but are carefully choreographed—they remind one of Cunningham's seemingly serendipitous meanderings—but with more pliable and fluid body parts (a bit like Forsythe, too). *Max* (2007) gives us more of the tension and intensity of Naharin's vision; the dancers take Graham's contraction and hold it tight, move it jarringly, throughout their bodies, not just in their torsos (www.youtube.com, search "Batsheva Dance Company–Max by Ohad Naharin").

Karole Armitage

Karole Armitage (b. March 3, 1954, Madison, Wisconsin) studied with the modern and tap dancer/choreographer Bill Evans[15] (b. 1940, www.billevansdance.org) at the University of Utah, then became a scholarship student at the School of American Ballet. She learned important Balanchine repertory from 1973 to 1976 at the Ballet du Grand Théâtre de Genève in Switzerland, and danced for the Merce Cunningham Dance Company from 1976 to 1981. She has had a similar eclectic career trajectory to that of Twyla Tharp. Going from a "Cunninghamian complexity" with her technique of "rangy reach and delicate control"[16] to her own punk-inflected full-length classic *Drastic Classicism* (1981). Complete with a feathery spiked hairdo, Armitage continues to take "the rigour and virtuosity inherent in classical dance and reshape it for the contemporary world. The result is sharp, jagged, invigorating and controversial, and is often danced to the sort of art-rock music that makes the loudest of discos seem as docile as a nursery at twilight."[17]

Collaborating with postmodern visual artists such as David Salle (b. 1952) and Jeff Koons (b. 1955), through companies such as the Paris Opera Ballet (origins: 1661), MaggioDanza (f. 1967, Florence, Italy), and her own ensemble, Armitage Gone! Dance (which returned to the United States in 2005), Armitage continues to carry her early "Punk Ballerina" title ever further out along the edges of controversy and provocation. She choreographed the MTV video *Vogue* (www.youtube.com, search "Madonna Vogue (Video)") for Madonna (b. Madonna Louise Ciccone, 1958) in 1990, and the steamy R & B/new jack swing single, "In the Closet," (www.youtube.com, search "Naomi Campbell In the Closet") for Naomi Campbell (b. 1970) and Michael Jackson (1958–2009) on Jackson's 1991 *Dangerous* album. She also choreographed the 40th Anniversary Central Park (New York City) Concert Performance of *Hair: The American Tribal Love-Rock Musical* in 2007 (Tharp, the earlier renegade, had choreographed the film, in 1979) and the 2008 Broadway musical *Passing Strange*.

A 2007 video ad for the Armitage company's January 2008 Joyce Theater (New York City) performance season features the quirky, Academy Award-winning actor Christopher Walken, himself trained at an early age as a dancer. (He can be seen tap dancing in Fatboy Slim's 2000 *Weapon of Choice* video at www.youtube.com,, search "Fatboy Slim - Weapon of Choice.") Armitage's video includes a humorous reference to her first work with the Paris Opera Ballet in 1983, when she was confronted by pointe-shoe-clad ballerinas, one of whom apparently threw a pair toward her from offstage. She then put on the shoes and reeled off some steps (www.youtube.com, search "Christopher Walken Wants Your Pointe Shoes").

Excerpts from the company's performance in April 2008 at Columbia College-Chicago include short sections of two other 21st century works, *Ligeti Essays* (2007) and *Time is the echo of an axe within wood* (2004), both full of her deliberate mixture of cocky, in-your-face pointed-ness (feet and staring eyes) and twisted classicism (www.youtube.com, search "Armitage Gone! Dance–Excerpt from Ligeti Essays"). The viewer can get a good idea of the breadth of her work by searching www.youtube.com, "Armitage Gone! Dance at the Joyce Spring 2011."

Armitage's own comments, in an interview for *Dance Magazine*, provide insight into the value of both modern and contemporary dance as they continue to evolve in the 21st century:

> [She] explained her aversion to aesthetic orthodoxy, the idea that danc-
> ers should bow to certain fixed ideals. "There is no such thing as pure,"
> she said. "The tradition of ballet, and all forms of dance, has been to
> incorporate what's going on around it. The Russians clearly took folk
> dances and stylized them so they became part of the ballet vocabulary.
> And Balanchine put jazz movements into ballet." Running her fingers
> through her spiky blond hair, she added: "We've got to have something
> that people recognize in their daily lives. Everything about life is more
> about cross-cultural influences, hybrid influences. That is to a great
> extent the history of art. The Renaissance, after all, was taking Greek
> ideas and updating them. That's really how art works."[18]

Meryl Tankard

Meryl Tankard, born into an itinerant Australian family on September 8, 1955, was a principal dancer with the Pina Bausch Tanztheater Wuppertal for six years (1978–1984), and has choreographed internationally with companies as diverse as The Lyon Opera Ballet (f. 1969), the mature dancers of Netherlands Dance Theater 3, and the Australian Ballet (f. 1962; Melbourne). Tankard's work can be characterized as grounded in classical ballet with a mix of contemporary dance and acrobatics (she likes to "fly"), and is often highly theatricalized and full of lighting and costume effects and video technology, such as rear projections and shadow play.

One can see excerpts from her 2007 *Kaidan: A Ghost Story* and the 1996 *Rasa*, reminiscent of Bausch's use of earth onstage beneath the dancers' feet, on Tankard's website (http://www.meryltankard.com/video.php). A short excerpt from her full-length *Wild Swans* (2003), all full of the above-noted effects, set on the Australian Ballet, and performed at the Sydney Opera House, is also available online [www.youtube.com, search "Meryl Tankard Wild Swans (trailer)"]. Tankard is particularly well-known for her creations at the opening ceremonies of the Sydney Olympics in 2000 (http://www.olympic.org/sydney-2000-summer-olympics) and Disney's Broadway production of *Tarzan* (2006).

James Kudelka

Born two days after Tankard and halfway across the globe, James Kudelka (b. September 10, 1955, Newmarket, Ontario) became one of his country's favorite sons in the contemporary ballet world, maintaining his role as Resident Choreographer with the National Ballet of Canada. The American Ballet Theatre website (www.abt.org) provides an excellent description of his style—a mix of Graham's dark and personal explorations with, perhaps, some leavening of emotions as in Lar Lubovitch's choreography.

> [Kudelka's] many works exemplify a tireless intelligence, probing and exploring the emotional and psychological avenues of the human condition with a vision at once forthright yet deeply compassionate. He terms himself a "conscientious observer" who gravitates in his work toward the themes of love, sex and death. Whether employing narrative means or the more elliptical strategies of abstraction, Kudelka's ballets show a choreographer at home equally in the vocabularies of classicism and modernism, but infusing everything he does with an arrestingly original and richly visual style. A remarkably prolific artist, his more

than seventy ballets have been staged by dance companies throughout the world.[19]

As a company supportive of both the classical canon and the commissioning of new contemporary ballets, ABT has a number of Kudelka pieces in its repertory, most famously *Cruel World*, from 1994 (2006, www.youtube.com, search "Pas de Deux from Cruel World"). Touching and yet troubling, the piece ends with ambivalence, a Kudelka trademark, leaving the audience uncertain how the characters got to that point or what might happen afterward—a reflection of the reality of many relationships. More purely classical but still poignant, his 1997 *The Four Seasons* (to the famous Vivaldi score) is excerpted at www.youtube.com, search "James Kudelka 'Four Seasons.'"

Stephen Petronio

Born the next year on March 20, 1956, in Newark, New Jersey, dance-choreographer Stephen Petronio was the first male dancer Trisha Brown hired in her company (1979–1986). He founded his own New York City-based Stephen Petronio Company in 1984 (http://stephenpetronio.com/). A collaborator with fashion designers (such as Benjamin Cho and Tara Subkoff), composers (especially Rufus Wainwright, Lou Reed, and Laurie Anderson), and visual artists (Cindy Sherman), Petronio

> makes dances that are aggressive, stylish, athletic, and highly sexed. His choreography surges with urban speed and power, but the individual movements are often both quirky and oddly juxtaposed. Unexpected tics and pauses texture and gnarl the rhythms of his hard-driving works…Perverse directional changes yank the dancers from the course of their momentum, while ungainly, but interesting positions misshape their bodies in the weirdest configurations imaginable, as when the torso arches back while the legs turn way, way in. In his choreography, says Petronio, "a verb follows straight after a verb." This description evokes well his action-packed dances, dense with an explosive accumulation of unlikely actions.[20]

To get a good sense of Petronio's high-octane energy, watch excerpts from the 2006 *BLOOM* or *Lareigne* (1996) (www.youtube.com, search "Stephen Petronio Company–Bloom–UK tour 2008" and "Stephen Petronio Company–Lareigne–UK tour 2008" respectively). His most famous work, *MiddleSexGorge* (1990), set to the driving music of the punk band Wire (f. 1976), is tightly packed with sexual power, movements initiated from the pelvic bone, and tension-filled partnering (excerpt at www.youtube.com, search "STEPHEN PETRONIO COMPANY Middlesexgorge").

Mark Morris

Original "bad boy" dancer-choreographer Mark Morris (b. August 29, 1956, Seattle, Washington) was known early on as the "long-haired, loud-mouthed, provocative [and] forthright homosexual."[21] As recently as 2004, interviewer Rose Eichenbaum could barely get him to talk for her book *Masters of Movement*.

Morris learned to read music as a child and studied flamenco, folk, and Balkan dance prior to entering the worlds of modern, ballet, and opera. Extremely musical as a choreographer and endlessly quirky, Morris's art is often one of irreverence and contradiction.

> While Spanish and Balkan dance, together with ballet, have been his major influences, he has also been deeply affected by Asian dance, European court dance, and indeed major figures of American modern dance: Isadora Duncan, Ruth St. Denis, Martha Graham, Merce Cunningham, Paul Taylor, Laura Dean, Lucinda Childs, Trisha Brown. Though music is the law of his mind, he is also passionately involved with stories, which work by an opposite logic. While his is a very modern mind—sophisticated, ironical, self-critical—he is also attached to old values and old music: Bach, Handel, and the things they felt were important…[His] habit has always been to join opposing things. This… produces a largeness of vision that has endeared him to the public.[22]

A true democrat with a small "d" since the beginning, Morris liberally reverses gender roles with parts and partners and has included dancers of all sizes, shapes, and weights. His art has one of the most diverse lists of musical accompaniment of nearly any choreographer—including Tahitian music, Antonio Vivaldi, Bob Wills and his Texas Playboys, Henry Purcell, George Gershwin, Stephen Foster, Yoko Ono—even though he favors Baroque composers. Morris tackles serious and humorous subjects with equal vigor.

The lovely and lively *Mozart Dances* (2006, excerpt at www.youtube.com, search "Mozart Dances (Mark Morris Dance Group)") contrasts hilariously with the high camp but respectful *Nutcracker* production *The Hard Nut* (1991, excerpt and discussion at www.youtube.com, search "The Hard Nut—A Look Back"). The genius of his full-length masterpiece *L'Allegro, il Penseroso ed il Moderato* (1988), set to Handel's rousing 1740 pastoral ode (excerpt at www.youtube.com, search "Mark Morris Dance Group—L'Allegro, il Penseroso ed il Moderato"), reconciles the *Sanguinic* and *Melancholic* variations of Balanchine's 1946 *The Four Temperaments* in exciting contemporary fashion—and with no less a complexity of patterns.

Equally brilliant, made 22 years later, is Morris's 2010 *Socrates* (set to many choreographers' favored abstract composer, Erik Satie) that, according to *The New York Times* critic Macaulay, is "the most sensuously attractive new choreography that I have seen by Mr. Morris in more than 10 years."[23] With both, as with so many of his works, the marriage of music and dance is astonishingly clear (also like Balanchine):

> As a choreographer, I am old-fashioned enough to believe in the deep relationship between dancing and music; I think they're part of the same thing. That's one reason I use vocal music so much because there's no equipment between the performer and the auditor; dancers and singers, to me, are the same species.... The reason I choreograph and have a dance company is the same reason I do everything—because of music. I love music in nearly every form and I choose music that is either overly familiar—to the point of irritation—or I've never heard it before in my life and it's a shocking revelation...and a bunch of things in between.[24]

One can see Morris himself in a four-minute excerpt from another of his acknowledged masterpieces, the deeply emotive and word-rhythm sensitive *Dido and Aeneas* (1989, www.youtube.com, search "dido en aeneas mark morris fr 3 ruzie"), set to the tragic opera of the same name (1689) by English composer Henry Purcell.

Directed by collaborator Barbara Willis Sweete, the three-minute "Gigue" (excerpt at www.youtube.com, search "Bach—Yo Yo Ma & Mark Morris—Falling Down Stairs") from the dance-for-film *Falling Down Stairs* (1994), is set to Johann Sebastian Bach's Third Suite for Unaccompanied Cello (c. 1717–1723) and played live by virtuoso cellist Yo-Yo Ma. This charming section clearly demonstrates the choreographer's skillful use of musicality, sophisticated patterning, and egalitarian partnering.

Founded in 1980, the Mark Morris Dance Group (MMDG, http://markmorrisdancegroup.org/) and the choreographer's work have extensively traveled the modern and ballet circuit through many residencies and commissions. Housed since 2001 in the state-of-the-art Mark Morris Dance Center in Brooklyn, New York, the company remains committed to the use of live music in all its touring productions and has maintained a West Coast home in Berkeley, California, and a Midwest home at the University of Illinois-Champaign. The prolific Mark Morris has already choreographed more than 120 works.

Nacho Duato

Nacho Duato (Juan Ignacio Duato Bárcia, b. January 8, 1957) was born and bred in Spain, studied with Maurice Béjart in Belgium and at the Alvin Ailey School in New York City, performed with the Swedish Cullberg Ballet for one year, and then with Nederlands Dans Theater and Jiří Kylián, for ten.

From 1990 to 2010, Duato served as the Artistic Director and Resident Choreographer of Spain's Compañía Nacional de Danza (CND, http:// cndanza.mcu.es/eindex.htm; f. 1979), one of Europe's finest contemporary ballet companies. The CND ensemble is truly international, boasting just half of the dancers from Duato's homeland and the other half from everywhere else. It is refreshingly endearing to hear many of them talk about being in such a diversified company between dances on the 2000 DVD *Three By Duato: Arenal, Duende, Por vos Muero.* Typical of contemporary ballet companies, CND frequently hosts guest international choreographers—well over a dozen in 2010—with a heavy slant toward the Europeans Ek, Forsythe, and Kylián.

In a 2001 *Dance Magazine* article, Duato and his interviewer discussed the company's versatile qualities:

> "I can do a period piece, such as Por Vos Muero [his 1996 masterpiece] inspired by fifteenth- and sixteenth-century Spanish music, but when you look at it, it is a contemporary work because I listen with my ears from today. We try to explain that music with our feelings as people of the twenty-first century." This approach has radically changed the company's image, and the Compania Nacional now plays to sold-out houses.
>
> Duato's choreographic style exhibits the impeccable balance of classical and contemporary technique characteristic of contemporary European ballet, especially the work of Jiří Kylián. It combines the choreographer's love for Spanish folk and period music. Using the traditional music of Spain helps lend the increasingly international company a profoundly Mediterranean character.[25]

One can get a good idea of Duato's fluid and sensual choreography, which clearly recalls the ten-year influence of Kylián's spare neoclassicism, through a ten-minute excerpt of his 1998 *Without Words*, a duet turned solo turned more duets becoming an octet, as set on the Berlin State Ballet (f. 2004) to music by Franz Schubert (1797–1828) (www.youtube.com, search "Without Words—Nacho Duato"). As with many contemporary companies in our current century, there is more and more of an amalgam of styles embodied in the CND (and the junior company, CND2, founded in 1999).

Consistent with Duato's mix of classicism, neoclassicism and his own country's regional styles, *Gnawa* (2005) draws on even deeper roots from North Africa's mystic Muslim brotherhoods of Morocco. Watching it, one can feel the piece build toward ecstasy as the insistent, bass-heavy music drives the dancers faster and faster toward the climax, a line of candles held aloft and gently glowing behind a statuesque tableau of a woman lifted up and reaching skyward (2009, www.youtube.com, search "Gnawa by Nacho Duato–Hubbard Street Dance Chicago").

The CND dancers developed under Duato's direction were powerful, men and women alike, reminding one of Ailey's lithe and luxuriant performers. Even in the more folkloric or liturgical Duato works, such as *Arenal* (1988), *Por Vos Mueros* (1996), and *O Domina Nostra* (2008), this physicality is deeply satisfying to audience members—we feel a part of the experience onstage due to the dancers' strong personalities. On the flip side, Duato's choreography also has a postapocalyptic streak as evidenced in such works as *Herrumbre (Rust)* (2004), *Alas* (2006), and *Hevel* (2007, in which dancers struggle against forces from within and without seemingly beyond their control).

With a bunker made of sand bags and a towering and twisted piece of fabric recalling a delicate skyscraper (or perhaps the twin towers) as the set, Duato's 2009 *Kol Nidre* (named after the prayer at the start of the Jewish holy day of Yom Kippur, a time to reflect and forgive; www.youtube.com, search "Kol Nidre–CND2") reflects a seriousness as it provides a harrowing look at what happens to children during war.

Duato headed to the Mikhailovsky Ballet (f. 1833) of St. Petersburg, Russia, at the beginning of 2011 as its Artistic Director, a move in keeping with today's growth of contemporary ballet on a global scale (www.youtube. com, search "Spanish choreographer Nacho Duato to head Mikhailovsky Ballet/euromaxx").

Angelin Preljocaj

Born the day after Duato, on January 9, 1957, in Sucy-en-Brie, France, the French Albanian Angelin Preljocaj founded Ballet Preljocaj in the lovely Aix-en-Provence area just north of the Riviera in 1984. Trained in ballet, Cunningham, and Noh (a type of Japanese theater), Preljocaj has created works not only for his company but all over Europe, Russia, and the United States for such companies as New York City Ballet, Ballet of La Scala in Milan (Italy), and the Bolshoi Ballet.

Favoring distinctive sets: monolithic walls straight out of the 1968 film classic *2001: A Space Odyssey* (*Eldorado*, 2007), large Noguchi-like rocks spread around the stage (*Blanche Neige*, 2008; www.youtube.com, search "Angelin Preljocaj–Blanche-Neige (Snow White)–Extract"), or a huge staircase framed with lit torches (*Fire Sketch*, 2006), Preljocaj keeps his dancers busy with highly theatrical floor work, numerous extensions, partnering, and patterns—with some confrontational vocalizations thrown in. Excerpts from these three dances and many others can be viewed on the Ballet Preljocaj website at www.preljocaj.org.

Suivront Mille Ans de Calme (And Then, One Thousand Years of Peace), from 2010, is typical—futuristic headdresses, movable and highly reflective all-steel walls, live sheep onstage—juxtapose sharply with the frantic, compelling movements of the many dancers (www.youtube.com, search "SUIVRONT MILLE ANS DE CALME–Angelin Preljocaj (2010)").

In contrast to similar dance institutions that host touring companies, choreographers, and residencies for a time, Ballet Preljocaj had famed architect Rudy Ricciotti build "The Black Flag" at the choreographer's home base in France in 2006. It is a place where the artists can both live in and create among four dance studios—a rare treat for the typically itinerant dancers in the 21st century.

In 2001 Preljocaj created his own *Rite of Spring* (2011, www.youtube.com, search "Angelin Preljocaj–'Le Sacre du Printemps,' 2001"), giving "a Berlin premiere to a new version whose shock value matches the original's. [The] new *Rite* features nudity, simulated rape and what one enthusiastic critic characterized as 'dance as eroticism.'"[26]

In watching Preljocaj's work set on the Stravinsky composition, one can see the total stripping down—in both a literal and metaphorical sense—of humanity into its worst impulses:

It has this barbarism, but at the same time it is constructed like a cathedral. That's its richness—a structured chaotic savagery. It's dangerous for a choreographer. Too much of the animal instinct, and you end up without any structure. Too much mathematical rigor, and you lose the human substance. You have to match the wildness, but you also have to give it coherence.[27]

Claude Brumachon

Also born in France, Claude Brumachon (b. May 2, 1959, Rouen), his body cut from the Greek Adonis mold, founded his powerful, rhythmically virtuosic, and at times extremely strenuous La Compagnie Claude Brumachon in 1984. Although it's clear his works are strongly grounded in classical ballet training, he remains a leading modern dance choreographer in France, heading the Centre Chorégraphique National de Nantes, one of dozens of nationally sponsored dance companies, since 1992.

His style is athletic and occasionally physically punishing. His works… have often been performed in nontheatrical spaces including museums, castles, even on a submarine base (*Emigrants*, 1993).[28]

This intensity—incredible body control, both in the varied tempos and partnering—can easily be seen in his signature eight-minute male duet, *Les Imdomptés* (The Indomitable Ones, 2008, www.youtube.com, search "les imdomptes avec Angelo Vergari").

Le Témoin (The Witness), from 2002, is harrowing. Performed in what looks like a furnace room or subterranean vault, with single bright lights blinding the audience, three dancers alternately crawl and smash their way around the space and on top of each other while one of the women shrieks hideously, all set to echoing hymnal music (www.youtube.com, search "Le Témoin–Claude Brumachon").

David Parsons

An enduringly popular modern dance choreographer, David Parsons (b. October 29, 1959, Rockford, Illinois) has created a powerful image that stands out and apart from any label. Founding Parsons Dance in 1987 (www.parsonsdance.org), his signature work *Caught* (1982) was choreographed while he was still a lead dancer for the Paul Taylor Dance Company from 1978 to 1987. The solo is set in the dark to music by electronic music innovator Robert Fripp (b. 1946) and, with impeccably timed flashes of strobe light, "catches" the lone dancer during the $1/10,000^{th}$ split-second illumination of the strobe at the pinnacle of each bounding leap or jump. The reader can view a one-minute excerpt of Parsons himself performing the solo at www.youtube.com, search "Caught," but you must see it live to believe it (www.youtube.com, search "David Parsons Caught"). Blinded by the darkness between jumps, the mind's eye is fooled into imagining the illusion of sustained human flight.

Parsons' nine years with Taylor were essential to his growth as a choreographer and bespeak the importance of that experience:

> Paul Taylor taught me how to live and think as an artist. His unconventional approach to life, his ability to craft brilliant dances, and his love of nature greatly influenced my life…Experimentation and taking risks is the basis of contemporary dance. The need to push boundaries is built into the art form. I started my company as a platform to take risks, to play with lighting, music, and sound. You can't discover new things about your soul unless you take risks. The performing artist delicately goes out on a limb.[29]

Pieces like the pajama-costumed *Sleep Study* (1986), the celebratory 1990 *Nascimento* (homage to the Brazilian guitarist Milton Nascimento), and the 2005 *In the End* (set to the Dave Matthews Band, excerpt at www.youtube.com, search "In the End David Parsons") showcase the stamina of Parsons' athletic, solid dancers. In some ways, his playful physicality recalls Lubovitch's lyrical strength while looking forward to Ohad Naharin's almost violent kinetic style.

Dance Funding

To a large extent, real help from governments defines a major difference between groups in the United States and other nation-based companies. In the 1960s, a Rockefeller report about the problems and possibilities of dance in America showed a real growth in audience numbers.[30] Soon after, the National Endowment for the Arts, during President Lyndon Johnson's administration, placed useful funding into the day-to-day operations of some of the nation's great companies. It also provided grants to states, companies, and individuals to increase audiences and promote creative works—not only in dance but in all the arts. Unfortunately, the dollar amounts have never significantly increased since then, while European governments continue to fund the arts to a much greater extent. It is difficult for United States-based companies to match the production standards of other country-based companies, although American choreographers have never allowed their creativity to be stifled by lack of dollars. Artists have needed to find and creatively solve artistic problems, especially by partnering with businesses and educational institutions.

Although many European companies receive more governmental support than American companies, hundreds of dance artist-teachers in the United States do receive state and private dollars not only for their productions, but for their very sustenance. These granting organizations are universities and arts magnet high schools. University dance professors and high school teachers receive a salary, benefits, and pensions commensurate with most state-supported dancer-choreographer-companies in Europe and elsewhere. Their main problem is that their works, by necessity and definition, are created mainly for and on students, and the rest of the world will probably never know if their works have artistic merit. Attend any regional or national festival of dance, the American College Dance Festival Association (f. 1973, www.acdfa.org) is the largest supporter of such conferences, and one can see dozens of dance artist-teachers who are earning enough to live decently.

During the 1970s and 1980s, professional dance was becoming more popular in big cities, and cities were building attractive and spacious fine and performing arts complexes to house local and touring dance and opera companies. (New York City's Lincoln Center for the Performing Arts was begun in 1959.) Universities were able to partner with the state and federal matching grants to employ National Endowment of the Arts (NEA)-approved dance touring companies—and there were many. The companies were able to take up residence, teach, and perform for a week or more, and two or more institutions could share one residency to reduce the cost of travel. These were the halcyon days of dance when a generation of college students and university audiences were able to see one or more of the best of American dance companies right in their own backyards. Professors of the arts are still dependent on their university sources, while NEA funds have dried up to a trickle.

The same professors and, at times, guest choreographers, are also able to use departmental, college, and university funds to defray the cost of productions. Telephones, student assistant salaries, and help with costumes and lights are all part of a university structure which supports the dance arts in the 21st century. Because colleges and universities may be found in urban, suburban, and rural settings, adequate funding for their events partly depends on healthy local public support. More audiences have the opportunity to see dance concerts in the halls of higher education, however, than are able to attend concerts in such prestigious performing arts centers as New York, Chicago, and San Francisco.

Selected Videos/DVDs/Films

Karole Armitage
Alive and Kicking (Program #96): Armitage Gone! Dance Visual Art & Dance: The Collaborations of David Salle and Karole Armitage (2009; 2 Volumes), Charles Dennis Productions.

Claude Brumachon
ADFV-5 Dancing on The Edge, Volume One (1992), American Dance Festival.

Siobhan Davies
Siobhan Davies DVDs: Siobhan Davies Dance.

Nacho Duato
Three by Duato: Arenal, Duende, Por Vos Muero (2000), Image Entertainment.

James Kudelka
The Firebird (2003), Rhombus Media.

Bill T. Jones
Bill T Jones: Dancing to the Promised Land (1994), Dance Horizons.

Mark Morris
Dido and Aeneas: A Danced Opera (1995), Amazon.com.
Falling Down Stairs (Yo-Yo Ma and Mark Morris) (1997), Amazon.com.
The Hard Nut (1991), Amazon.com.

David Parsons
Behind the Scenes with David Parsons (1999), Insight Media.
The Parsons Dance Company (2010), Dance Horizons.

Stephen Petronio
Stephen Petronio Company (2010), NTSC Company.

Angelin Preljocaj
Paris Opera Ballet Boxed Set (2010), Dance Horizons.
Siddharta (2010), Dance Horizons.

Elizabeth Streb
Alive and Kicking, Program 97 Streb (2009), Charles Dennis Productions.

Meryl Tankard
Black Swan (1995), ABC Shop.
Meryl Tankard (1995), Insight Media.

Notes

1   Elizabeth Streb, "The Vision: The Future," http://www.streb.org/V2/vision/index.html.

2   Rose Eichenbaum, *Masters of Movement: Portraits of America's Great Choreographers* (New York: Random House, 2004), p. 153.

3   "STREB Talks: PowerPoint," http://www.streb.org/V2/vision/powerpoint.html.

4   Julie Scelfo, "A High-Level Collaboration on a SoHo Loft," *The New York Times*, December 15, 2011, http://www.nytimes.com/2011/12/15/garden/elizabeth-streb-and-laura-flanders-at-home-with.html?partner=rss&emc=rss.

5   Stephanie Jordan and Sarah Whatley, "Siobhan Davies," in Martha Bremser, ed., *Fifty Contemporary Choreographers* (London, UK: Routledge, 1999), pp. 81–82.

6   "Title: Dance Work, Work: 13 Different Keys," http://www.siobhandaviesreplay.com/record.php?id=43.

7   "Siobhan Davies Replay: About the Archive," http://www.siobhandaviesreplay.com/index.php?view=sddda.

8   Debra Craine and Judith Mackrell, eds., *The Oxford Dictionary of Dance*, 2nd Ed. (Oxford, England: Oxford University Press, 2010), p. 243.

9   Bill T. Jones, with Peggy Gillespie, *Last Night on Earth* (New York: Pantheon, 1995), p. 252.

10 Donald Hutera, "Bill T. Jones," in Martha Bremser, ed., *Fifty Contemporary Choreographers* (London, UK: Routledge, 1999), p. 125.

11 Craine and Mackrell, *The Oxford Dictionary,*,pp. 316–317.

12 None of these nonsense wordplay phrases should be confused with the Swiss-born cultural movement Dada, which reached its peak from 1916 to 1922 and "concentrated its anti-war politics through a rejection of the prevailing standards in art through anti-art cultural works. Its purpose was to ridicule what its participants considered to be the meaninglessness of the modern world. In addition to being anti-war, dada was also anti-bourgeois and anarchist in nature" (http://en.wikipedia.org/wiki/Dada).

13 http://en.wikipedia.org/wiki/Gaga_(movement_language).

14 http://www.batsheva.co.il/en/Gaga.aspx/gaga-in-new-york.

15   The dancer/choreographer Bill Evans should not be confused with the great jazz pianist Bill Evans (1929–1980).

16   Robert Greskovic, "Karole Armitage," in Bremser, *Fifty Contemporary Choreographers*, p. 22.

17   Allen Robertson and Donald Hutera, *The Dance Handbook* (Boston: G. K. Hall., 1988), p. 226.

18   Christopher Reardon, "Return of the PUNK Ballerina—Karole Armitage," *Dance Magazine*, January 2001; http://findarticles.com/p/articles/mi_m1083/is_1_75/ai_68618185/.

19   "James Kudelka: biography," http://www.abt.org/education/archive/choreographers/kudelka_j.html.

20   Nicole Dekle Collins, "Stephen Petronio," in Bremser, *Fifty Contemporary Choreographers*, p. 189.

21   Joan Acocella, "Mark Morris," in Bremser, *Fifty Contemporary Choreographers*, p. 164.

22   Ibid., pp. 167–168.

23   Alastair Macaulay, "Cheekily Defying Expectations," *The New York Times*, February 24, 2010, http://www.nytimes.com/2010/02/25/arts/dance/25socrate.html.

24   "Mark Morris Dance Company: The Influence of Music," *Dance Consortium*, 2007, http://www.youtube.com/watch?v=yqnOhZgeZkO.

25   Laura Kumin, "Nacho Duato and the Compania Nacional de Danza: Contemporary Dance with a Spanish View—Interview," *Dance Magazine*, June 2001; http://findarticles.com/p/articles/mi_m1083/is_6_75/ai_75089723/.

26   Margaret Regan, "Rite Turn," *Tucson Weekly*, October 31, 2002, http://www.tucsonweekly.com/tucson/rite-turn/Content?oid=1071218.

27   Nadine Meisner, "The Rite Stuff," *The Independent*, April 20, 2002, http://www.independent.co.uk/arts-entertainment/theatre-dance/features/the-rite-stuff-658529.html

28   Craine and Mackrell, *The Oxford Dictionary*, 2010, p. 81.

29   Rose Eichenbaum, *Masters of Movement: Portraits of America's Great Choreographers* (New York: Random House, 2004), pp. 54–55.

30   The performing arts: problems and prospects; Rockefeller Panel report on the future of theatre, dance, music in America, 1965; www.nla.gov.au.

Chapter Eight
1960 to 1970

Anne Teresa De Keersmaeker, Philippe Decouflé, Michael Clark,
Postmodern Dance, Contemporary Technique I, Tero Saarinen, Sylvie Guillem,
Lightfoot León, Dance Theater Workshop, Mia Michaels, Helen Pickett,
Shen Wei, Alexei Ratmansky, Pam Tanowitz, Trey McIntyre

Anne Teresa De Keersmaeker

Anne Teresa De Keersmaeker (b. June 11, 1960, Mechelen, Belgium), the
next generation choreographer based in Belgium after Maurice Béjart
(she studied for two years at his Brussels school, Mudra), founded the all-
woman company Rosas in 1983, adding men after 1990 (www.rosas.be). De
Keersmaeker then became artist-in-residence at the Théâtre de la Monnaie in
1992 soon after Mark Morris's group (in residence from 1988 to 1991) had
moved back to the United States. Her work "…fuses the rigors of American
minimalism (built on repeating patterns in the style of Lucinda Childs) with
the emotive European expressionism spawned by Pina Bausch. The outcome
is a compelling, exhaustive display of relentless energy deepened by De
Keersmaeker's invitation to see her dancers from a dramatic point of view."[1]

The 1990 *Achterland* (filmed in 1993) includes many of De Keersmaeker's
typical themes such as repetitious patterns, a sense of community (especially
among the women), the use of stiletto heels and chairs, gender issue invoca-
tions, dramatic expressionism (particularly in her use of detailed gestures in
isolated body parts such as hands, hips, head, and feet), and a complex musicality. In this work, one hears the hollow echoing of thudding shoes, stomping
bare feet, and pounding hands as they resound on the wooden platforms upon
which eight dancers perform. These five women and three men laugh and
frown and whoop and gesture to live violin and piano, alternately performed
alongside and behind them by solo virtuoso musicians. The men are dressed
in the long pants, tight belts, and rolled-up sleeves of businessmen on a lunch

break—but are barefoot—while the women are in pant suits and stiletto heels; their underwear flashes as they fling themselves about, as does their loose, hanging-straight, sweat-drenched hair. Jump rope and hopscotch-like jumps accompany nonstop floor drops, turning *chassés*, body rolls, and insect-like push-ups for the men. At one point we see the women wisely pull on knee-pads. Many of the falls hearken back to Taylor's groundbreaking *Esplanade* (1975) (2010, www.youtube.com, search "Achterland, Anne Teresa De Keersmaeker 1 de 7" and 2010, www.youtube.com, search "Paul Taylor's Esplanade").

Inscrutable hand and head gestures intermingle with the breakneck fury, punctuated by pregnant pauses and pedestrian strolls performed in silence. The men, internalized, insular, and asocial, remain wholly unaware of anyone but themselves throughout most of the seventy-minute, full-length performance, while the women, eyes bright and flashing, share a flirty, genuinely happy camaraderie directly with the audience. At one point one man hysterically attempts to join the club with a mock, gender-reversal solo of the women's movements; he is frowned upon and walked away from to be left alone, with just the pianist sardonically laughing at him. The only partnered lift in the whole evening—it's barely more than a woman's dive into a man's arms, and he immediately sloughs her off—occurs an hour into the program. In *Achterland*, the men and women clearly live different lives and inhabit different worlds.

As in much modern dance that willingly shares the process alongside the product, we see the performers themselves move the platforms and chairs on and off the largest platform (this choreographer loves to use chairs in her work) and dress and undress before our eyes, boldly exposing the transitions. Sometimes the dancers nod to the musicians to begin certain solos, and the musicians often nod back.

A Belgian television promotional video (www.youtube.com, search "Rosas gaat op zoek naar contrasten, TV1") includes some interview fragments with De Keersmaeker, as well as an excerpt from the 2006 *D'un Soir un Jour* (Of a Night a Day), set to Claude Debussy's score *Prelude to the Afternoon of a Faun* (1894) and complete with her trademark props (two benches).

Sanjoy Roy of London's *The Guardian* concisely tells us more about her early work and general approach to choreography:

> In the company's early years, De Keersmaeker made distinctive all-female quartets, their drilled discipline offset by displays of "femininity": tip-toe strutting, swishy skirts and swinging hair…She also

developed a vigorous, sometimes violent style of action that she has since left behind, although many of her pieces still require a great deal of stamina.

She also began to add more layers to the work—text, voice, film—sometimes producing work that was closer to experimental theatre than dance… The composer she is most closely associated with is Steve Reich [in large part because her earliest influences involved minimalism].

Composition is key. In many of De Keersmaeker's works, there is a tension between order and disorder—complexity glimpsed at the chaos like patterns in rain, or disturbances appearing in machine-like patterns as if spanners thrown into works. Don't expect an easy time with De Keersmaeker. She can be high-minded and demanding—and you'll need to be attentive—but the rewards are great.[2]

In a variation to the commissioning of composers to create music for a choreographer's new work, De Keersmaeker commissioned several different composers to create works for an existing piece of choreography, her 2000 *Counter Phrases*. Excerpts of the work can be seen in a 2004 film of the dance performed in a square between buildings on a tiny, oval "island" surrounded by water at www.youtube.com, search "Counter Phrases De Keersmaeker" and, with ambient woodland sounds, by searching "Rosas Counterphrases Marta Coronado's Solo."

While her colleague in Germany, Pina Bausch (discussed in Chapter 6), focused primarily on women in opposition to men, De Keersmaeker's attention is solely on women with a far more empowering and less oppressive perspective.

Philippe Decouflé

Mime and Nikolais-trained Philippe Decouflé (b. October 22, 1961, Neuilly-sur-Seine, Paris) has found ways to make contemporary dance great fun, something not always possible or appropriate with many of the serious issues addressed by the modern world. His accessible mix of dance and theater is created out of "arresting stage images…optical illusions…video imagery, lighting effects, mirrors, stage machinery, and elaborate costumes."[3] His short film *Le Petit Bal Perdu* (1994, www.youtube.com, search "le petit bal perdu decouflé") presents an almost slapstick version of the illogical logic of a dream, giving the audience a clear insight into his witty, prop-filled, gestural language. Decouflé and his dancers (his company, Decouflé Company of Arts, or DCA, was founded in 1983, www.cie-dca.com) understand commitment, the mesmerizing contrast between sustained and sudden movement, the juxtaposition of close-ups and long shots, and extreme facial expressions. Decouflé's dances remind the viewer of the work of the Dada movement (1916–1922) photographer Man Ray, whose surrealist images shocked with their audacity.

In *Three Boys Dance Fight* (2007, www.youtube.com, search "Philippe Decouflé 3 Boys Dance Fight"), three boys dance and fight while sitting next to one another in a coolly choreographed vaudeville number. The 1986 *Codex* (excerpt at www.youtube.com, search "Philippe Decouflé—Codex1") involves full-bodied creatures, wearing unitards and flippers, flapping about to ecstatic Middle Eastern music. The piece was inspired by Italian artist-naturalist Luigi Serafini's (b. 1949) *Codex Seraphinianus* (1981), a famous encyclopedia of mythical plants, animals, and insects.

Decouflé's popularity became solidified when he was asked to choreograph for the 1992 Winter Olympics opening and closing ceremonies in Albertville, France. An extraordinary montage of those ceremonies can be seen at www.youtube.com, search "Decouflé Crazy Zawinul 'Albertville Procession.'"

Michael Clark

Nineteen sixties' "bad boy" Michael Clark (b. June 2, 1962, Aberdeen, Scotland), who founded the Michael Clark Company (http://www.michaelclarkcompany.com/) in 1984 and has lived through the loss of a close partner (as did Bill T. Jones, who lost his partner Arnie Zane), excessive clubbing, heroin addiction, and depression, continues to push the envelope.

> [He has] built himself a cult following thanks to his punk rock persona, fashionable friends, cool collaborators, and a little personal scandal on the side. But despite all this cutting edge anarchy, his choreography sticks close to its classical roots. He may have a devilish spirit but he's a sucker for beauty. And all the better for it.

> "*Oh My Goddess*," which premiered at last year's Dance Umbrella (2004), sees him in fine form and doing everything on his own terms. In a witty opening, the dancers come scurrying on lemming-like, wearing paper bags on their heads. *Clark carries off such moments of lunacy with complete conviction, which is always the secret to getting away with it.* [Italics added]

Music from krautrockers Can, Sex Pistols, The Human League, and T Rex rattles the Sadler's Wells theater speakers, but it's a section set to Erik Satie's sparse, slow, spacious piano pieces that is most striking.

A slow chain of chords chimes from the four pianos at the back of the stage, ringing into silence, create a barren backdrop. Tom Sapsford starts dancing, making a succession of angular statements. Everything is equally spaced, in perfect lines and 90-degree angles. The body is open, like the modal harmonies.

Sapsford is followed by two dancers, then three, moving in unison to Satie's music. The choreography is perfunctory almost, unsentimental but strangely absorbing. Very Zen. When the four pianists play their pieces concurrently, the bare chords overlay each other to become clashing and antagonistic. The dancers do the same, clashing silently as they perform their different pieces simultaneously, mixing up the signals. It's a very simple idea, but sometimes the simple ones are the most effective.

...Michael Clark's brilliantly British fudge of classicism, rebellion, superiority, and self-deprecating humour makes him something to be thankful for.[4]

The London dance critic Sanjoy Roy aptly calls Clark an "iconoclassicist," yet contends that

...classical ballet remains at the heart of Clark's choreography, even as he works to disrupt it. You recognize classical steps, positions and sequences, with balletic lines of beauty made kinky by unexpected angles, torques and changes of direction (in this, you see the influence of Merce Cunningham). This makes his choreography look highly controlled and technical. You notice it most in his trio of Stravinsky works and Swamp [1986], but even at his most theatrically anarchic there is a sense of strictness in the dancing.

You might (as many dance critics do) prefer the pieces with less of an up-yours attitude, or you might (like many audiences) prefer the punch of provocation. It's the tension between them that marks Clark's iconoclassicism.[5]

In 1992, Clark did his version of *Rite of Spring*, cryptically called *mmm...* as one-third of his three-part homage to Stravinsky. A short one-minute excerpt gives the viewer just a taste of the piece (www.youtube.com, search "Dance:

Michael Clark Company"). Set to the familiar score but played live onstage by two pianists, this version of the music brings freshness to the dance that keeps it raw—the way Clark likes it.

> Once the driving chords of the Augurs of Spring began, it was evident that this staging would take the viewer far from pagan Russia to a distant planet inhabited by bald-patched men and women in "pleather" skirts, an ensemble of black toilet-seat-collared dancers, a skull-bearing sage with a lace veil, an enormous marshmallow Gumby figure, "flower people" in crotch-less green tights over a standard leotard, and a Chosen One who ensures the return of Spring by performing a sort of extreme yoga in solitude. All of this occurs in a spotless white room in front of a hall of eight large revolving mirrors.[6]

Clark's anarchic *Hail the New Puritan* (1986) is a film about Clark directed by video pioneer Charles Atlas (b. 1958, excerpt at www.youtube.com, search "The Fall and Michael Clark"). Its punk rock band blares and cut-out pants reveal naked rear ends on some dancers.

Postmodern Dance

One might consider the postmodern era in dance just another period of innovative experimentation, reacting to its modern antecedents, but at Judson Memorial Church (New York City) on July 6, 1962, a new generation of revolutionaries expanded our consciousness about the very meaning of dance. Audiences had to find their own ways toward understanding, let alone embracing, these new and challenging performances.

Most postmodern dancers tested their audience's comprehension and acceptance on purpose. Yvonne Rainer's (b. 1934) pedestrian *Trio A* (1966, see a 1978 filming of one version of the piece at www.youtube.com, search "Yvonne Rainer Trio A") goes nowhere slowly, an attempt by the choreographer to "eliminate all sense of learned technique and polish from her movement."[7] The audience for Lucinda Childs' (b. 1940, www.lucindachilds.com) *Street Dance* (1966) sat in loft windows listening to an audiotape explaining the piece and looking out at the dancers who moved among the city crowd, only partially visible. Steve Paxton's (b. 1939)[8] *Backwater: Twosome* (1977) incorporated the dance form called contact improvisation (http://www.contactimprov.net/). Watch a 2007 YouTube video of Paxton himself in a solo improvisation dance called *Material for the Spine* (www.youtube.com, search "Steve Paxton Material for the Spine—DVDrom Trailer").

Judson Church choreographers explored many questions about the very nature of performance, such as: Is a theater necessary? Are performers necessary? Is planning necessary? Are dance-trained professionals necessary, or may we use nondancers? Can visual artists create performances? When does a performance begin or end? May audience members actually be participants in a work? May there be same-sex dance partners? Can dances be improvised in whole or in part? Are there structures in time that can be created just once to provide a foundation for a new work? And are turtles moving in the dark with flashlights attached to their shells–dance? Answers to these and many more intriguing questions provide grist for the experiments of many of the choreographers and nondancers who came out of the Judson camp.

Defying categorization, the postmoderns appeared at unique times (midnight, early morning, unexpectedly), places (city squares, subway platforms, building tops), and theaters, with performers sometimes technically proficient and, other times, wholly (and deliberately) untrained in either the *danse d'école* or any of the modern dance techniques previously mentioned. The dances of the postromantics and postclassicists that came to be called modern in the early part of the 20th century were no less avant-garde than the nascent postmodern performers of the 1960s, but historical memory is always short, and this was a new generation searching for its own answers.

However, the idea that there might exist a particular postmodern dance technique counters the frequent questioning of some postmoderns about the use of "traditional" dance technique at all. In general, postmodern art (including dance) is more focused on finding ways to deconstruct, understand, and articulate the depersonalizing aspects of today's society through experimental applications of theories such as existentialism, intellectualism, and commercialism to both movement and theater. In an ostensible effort to evoke the humanizing truths lying dormant beneath today's surface complexities, resulting in significance at least as discordant as it is enlightening, postmodernism has employed established techniques such as ballet, modern dance, jazz, and styles from various cultures. It has even used visual artists as movement performers, who had never studied dance, to forward their challenging agendas. Do they accomplish their goals? The postmodernists do not offer easy answers.

The priority of these postmodern revolutionaries seems to be choreography that can be created through a group effort (rather than by just one person) and no particular technique, form, performance space, aesthetic, tradition, culture, style, or boundary. In the 1960s, they were led by

choreographers such as Yvonne Rainer, Steve Paxton, David Gordon
(b. 1936), and Lucinda Childs, and painter-performance artist Allan
Kaprow (1927–2006), among many others.

An excerpt from the 1984 Brooklyn Academy of Music re-creation of
the opera *Einstein on the Beach* (1976), with music by Philip Glass, highlights
movement contributions of Childs (www.youtube.com, search "Einstein on
the Beach, Segment I"). One cannot describe this work only in the genres
of dance, theater, art, or music. Childs followed up her *Einstein* collaboration
with Glass three years later in *Dance*, this time with geometric minimalist
artist and filmmaker Sol LeWitt (1928–2007), in a full-length work that
mesmerized viewers with the three artists' overlapping and accumulating
patterns. Childs herself says:

> This magnificent artist, this minimalist artist, [has] an aesthetic not so
> different from mine in the sense of pure geometric shapes…and all of
> these shapes correspond to the patterns that the dancers are dancing.
> And I came back to Sol LeWitt and he said "I think the décor should
> be the dancers dancing in the film and we could do a big screen
> downstage with a film of the dancers dancing so that you have the
> dancers dancing in film and the same dancers dancing on the stage,
> completely synchronized.[9]

It was heady work. Childs' *Dance* was reconstructed with some slight
changes thirty years later, in 2009, and was still touring the world the following
year. See an excerpt of the performance from the Museum of Contemporary
Art-Chicago (MCA) at www.youtube.com, search "Lucinda Childs' DANCE."[10]

With nihilistic dance events often called "happenings," the postmodern
experiments of the sixties and beyond countered the solidifying modern
dance philosophies and the increasing theatrical capacities of the modern
dancers of the 1950s. These programs were structured to varying degrees
in ways that made it impossible to ever be exactly repeated. Dance makers
often included untrained dancers, pedestrian movements, and improvisation
in tandem with visual and musical artists with the same sensibilities. The
experiments were intellectually challenging and revolutionary. They were
also exciting. In fact, these experimentalists have rightly been recognized
for their important, continuing contributions. Within fifteen years of Judson
Church, the term "postmodern dance" had become affixed to their endeavors.
Even though their work represented the very latest "modern" incarnation,
that term had already become too closely identified with the earlier modern

dance pioneers and their followers, and so its use could only be confusing. The term "postmodern dance," then, although connected philosophically to concurrent aesthetic forms among the other arts, was originally and simply intended to mean choreography done *after* the earlier modern dance era, and with the passage of time can now be viewed in an historical sense.

Contemporary Technique I

In contrast to the postmoderns' disassociation from technique, the technical capacities of dancers and the demands on their artistry have increased exponentially over the past decades, offering choreographers opportunities to expand and heighten images—visual, auditory, and, of course, kinesthetically.

Today's contemporary explorations by choreographers require dancers of unbridled technical virtuosity to improve their skills in acting, music, and other dance styles, further erasing the demarcations between the capabilities of modern and ballet dancers. In addition, improved techniques of ballet dancers, modern dancers, and athletes elicit some interesting parallels. In general, people jump higher, turn more times, have more stamina, and are stronger, faster, and more flexible today than their forbearers. This is partly due to our increased knowledge and its application about better diets, dietary supplements, injury prevention and therapies, and more scientific training methods for both athletes and dancers.

Our society has a reverence for technology and the philosophy that a somehow perfect technical creation, human or otherwise, can be achieved. Many feel that a dancer's unbridled passion for putting across dance as an art form has been usurped by the overwhelming need for technical achievement in a highly competitive market. Today's audience member can (and perhaps should) demand both passionate involvement *and* exquisite technique from all dance performers.

The similarities among the modern, postmodern, and always-new alternative art forms seem to be in their choreographic singularity—the notion of an individual's right to create whatever she or he wishes. In 1966, dance historian Selma Jeanne Cohen referred to the field of modern dance as an "art of iconoclasts."[11] It still is.

Irrespective of the techniques used, the artistic currents that have been flowing since the time of Isadora Duncan embrace whatever style is appropriate for the choreographer's expression. New ballet works that combine diverse traditions, such as in the Alonzo King (birth date not available) LINES Ballet (f. 1982, http://www.linesballet.org), Australian Dance Theatre (f. 1965, www.adt.org.au), and Les Ballets Africains (f. 1952, www.lesballetsafricain.com), among many others, use everything from classical ballet to hiphop, modern dance to yoga.

Tero Saarinen

Tero Saarinen (September 7, 1964, Helsinki, Finland) was born just over two years after the Judson Church postmodern movement began. Training at his native Finnish National Ballet in the eighties and studying Butoh, martial arts, and Kabuki in Japan in the nineties, Saarinen founded the Tero Saarinen Company in 1996 in Helsinki (http://www.terosaarinen.com/en). Besides his own company, he has choreographed at Nederlands Dance Theatre, Batsheva, and Ballet Gulbenkian (Portugal), among many other companies. His full-length 2008 *Next of Kin* (excerpt on www.youtube.com, search "Saarinen Next of Kin") is dark and moody, and that's just what we get: sharply angled lights and shadows, flickering screen images projected through the beams of strobe lights, darkened hallways with staggering bodies passing along them.

Saarinen loves live music and collaborates very closely with his sound, costume, and lighting designers to create wholly believable, yet fantastic expressionistic worlds—worlds that are in demand everywhere (an early 2009 tour included theaters in Australia and New Zealand). Set to the Don Johnson Big Band (a Finnish hip hop group founded in 2000) and reminiscent in tone and body type of some of David Parsons' work for Paul Taylor (for example, Parsons' solos in Taylor's 1985 *Last Look*), Saarinen's 2009 *L.L.H.* embodies the choreographer's quirky and intense sojourns, done solo by Saarinen himself. Desperately trying to escape the "trap" of his business attire in what appears to be an all-white warehouse, he staccato-strips the suit off piecemeal, interrupted at one point by the projected face of Don Johnson singing his song while superimposed onto various body parts of Saarinen (excerpt at www.youtube. com, search "Don Johnson Big Band LLH w/Tero Saarinen"). Saarinen's blue-eyed Nordic good looks mirror the choreography's ferocity.

Sylvie Guillem

Sylvie Guillem (b. February 23, 1965, Paris, France), famous first as an *étoile* at the Paris Opera Ballet under Artistic Director Rudolf Nureyev during the 1980s, loaned herself out by the 1990s so often to so many different choreographers that she became known as "*Mademoiselle Non*" (as in, "No, I do not work for any one dance company!"). By early 2009, however, Guillem had become an Associate Artist at the famed Sadler's Wells Theatre, London, although continuing her peripatetic approach to dance.

Like Mikhail Baryshnikov before her (or Rudolf Nureyev, Anna Pavlova, and hundreds of other performers) and ABT's David Hallberg after her, Guillem is representative of not companies nor choreographers but highly individual dancers wholly intent on exploring a myriad number of styles and genres. As the 21st century progresses, more and more extraordinarily talented dancers like her feel compelled to strike out on their own, sometimes starting companies, sometimes just going where the jobs are. Famous for her extraordinary flexibility, hypersensitive musicality, and astonishing balance skills on and off pointe, Guillem has justly been sought out to perform some of the most cutting-edge, physically challenging dances ever created. William Forsythe (see Chapter 6) used her in his famous 1987 *In the Middle, Somewhat Elevated*, set to music by his frequent collaborator, the Dutch electronic and instrumental composer Thom Willems (brief excerpt at www.youtube.com, search "Sylvie Guillem in the Middle Somewhat Elevated"). Mats Ek (see Chapter 6) created *Wet Woman* for her in 1996; the original recording, set beside a bare table, can be seen in its totality at www.youtube.com, search "Modern Dance—Wet Woman (full Ver)–Sylvie Guillem." Companies around the world have engaged her and, even nearing her fifties she was still all over YouTube. Like Baryshnikov (b. 1948) did in the 1970s and 1980s, Guillem regularly embodies that rare successful—and transcendent—application of classical ballet technique to the service of increasingly varied and challenging contemporary sensibilities.

In a solo, the eight-minute *Two* by Russell Maliphant (b. 1961 in Canada but studied at Sadlers Wells), Guillem easily holds our attention without ever traveling outside of a 4' x 4' center stage, down-lit square box [www.youtube.com, search "Sylvie Guillem—Two (Rise and Fall)"].

Lightfoot León

Lightfoot León (a perfect dance name!), otherwise known as the choreographic and dancer team of British-born Paul Lightfoot (b. August 31, 1966, Kingsley, England) and his Spanish-born female partner, Sol León (birth date unknown, Córdoba, Spain), have been collaborating together since 1991, resident artists since 2002, and artistic advisors since 2003 at the Nederlands Dans Theatre (NDT). Both trained at NDT and, amplifying Jiří Kylián's style, the couple creates fascinating worlds of virtuosic and grounded balletic movement, alongside often startling vocalizations.

In their 2003 *Shutters Shut*, set to playful poet Gertrude Stein's (1874–1946) own recorded voice of her stream-of-consciousness word-portrait *If I Told Him: A Completed Portrait of Picasso* (1924), "the choreography sets lightning-fast gestures, wriggles and shifts of direction to the nonsensical wit of [the poem]…The effect is improbably funny and charming."[12] A mesmerizing excerpt can be viewed at www.youtube.com, search "Shutters Shut by Lightfoot León."

Lightfoot León created an homage to silent movies in their 2005 *Silent Screen*, set to the music of composer Philip Glass (excerpt at www.youtube.com, search "Silent Screen by Lightfoot León"). An excerpt of the poignant *Subject to Change* (2003), set on and around a large red rug and choreographed to music by Franz Schubert, can be seen at www.youtube.com, search "NDTII Subject to Change Lightfoot/León pas de deux." Their work is alternately serious and light but always full of musical, engaging, and fun-to-watch dance.

Dance Theater Workshop/New York Live Arts

Welcoming homes that consistently support contemporary dance began to spring up like wild flowers in the 1960s. The list includes the invaluable Dance Theater Workshop (DTW, f. 1965, http://www.dancetheatreworkshop.org/), based on West 19th Street in the Chelsea district of downtown New York City, which since 2002 has had its own 180-seat theater showcasing the many dance works that pass through its doors.

DTW has been "the Chelsea institution that has been at the forefront of contemporary dance for over forty years," states Melena Ryzik from *The New York Times* UrbanEye, "a free e-mail newsletter."[13] Bill T. Jones was honored at DTW's June 5, 2008 gala benefit inside the Skirball Cultural Center (f. 1996) at New York University. He had gotten a big push back in 1977 at DTW (along with his late co-choreographer/partner Arnie Zane), his first visit to the space. In his interview with Ryzik, Jones said, "Dance has to prove itself again and again. It's an esoteric branch of the entertainment industry."[14]

The small size of DTW's original 20th Street loft was offered free of charge for many choreographers. No single style emerged, but the post-1950s pioneers such as Jeff Duncan, Jack Moore, Art Baumann, William Dunas, Deborah Jowitt, and Kathryn Posin accelerated the acceptance of "experimental" solo, duet, and small-cast dances of many postmodern era choreographers not associated with the postmodern Judson Church philosophy. Choreographers Ronald K. Brown, Donald Byrd, H. T. Chen, David Dorfman, Molissa Fenley, David Gordon, John Jasperse, Ralph Lemon, Susan Marshall, Bebe Miller,

Mark Morris, David Neumann, Pepón Osorio, David Parsons, and Tere O'Connor, among dozens of others, found an artistic home at DTW.

In April 2010 it was announced that DTW and the Bill T. Jones/Arnie Zane Dance Company would merge, a unique union of two distinct dance visions. In February 2011, its new name became New York Live Arts (http://newyorklivearts.org). Consider that NYLA continues to hold more than 100 performances annually with nearly half that many artists and companies connected to it, while Bill T. Jones/Arnie Zane involves an entourage, including the dancers, of more than 25. Intriguing marriages such as these in the dance world seem to be one of the 21st century's answers to decreased funding.

Mia Michaels

Modern dance as a serious commercial enterprise has been around since at least the time of Denishawn, although all dance, like all art, has had to find monetary support for centuries. The rapidly evolving 21st century dance world has broken into television with a huge bang with choreographers born in the 1960s through 1980s taking to the airwaves. Pop-TV star choreographers such as Mia Michaels and Sonya Tayeh (see Chapter 9) on shows like Fox's *So You Think You Can Dance* (f. 2005, SYTYCD, http://www.fox.com/dance/), MTV's *Randy Jackson Presents America's Best Dance Crew* (f. 2008; http://www.mtv.com/shows/dance_crew), and ABC's *Dancing with the Stars* (f. 2005, http://abc.go.com/primetime/dancingwiththestars), reflect this rapid growth.

Mia Michaels (b. 1965, Coconut Grove, Florida) grew up in a family of dancers and directed and created her own New York-based company, RAW (Reality At Work), in 1997. She has choreographed works for Madonna (the 2001 "Drowned World" tour), Celine Dion (the 2002 "A New Day" Las Vegas concert), Prince (his 2000 concert tour), Cirque du Soleil (the 2006 "Delirium" tour), and commercials (especially for Ziploc bags and the realtor Coldwell Banker). She is best known, however, as a judge and choreographer on *So You Think You Can Dance*. Michaels won an Emmy for her "Park Bench" duet for Heidi and Travis during Season 2 set to Celine Dion's "Calling You" (complete duet at www.youtube.com, search "Travis & Heidi—Contemporary"). Her ensemble work for the 2007 SYTYCD Season 3 dance *The Moment I Said It*, set to music by Imogen Heap (b. 1977), can be viewed at www.youtube.com, search "Mia Michaels—The Moment I Said It."

Using a condensed fusion of athleticism and hip hop, ballroom, lyrical, and virtuosic classical technique, Michaels's choreography is rhythmically complex (note the extremes of speed juxtaposed with occasional stillness) and full of traditional balletic partnering and corps patterning work (in unison, canon, alternation, mirroring). Whether she would agree or not, her choreography borrows liberally from the modern dance lexicon of Doris Humphrey's fall-and-recovery style; Taylor's free-flying *Esplanade* (1975) jumps; frequent use of trust dives, leaps, hard knee drops, shoulder rolls, crawls, and floor drags; the breaking of the fourth wall of the proscenium arch (or, more precisely, with SYTYCD, their circular stage); facial and body gestures; far-off-balance tilts, women partnering men.

Within the 90-second time restraint, Michaels's dances are Tharp-Armitage-Taylor amalgams; she learned her lessons well. A valid complaint might be that the taste of these pieces tends toward the sentimental, but that seems to be what the audience likes.

Nevertheless, Michaels herself can help the reader better understand the risk, motivation, and sensibility of a current choreographer working hard to both entertain and challenge her dancers and audience:

> My energy and way of movement pushes [students] to a place that is a little bit uncomfortable; which is what I experience every time I get into the studio. It's so easy for great technical dancers to hide behind steps. I try to open up and free them…. If an artist or dancer leaves the room [and is] the same person who walked in, it was a waste of time. It's all about growth.[15]

Helen Pickett

Articulate dancer, actress, choreographer, and published writer Helen Pickett (b. July 6, 1967, San Diego, California), a welcome female addition to the mostly male choreographic contemporary ballet scene, brings ambition, accessibility, formality, improvisation, and a distinctive (and highly distorted) liveliness to the genre. Her rapid-fire 2008 *Eventide* (www.youtube.com, search "Boston Ballet in Helen Pickett's 'Eventide'") and fluid *Etesian* (2006, www.youtube.com, search "Christian Squires") embody that singularity.

Having trained with the classical ballet-musical-nightclub dancer-choreographer Michael Smuin (1938–2007) and the San Francisco Ballet in the 1980s, and studied with and performed for William Forsythe's Ballet Frankfurt from 1987 to 1998, it is easy to spot Pickett's next-generation mix of Forsythe's organic technical virtuosity and deconstruction of classic ballet vocabulary. Pickett was one of the *Dance Magazine's* "25 to Watch" in January

2007. (*Dance Magazine* is a wonderful starting place for the latest news about up-and-coming dancers, choreographers, and companies in all styles all over the world.) (www.dancemagazine.com)

> Given all the hand wringing about the dire state of contemporary ballet, it is good to be reminded that new work is being made all the time and that much of it is of at least some interest. Genius choreographers might not come around very often; choreographers with potential do.
>
> Helen Pickett is one, judging by "Petal," which had its New York premiere on Wednesday at the Joyce Theater courtesy of the Aspen Santa Fe Ballet… "Petal" combines a sophisticated sense of spacing with a resonant exploration of emotional discovery. Eddies of social groupings swirl within a stage bounded by large white screens and suffused by Todd Elmer's gorgeously lush lighting design of Easter-egg yellows, pinks and oranges. A sense of restless female desire pervades the choreography, which sets intimate duets and solos within more formal group patterns, much as pockets of tenderness bloom within the relentless music by Philip Glass and Thomas Montgomery Newman.
>
> There are many styles in play here, including Twyla Tharp's tough, sexy female athleticism and, most strongly, the aggressively buckling, rippling movement language of William Forsythe, in whose company Ms. Pickett danced for many years.[16]

The 2009 work was set on the Atlanta Ballet in 2011, a rehearsal excerpt of which, with Pickett's voice-over, can be seen at www.youtube.com, search "FUSION: Petal by Helen Pickett."

Shen Wei

Mainland China-born choreographer, director, dancer, painter, and designer Shen Wei (b. 1968, Hunan) founded the first modern dance company ever in his homeland in 1991, the Guangdong Modern Dance Company, before taking up training in New York City in 1995 with Murray Louis. Five years later he opened Shen Wei Dance Arts (www.shenweidancearts.org) in the same city and his work has since caught on internationally, with the choreographer receiving numerous commissions and awards.

Because he grew up learning a variety of art forms at the same time, especially Chinese opera, Wei does not separate them in his work, often designing the costumes, makeup, and sets for his pieces. Reminiscent of how the traditional Navajo Indians erase their sand paintings after spending upwards of a week or more creating them, *Re-(Part I)*, from 2006, incorporates a full-stage Tibetan Mandela made of paper shards that eventually becomes indecipherable, the pieces partially stuck to the dancers' costumes as the movements destroy the powerful image. The work can be seen in excerpt form at www.youtube.com, search "Re-(Part I) and Re-(Part II)."

Not wed to the often breakneck speed of American contemporary dance and ballet—although all fourteen of Wei's dancers can move at top speed when necessary—the choreography usually takes its time getting somewhere, building incrementally in momentum from near stillness.

In the 2004 full-length work *Connect Transfer* (performed November 26, 2005),

> …the energy seems to spring from the choreography, particularly when the dancers start to paint the stage-canvas. It comes as a surprise: one of them enters the stage and after moving down on the stage, he performs circular movements wearing a special glove on one of his hands. Movement [of dancers usually] paints the space but it does not leave any tangible trace—in this case, however, a mark is being left. Others are added in various colors, black, blue, green and red. The result is an abstract painting whose fragments will be sold in future performances in order to keep a connection with the previous one— here, connection is a concept that refers not just to the dancing bodies on stage but also to their relationship with the visual elements in the piece and with the audience.[17]

Invited back to China by its Olympic Committee to choreograph (brilliantly) the Opening Ceremonies of the 2008 Summer Beijing Games, Wei expanded the brush-dancing from *Connect Transfer* by embedding the idea within a huge opening scroll and then using his dancers to paint like giant calligraphers (Wei's contribution starts near the six-minute mark at www.youtube.com, search "Beijing Olympic Opening Ceremony Part 2").

In 2003 he created his own *Rite of Spring* to the momentous Stravinsky work. In it, Wei

> stripped "Sacre" of much of its historical baggage and made it possible for audiences to really feel Stravinsky's genius. Wei's work, called "The Rite of Spring," begins even before the audience knows it as the danc- ers calmly walk to their places on stage before the house lights have dimmed. Fazil Say's recorded pianos thunder out from speakers to put

the dancers into motion—tumbles, leaps, twists, falls, jazzy isolations, voguish arms—and all to an eerie deadpan face held stoically through the entire work. No hunters in bearskins, no Chosen One, no human sacrifice, no riots at the Théâtre des Champs-Elysées. Without the distraction of its celebrity baggage, Wei leaves us only the polyrhythms of Stravinsky's majestic score but visually amplified by the movement. It's "Sacre" unplugged.[18]

A three-and-a-half minute excerpt of the work can be seen at www.youtube. com, search "Shen Wei Dance Arts Rite of Spring." Unfortunately in silence, it still gives the viewer an idea of Wei's pure-rhythm approach.

Limited States, commissioned by the American Dance Festival for its 2011 summer season, is characterized by a fascinating mix of projected video, body sculpture, and his now patented dance painting (www.youtube.com, search "Shen Wei Dance Arts–2011 ADF–Limited States").

Alexei Ratmansky

Contemporary ballet choreographer Alexei Ratmansky (b. 1968, St. Petersburg, Russia) served as Artistic Director of the famed Bolshoi Ballet (f. 1776) from 2004 to 2009. In January 2009, he became Artist-in-Residence at the American Ballet Theatre and began setting his own unique mix of classical/ contemporary ballet pieces on that company's versatile dancers. Because he was born in the sixties,

> [Ratmansky is] part of a unique new breed of Russian ballet dancers who matured in the immediate post-Soviet era and were able to perform both the Russian and the Western repertories, from Petipa and Bournonville classics to Balanchine, Tudor, Maurice Béjart and Tharp. This training provided Ratmansky with a wealth of styles from which to draw later as a choreographer: the attack and freeness of Tharp, the speed and musicality of Balanchine, the unaffected demeanor and intricate footwork of Bournonville, the psychological depth of Tudor.[19]

Predating his invitation to the United States, Ratmansky was able to not only satisfy traditionalist Russian *balletomanes* but also to remind us of the old Soviet Union in works such as the 2006 *BOLT*. The choreographer cast 48 corps de ballet dancers in a piece set to the music of composer Dmitri Shostakovich (1906-1975), paying partial homage to the classical Petipa past while also including a contemporary *pas de deux* filled with accented hesitations and narrative [excerpt at www.youtube.com, search "BOLT (Bolshoi): Physical drill and Denis's split with Nastya"].

Certainly his thoughtful and ambitious approach to his own training at the Bolshoi helped set the stage for his choreography. *The New Yorker's* dance critic Joan Acocella interviewed him in 2011, revealing qualities of dance sensibility that give viewers and performers that essential in-the-moment, contemporary life necessary for any vital performance:

> "[My teacher Pyotr Pestov's] attention was the transitional step, the musicality," Ratmansky says. "He didn't teach us any tricks [but] instead we got the understanding of the phrase, the logic of the phrase, and strong backs and soundless landings and good pliés..."[20]

Seven Sonatas (2009), created at ABT, was set to solo piano pieces composed by Domenico Scarlatti (1685–1757) and played live upstage. Again, while rooted in the classical ballet idiom, one can easily imagine any number of modern dance choreographers creating such a dance, as recounted in Alastair Macaulay's *New York Times* review:

> Mysterious suggestions of personal emotion—gestures of swooning, collapse and death, as well as delight and tenderness—dot several of the dances; these fascinate and yet are not the central point. Mr. Ratmansky has created a world in which we hardly know what the binding thread is: The clear sense of community between these six dancers? The fragments they offer of unexplained feeling? The multilayered sense of form and formality among them? As we feel its rightness for the music, the ballet's ambiguities bring satisfaction.[21]

Ratmansky is primarily a classical ballet choreographer [in Spring 2010 he was a Guest Artist working on his own version of Petipa's classical *Don Quixote* (1869) for the Dutch National Ballet], but his association with ABT is helping to bring his sensibilities even further into the contemporary world. The company has long encouraged new works by modern creators such as diverse as Nijinska, Tharp, Kudelka, and Ailey.

Middle Duet, from 2006 and set on the New York City Ballet, is a delicious and luxurious ten-minute *pas de deux* full of Ratmansky's classical-contemporary investigations [www.youtube.com, search "Middle Duet (Contemporary Ballet by Alexei Ratmansky)"].

One would not normally think of the classical fantasy *The Nutcracker* (1892, Petipa/Ivanov; 1954, Balanchine) as a contemporary work—except in perhaps Mark Morris's hands with *The Hard Nut* (1991)—but Ratmansky's 2010 version for ABT (www.youtube.com, search "ABT's New Nutcracker"), with sets and costumes by Richard Hudson, Tony Award-winner for *The Lion King* (1997), finds ways to imagine the younger and older Clara and Nutcracker Boy in realistic relations with each other, and even the almost unchangeable Snowflakes scene progresses from

> …images of lovely, artless innocence, by way of alluring beauty, to stormy, mazelike furor, to designing, vengeful cruelty. Mutating with the music, they show us the different faces of snow itself.
>
> The wordless choir that joins this waltz becomes, as in no other version, an expression of some Snow Queen's siren voice: as if saying, "Lose yourselves in my pure white beauty—stay in my realm forever." When the two children begin the scene, they've found a playground; they end it fleeing in terror.[22]

Already, Ratmansky seems to be the most promising contemporary heir to his modern and classical and neoclassical ancestors the world has seen yet in this second decade of the 21st century (along with, perhaps, Christopher Wheeldon; see Chapter 9).

Pam Tanowitz

Born in 1969 in the Bronx borough of New York City, Pam Tanowitz "has an instinct for the contrasts that make dance count: stillness against motion, small against large, slow against fast, the individual against the group."[23] In her own words:

> My dances are deeply personal explorations on movement, grounded in tradition, that comment on history—revering and revising its legacy. I play with classical vocabulary, not as parody, but out of respect for the dances from which I have learned so much. I take ballet steps and alter them into modern forms: traditional movement is twisted and thrown off-center, challenging the expectations of the viewer. I want the audience to observe the seams of my work, momentarily taking the "magic" out of theater and revealing the mechanical gears of performance.[24]

These comments are true about Tanowitz's art—she clearly and carefully juxtaposes all sorts of bits and pieces from classical and modern history. In the 2009 work *Be in the Gray with Me*, these elements include Cunningham's penchant for dancing near the wings (or partly in them), balletic *fouettés* and *arabesques*, duets and trios and ensembles in unison, and neoclassical references to Balanchine.

What makes Tanowitz stand out from her contemporaries? Her work is full of pure dance steps! Watch endless varieties of those steps at www.youtube.com, search "Pam Tanowitz Fragment of Ballet Be in the Gray with Me 2009." Tanowitz is in great demand on college campuses like the State University of New York (SUNY) at Purchase, which has a thriving dance program, and regularly at Dance Theater Workshop/New York Live Arts) and Danspace Project. One can follow her evolution on her website at www.pamtanowitzdance.org/.

Trey McIntyre

A choreographer with Irish ancestry born the same year as Tanowitz, Trey McIntyre (b. November 12, 1969, Wichita, Kansas), founded his own company, the Trey McIntyre Project (http://treymcintyre.org/) in 2005 and moved it to Boise, Idaho, to make that outlier city his company's home three years later.

McIntyre has launched a full-scale assault on the "purity" of classical ballet with extreme (and wickedly fast) tilts, simultaneous counterpointing polyrhythms, pelvic jazz-inflected wobbles, props (furs, paper cut-outs, crowns), and stage effects (falling-from-the-fly fabrics, rapid light changes), all the while grounded in that technique (pirouettes on pointe, *pas de deux*, turn-out). Think of hyperactive Tharp together with Kylián-like quirkiness and humor. Set to everything from classical (Dvorak, Beethoven, Bach) to pop (The Beatles, Grand Funk Railroad, Regina Spektor, Beck), McIntyre is, like Christopher Wheeldon (discussed in Chapter 9), one of the most highly visible contemporary ballet choreographers working in America today. You can view a two-minute clip of a host of McIntyre pieces spliced together with his whiz-bang style at www.youtube.com, search "Trey McIntyre Project Montage." If the reader still needs a clear example of why dancers today need to be able to do just about anything onstage, this video is a great one.

Selected Videos/DVDs/Films

Clark, Michael
Legend of Leigh Bowery (2003), Palm Pictures.

De Keersmaeker, Anne Teresa
Achterland (1994), Dance Horizons.

Decouflé, Philippe
The Planet Decouflé (2009), Amazon.com.

Guillem, Sylvie
Sylvie Guillem At Work and Portrait (2012), Dance Horizons.
Sylvie Guillem: On the Edge (2011), Deutsche Grammophon.
The Paris Opera Ballet: Seven Ballets (2008), V.I.E.W. Video.

Postmodern Dance
Post-modern dance: Judson Theatre & Grand Union (1990), Arc Videodance.

Ratmansky, Alexei
Bolt (2007), Dance Horizons.

Tanowitz, Pam
Pam Tanowitz: Be in the Gray with Me (2009), NTSC Color Broadcast System.

Wei, Shen
Beijing 2008 Olympics Complete Opening Ceremony, Amazon.com.

Notes

1   Allen Robertson and Donald Hutera, *The Dance Handbook* (Boston: G. K. Hall., 1988), p. 235.

2   Sanjoy Roy, "Step-by-Step Guide to Dance: Anne Teresa De Keersmaeker and Rosas," *The Guardian*, September 8, 2009, http://www.guardian.co.uk/stage/2009/sep/08/dance-anne-teresa-de-keersmaeker-rosas.

3   Debra Craine and Judith Mackrell, eds., *The Oxford Dictionary of Dance* (Oxford, England: Oxford University Press, 2010; 2nd ed.), p. 126.

4   Lindsey Winship, "Michael Clark: 'O My Goddess,'" *Dance Magazine Online*, May 11, 2004, http://www.ballet-dance.com/200406/articles/michaelclark20040511.html.

5   Sanjoy Roy, "Step-By-Step Guide to Dance: Michael Clark," *The Guardian*, August 27, 2009, http://www.guardian.co.uk/stage/2009/aug/27/guide-dance-michael-clark.

6   Theodore Bale, "Michael Clark Company," *Dance Magazine*, July 2008, http://www.dancemagazine.com/reviews/July-2008/Michael-Clark-Company.

7   Robertson and Hutera, *The Dance Handbook*, 1988, p. 216.

8   http://www.facebook.com/pages/STEVE-PAXTON/50338616026.

9   "Lucinda Childs' DANCE @ MCA Stage." http://www.youtube.com/watch?v=B_uHPXMsuX8.

10   "Lucinda Childs' DANCE @ MCA Stage." http://www.youtube.com/watch?v=B_uHPXMsuX8.

11   Selma Jeanne Cohen, *The Modern Dance: Seven Statements of Belief* (Middletown, CT: Wesleyan University Press, 1966), p. 14.

12   Stein's poetry is often understood as the literary equivalent of Picasso's cubist art or Steven Reich's and Philip Glass's minimalist music. The poem starts with: "If I told him would he like it/Would he like it if I told him/Would he like it/Would Napoleon/Would Napoleon would/Would he like it" and then begins to move more quickly, words piling onto words, onto words, piling.

13   http://www.youtube.com/watch?v=Nphmlk077c0.

14   Ibid.

15   Jen Jones, "Mia Full of Grace," *Dance Teacher*, November 2006; http://www.dance-teacher.com/content/feature-mia-full-grace.

16   Claudia La Rocco, "Evening of Adventuresome Premieres," *The New York Times*, February 19, 2009, http://www.nytimes.com/2009/02/20/arts/dance/20aspe.html?ref=dance.

17   Rosella Simonari, "Shen Wei Dance Arts—'Connect Transfer': When Dance Paints Movement," *Dance Magazine*, February 2006, http://www.ballet-dance.com/200602/articles/ShenWei20051126.html.

18   Jeff Kuo, "Shen Wei Dance Arts: Austerity and Exoticism at the Music Center," *Ballet-Dance Magazine*, April 2004, http://www.ballet-dance.com/200404/articles/ShenWei20040319.html.

19   Marina Harss, "Ratmansky Takes Manhattan," *The Nation*, September 23, 2009, http://www.thenation.com/article/ratmansky-takes-manhattan.

20   Joan Acocella, "Dance with Me," *The New Yorker*, June 27, 2011, p. 37.

21   Alastair Macaulay, "Three Choreographers, Bound by Their Way With a Ballet Twist," *The New York Times*, January 28, 2010, http://www.nytimes.com/2010/01/28/arts/dance/28triple.html?ref=dance.

22   Alastair Macaulay, "What if You Could Meet Yourself as an Adult? These Children Do," *The New York Times*, December 16, 2011, http://www.nytimes.com/2011/12/16/arts/dance/alexei-ratmanskys-nutcracker-at-bam-review.html.

23   Alastair Macaulay, "Puzzles in Layers of Cool Suspense," *The New York Times*, May 21, 2010, http://www.nytimes.com/2010/05/22/arts/dance/22wanderer.html?ref=alastair_macaulay.

24   http://contemporary-arts.org/grant_recipients/pam-1.html.

Chapter Nine

1970 to 1980

Wayne McGregor, Santee Smith, Pilobolus, The Kitchen and The Yard,
Cloud Gate Dance Theatre of Taiwan, Christopher Wheeldon, Robert Battle,
Danspace Project, Akram Kahn, Hofesh Schechter, Sidi Larbi Cherkaoui,
Cedar Lake Contemporary Ballet, Sonya Tayeh, Kyle Abraham,
Hubbard Street Dance Chicago, Dance Umbrella,
River North Chicago Dance Company

Wayne McGregor

British-born Wayne McGregor (b. March 12, 1970, Stockport, England)
is another of the world's contemporary choreographers who cannot be
pigeonholed into any one style or approach. McGregor ably employs a
generous mix of classical ballet virtuosity (often on pointe) with modern
contractions, gestures, abstracted imagery, and even vogue dance, all at a
hyperkinetic pace and in collaboration with visual artists, commissioned
composers, and technology whizzes.

In 2006, he became the Royal Ballet's (England) first-ever Resident
Choreographer from the contemporary dance world, an impossible-to-
imagine marriage even ten years ago. In his twenty-five minute *Infra* (2008,
excerpt at www.youtube.com, search "Infra–Wayne McGregor–Part 1") for
that company, ethereal images of walking business people projected onto
an 18-meter LED screen set high above the stage, created by visual artist
Julian Opie, are juxtaposed with McGregor's manic, precise onstage soloists,
duets, trios, and sextets, as well as the occasional offstage (in the audience)
performers. A believable illusion of three "cinematic" events occurring
simultaneously is effected, even if the audience must happily multitask to
keep up with the action. Composer Max Richter's (b. 1966) forlorn mood
piece provides just the right touch of uncertainty to the characters' inability
to connect.

The danger of mixed media work is that it can detract from each of the numerous individual genres on view, making the whole less than the sum of its parts. So, for every complex but cohesive Bill T. Jones *Still/Here* (1994) or William Forsythe *Kammer/Kammer* (2000) there are the increasingly incoherent *Chapel/Chapter* (2008) and *Decreation* (2009), by the same choreographers respectively. (Of course, as noted in earlier paragraphs on Meredith Monk or Laura Dean, one person's pleasure is another's pain.) The same is true for some of McGregor's more extravagant mistakes. *New York Times* critic Gia Kourlas makes that argument about one of his 2010 works:

> Much has been made of Mr. McGregor's fascination with cognitive science and how "Entity" is, in part, an exploration of the body-mind relationship. But that notion seems at odds with the theatrical picture, which aims for a kind of idiosyncratic sexiness, no matter how many harsh angles there are to keep the movement from looking too blatantly alluring. Just as Mr. McGregor builds momentum and erases it in quick, agitated sparks, the monotony of watching a woman's legs split apart can't be underestimated.[1]

Nevertheless, the piece is a crowd pleaser, and while marrying neuroscience to dance sounds almost too esoteric to imagine—the dancers' own DNA patterns are imprinted on their ripped T-shirt costumes, yet another conceit—McGregor is breaking boundaries, particularly at The Royal Ballet.

In 2010 he created a similarly distinctive piece for New York City Ballet with *Outlier*—full of head jerks, no makeup, stark lighting, and his typically multifocal antics, all set on the classically trained NYCB. Inspired in part by the angular glass structures of architect Philip Johnson (1906–2005), who designed the original Lincoln Center New York State Theater (constructed in 1964 and renamed the David H. Koch Theater in 2008), the work is consistent with the title of NYCB's Architecture of Dance festival and recapitulates some of Johnson's sharp and spare tectonics (which are reminiscent of Balanchine's own deceptive and angular "simplicity.") Likewise, the 2008 *Entity* keeps the audience guessing who is going to dance with whom and where (www.youtube.com, search "Entity–Wayne McGregor Random Dance").

Again, McGregor's next wave does not appeal to everyone, and his work can just look busy rather than "Diaghilev new."[2] He is prolific, having worked in film (*Harry Potter and the Goblet of Fire*, 2004), theater, and opera, and the groundbreaking *53 Bytes* (1997), a dance work simultaneously performed and telecast via satellite link in Germany and Canada.

Nevertheless, even though *New York Times* critic Roslyn Sulcas was pleasantly surprised by the "beguilingly simple [and] pellucid" *Undance* (2011), partly based on the motion-study photographs of Victorian-era Eadweard J. Muybridge, she still felt compelled to note that, "[f]or better or for worse, there is usually a great deal going on, both physically and conceptually; this intellectual and sensory overload can be thrilling or frustrating, or both at the same time."[3]

Santee Smith

A member of the Mohawk Nation and Artistic Director of the Kaha:wi Dance Theatre in Ontario, Canada, Santee Smith (b. 1971) creates potent mixes of native and contemporary movements in pieces like the full-length *Here on Earth* (2005, excerpt at www.youtube.com, search "Santee Smith at NMAI"), performed at the National Museum of the American Indian (NMAI) in Washington, D. C. (the NMAI has its other home in New York City). Calling her company a contemporary indigenous Aboriginal ensemble, Smith entrancingly fuses 21st century culture with her embodied history. Her work is gorgeous, spiritual, welcoming, bracing—and long overdue by simultaneously honoring tradition, engagingly educating non–Native Americans, and pushing the contemporary envelope.

Audiences in our century are already seeing more and more mixes of authentic and staged ethnic dance forms by choreographers from many lands and ethnicities. Authentic dances from throughout the world have become more available and familiar to us because companies and dancers travel everywhere by air, immigrate to many countries, post their work on the internet, and study dance at the same studios, conservatories, colleges and universities that traditional theater dance students attend.

Pilobolus

Pilobolus, a collective company of dancers and gymnasts that started at Dartmouth College in 1971, as well as their offspring MOMIX and ISO, founded in 1980 and 1987 respectively, continue to create complex, visually compelling, often humorous mobile-like structures through the muscular strength and proximity of the bodies of two or more of their dancers. Critic Alastair Macaulay captures the collective's artistry perfectly in a review of *Darkness and Light* (2008), their collaboration with puppeteer Basil Twist:

> Pilobolus, like any dance company, has several styles. Some of its works are visions of imaginary biology, some are human dramas,

some are about clowning. But since its early years the purest Pilobolus experiences have involved metamorphosis. We see both physicality and illusion. Bodies become imagery, and one image merges into another, organically, poetically, inexplicably.[4]

Androgynous body sculptures and offbeat creations such as *Ocellus* (1972, by Pilobolus), *Untitled* (1975, by Pilobolus), and *MOMIX in Orbit* (2002, by Momix), performed with and without props and clever costuming, continue to delight and surprise audiences. Late-night television host Conan O'Brien invited Pilobolus to perform in July 2008, which gave viewers an excellent idea of the kind of striking visuals (this time using all shadows) one can enjoy at a Pilobolus concert (www.youtube.com, search "Pilobolus on Late Night with Conan O'Brien"), as did their near-naked 2007 duet *Symbiosis* (www.youtube.com, search "Pilobolus: A performance merging dance and biology") for TEDTalks (http://www.ted.com/talks).[5]

Where do the ideas for Pilobolus come from? What do they want to say? Pilobolus members Michael Tracy and Robby Barnett helped interviewer Rose Eichenbaum get a better understanding of its agenda:

> **Michael Tracy and Robby Barnett:** "Ours is more an innocent approach to movement in that it allows us to respond freshly to things—or try to. One might call it cultivated ignorance or belief in naiveté."

> **Rose Eichenbaum:** "So the work is not intended to inform or influence others?"

> **MT/RB:** "We try to put together something that is rich enough that there may be ambiguities about what it means, so that each person in the audience will be interested in it," said Robby. "We have very specific ideas about what we put into the choreography, but we don't have faith that these ideas will read to an audience. We are not inherently didactic. We very rarely develop a political stance and then create movement to elicit that. We don't know the answers to life's questions."

> **RE:** "How do you conceptualize work? Where do the ideas come from?"

> **RB:** "Everyone in the group has what I call restless intelligence," said Robby. "We are fairly discursive people with lots of interests. We read a great deal and listen to music diversely. All that stuff goes back into the pot, rattles around in there, and is available for us to draw upon. Art

is created out of things you're reminded of. It's associative. Movement without reference has little interest to me. The more references you have, the more likely you are to experience an emotional response."[6]

Early-Pilobolus member Martha Clarke (b. June 3, 1944, Baltimore), who studied with Tudor and performed with Anna Sokolow in the 1960s, "credits Louis Horst with teaching her how to use preexisting art to make new art."[7] A recent work, *Angel Reapers* (2011; www.youtube.com, search "Martha Clarke, Alfred Uhry: Angel Reapers" and "Dance Talks: Angel Reapers"), based on the Shakers and created in collaboration with Pulitzer Prize winner Alfred Uhry (the author of *Driving Miss Daisy*, 1987) is typical of her productions, which "are like lovingly prepared stews of tableaux, dance and movement, text and music."[8]

Two Dance Spaces: The Kitchen and The Yard

The Kitchen (http://thekitchen.org/), a nonprofit, interdisciplinary arts collective founded in 1971 on Mercer Street in Soho in Manhattan but currently in Chelsea, primarily supports experimental work in video and performance art but also in literature, the visual arts, and dance. Famed artists as varied as Charles Atlas (film), Meredith Monk (dance/performance art), Kiki Smith (visual art), Philip Glass and Laurie Anderson (music), and Elizabeth Streb and Bill T. Jones (dance) developed their artistry at The Kitchen and other similar safe havens.

Conversely, The Yard (http://www.dancetheyard.org) was founded solely for dance in 1973 on the island of Martha's Vineyard in Massachusetts. It remains a retreat from the everyday bustle of city life for artists such as David Dorfman, Gus Solomons, Jr., and Jawole Willa Jo Zollar, who usually stay one month alone or with their current company to create and then perform work. In 2006, The Yard expanded its mission to also include nondance arts with their YardArts! Festival of Dance, Theater, Music and Opera, hosting actors, singers, and spoken-word poets.

There remains something fascinating and empowering about the 1970s, which, through collectives such as these, took the counter-culture energy of the sixties and tried to create havens for dancers to stay true to a spirit of adventure and integrity. In talking primarily about performance art in the November 2011 issue of *ARTnews*, feminist Judy Chicago (b. 1939) most assuredly was alluding to places like The Kitchen and The Yard that started during that decade: "It wasn't about making money; it wasn't about careerism.

It was about making art that mattered. We believed we could actually impact the world."[9]

Cloud Gate Dance Theatre of Taiwan

Founded half-way across the globe, also in 1973, the China-based dance company called Cloud Gate Dance Theatre of Taiwan claims to have legendary roots in ritual dance 5,000 years old and practices its own singular mix of tai chi, modern dance, ballet, martial arts, meditation, Chinese Opera, and calligraphy. It maintains itself in Taiwan as the first contemporary dance company in any Chinese-speaking community (www.cloudgate.org.tw) and regularly tours the world.

Moon Water (http://www.youtube.com, search "Cloud Gate - Moonwater"), a signature work from 1998, literally shines and shimmers as dressed-all-in-white dancers perform with water all over the stage, reflected in overhead mirrors to a transported audience. Choreographed by Cloud Gate's Lin Hwai-min, founding Artistic Director, practicing Buddhist, and frequently published writer (b. February 19, 1947, Taiwan), *Moon Water* is set to the glorious *Six Suites for Solo Cello* by J. S. Bach. The full-length dance has no intermission and has left countless audience members in the same state of transfixed meditation from which its energies originate.

As Pina Bausch often did, Cloud Gate brings the natural world onto the stage: in addition to the water of *Moon Water*, the 1995 *Songs of the Wanderers* incorporated three tons of rice. Unlike the long, glacial Butoh movement performances of ensembles like Sankai Juku (that can push speed-oriented Western sensibilities past the breaking point), the tai chi-inflected movements of Cloud Gate are slow but discernible, prompting audiences to consider the Chinese proverb: "If you are in a hurry, you will never get there." (http://www.youtube.com, search "Cloud Gate Dance Theatre of Taiwan: Songs of Wanderers")

In an interview for the German online, onscreen and on air *Deutsche Welle Arts.21* cultural magazine,[10] Lin Hwai-min concisely encapsulates Cloud Gate's philosophy: "The way we dance is fundamentally different [from] Western ballet. Western dance works against gravity; we work with gravity. Western dance is extroverted, while we concentrate on our inner energy. We don't dance for an audience; we simply invite an audience to watch us perform and be privy to our movements and our breathing."[11] (www.youtube.com, search "Arts.21 Straddling East and West")

One might notice similarities with the philosophy of American modern dancer Erick Hawkins, who greatly respected the "now" of Eastern perspectives and the subtle connections his performances had with the audience.

Christopher Wheeldon

British-born choreographer Christopher Wheeldon (b. March 22, 1973, Somerset, England) remains one of the most highly visible contemporary ballet choreographers working in America today. He trained at The Royal Ballet and then was accepted into New York City Ballet in 1992, choreographing for the company beginning in 1997 and then becoming a resident choreographer in 2001. Wheeldon has received repeated (and, at times, just) comparisons to Balanchine, Ashton, Jerome Robbins and Kenneth MacMillan (1929–1992). Wheeldon himself has said as much:

> In the past couple of years I've learned a great deal about the shape and quality of movement, and I prefer to focus on that rather than production values like theatrics, scenery, and costumes. I'm more interested now in stripping away to the movement, to the purest dance. In the tradition of George Balanchine, I try to communicate to an audience without relying on spectacle..."Polyphonia" [2001], set to the piano music of Györgi Ligeti...was created along the lines of *Agon* [1957] or *Episodes* [1959], a plotless ballet with pure dance at its core.[12]

Having rocked New York the year it first appeared, *Polyphonia* continued receiving praise years later when performed during Wheeldon's own company's premiere in Vail, Colorado:

> From the first, it combines acrobatic and technical excitement with intricate classical order; in Vail you could feel how immediately it commanded the audience's attention and respect. Amazingly, it achieves this to a collage of intensely modernist piano pieces by Ligeti. The first of these is "Désordre," and Mr. Wheeldon's mastery is unmistakable in the way he sets four couples in elaborate choreographic order to its near-cacophonous organized disorder. When "Polyphonia" was new, it was just what the doctor ordered for ballet worldwide. It handled the classical vocabulary of Balanchine (in particular), Ashton and others without being inhibited or retro; it has a constant supply of inventiveness. And it is unmistakably well built: here, as elsewhere in Mr. Wheeldon's repertory, you see motifs returning when you least expect them, so that you feel the happy surprise of pattern falling into place.[13]
> (www.youtube.com, search "PNB's Polyphonia excerpts")

His 2009 *Within the Golden Hour,* set on San Francisco Ballet, a company that has commissioned several of his works, is another neoclassical virtuoso piece (excerpt at www.youtube.com, search "SF Ballet—Wheeldon's Within the Golden Hour in HD").

With the 2010 premiere of *Ghosts,* also for the San Francisco Ballet, much of his signature style is on display:

> The upper and lower bodies of his dancers frequently move in urgent opposition. The torso stays lively, bending forward and backward or twisting right and left, then the entire physique is involved…Feet make a vivid contribution: they are flourished expressively in the air; pointwork is deployed both powerfully and lusciously; and unpointed, near-flexed feet also make memorable appearances.[14]

In 2006 he cofounded the contemporary Morphoses/The Wheeldon Company, but the economy and other factors compelled him to take himself and the second half of the title off the marquee in early 2010 (www.morphoses.org). For its first three years it held the unique position of Guest Resident Company at both New York's City Center and Sadler's Wells in London. Since his departure, Morphoses, with Havana-born New York City Ballet-alumna Lourdes Lopez (b. 1958) at its helm, has become more multidisciplinary, especially with its live-performance streaming telecasts to bistros as well as theaters. Ms. Lopez subsequently took over Miami City Ballet's reins from Edward Villella in 2012.

Wheeldon continues to be one of the most sought-after young choreographers in the world, setting works on the San Francisco Ballet, Pacific Northwest Ballet, and the one-act *Miséricordes* on the famed Russian Bolshoi Ballet in 2007 (excerpt at www.youtube.com, search "Dmitri Gudanov in Misericordes (Elsinore) Bolshoi Ballet"):

> In the space of a mere twenty minutes, Wheeldon manages to create an entire world, a shadowy, medieval place suggested by Shakespeare's "Hamlet" and by the solemn, often clangorous orchestral score that contemporary Estonian composer Arvo Part based on his studies of music from the Middle Ages. On stage are four couples dressed in various dark colors, plus a brooding figure—perhaps the Prince of Denmark himself—in a pale-color costume. Wheeldon's choreography, though essentially classical, bends and wrestles the dancers' bodies to the very limit. Emotions surface and disappear. Love, hate and hints of

doom all seem to be present. The result is a marvelous piece of theater for which each viewer is free to create his own plot. And as with Balanchine, with whom Wheeldon has often been compared, all that takes place in the dancing seems to arise directly from the music, as if Part had written his Symphony No. 3 nearly four decades ago with Wheeldon's ballet in mind.[15]

After the Rain (2005), performed by Damian Smith and Yuan Yuan Tan of the San Francisco Ballet during the Fire Island Dance Festival in 2010 with the setting sun over the Atlantic ocean behind them, typifies Wheeldon's musical sensitivity and moving contemporary qualities that transfer easily to an audience (www.youtube.com, search "Damian Smith and Yuan Yuan Tan in Christopher Wheeldon's After The Rain"). Insights into Wheeldon's thinking behind a number of his ballets can be found at www.youtube.com, search "PNB's Lecture Demonstration with Christopher Wheeldon."

Robert Battle

Robert Battle (b. 1973, Jacksonville, Florida) has a number of works in many company repertories around the globe. Having performed with Parsons Dance Company from 1994 to 2001 and founded Battleworks Dance Company in 2002, he was chosen to become Artistic Director of the Alvin Ailey American Dance Theater in 2011, huge shoes to fill after Ailey himself and Ailey's personally chosen successor, Judith Jamison (b. 1943).

Battle's work is characterized by audience-friendly, bravura explosions of polyrhythmic, multigestural, and multidirectional movements. His *Three* (2010) is a perfect example. Maintaining hypnotic repetitions at top speed and five times longer than one would expect, he keeps his audience guessing what pace, spatial placement, and numbered groupings will come next. Likewise, the 1998 *Strange Humors*, set to music by his longtime collaborator John Mackey, is endlessly eruptive, the dancers (and audience) exhausted by its end (excerpt at www.youtube.com, search "Battleworks Dance Company").

An October 2008 interview during a week-long residency at Southeast Missouri State University revealed several important influences in Battle's professional life:

- Graham's *Night Journey* (1947) and *Cave of the Heart* (1946);

- Parson's 1990 *Nascimento*: his "sense of theater has influenced my work greatly";

- Ailey's 1960 *Revelations:* "the quintessential genius who brought the humanity to dance…the thing that ties us all together…he transcended race, social status. His work celebrates our common humanity. I always try to find that in my work. It's always the human effort [that matters]; the human hand should always be evident";

- Taylor: "he gave us the dark and light";

- And Doug Elkins who "fused hip hop and modern dance together."[16]

Battle's personal mentors include the "great" Paul Taylor dancer Carolyn Adams,[17] and especially Benjamin Harkavy from Juilliard,[18] who always said that good choreographies must have a "resistance," a "grounded idea [that] always [has] a sense of corseted, constructed, restrained energy."

Such a potent lineage makes perfect sense, in retrospect, for why Battle was chosen to take the helm at Ailey, and his background, discipline and intensity seemed to be helping the company become more popular, if not versatile, than ever.

Danspace Project

An important organization that has hosted hundreds of companies like Battleworks over the years—often in their infancy, before celebrity status catches up with them (or not)—is Danspace Project (www.danspaceproject.org), centered in the lovely stained-glass lighted open space of St. Mark's Church-in-the-Bowery in the East Village of Manhattan. It was founded in 1974.

Often just called Danspace, the variety and depth of the dance programs reflects Danspace's highly attuned sensitivity to dance, dancer, and choreographer needs. Recent and ongoing programming includes the biannual Food for Thought, the dance section of the global initiative Arts Against Hunger which distributes food in the neighborhood while building arts audiences, as well as "the City/Dans series (featuring the work of New York City choreographers), Global Exchange (international choreographers), Danspace@ (performance at alternative sites and a semiannual showcase series at BRIC Studio in Brooklyn), DraftWork (free informal performances followed by moderated dialogue and a reception), and Rap-Ups (postperformance discussions with the artists)" (http://en.wikipedia.org/wiki/Danspace_Project).

A recent season saw dozens of current "unknowns" present dance via the DraftWork and City/Dans series, veterans Eiko and Koma celebrate their 40th year retrospective, relative newcomer Pam Tanowitz and her company in a premiere work, and a new series launched, Platforms, which invites recognized artists to curate concerts. The first "platform" was called *i get lost*, all dances chosen by choreographer and multimedia artist Ralph Lemon (b. 1953).

Akram Khan

Born the same year as Danspace was founded, Akram Khan (b. July 24, 1974, London, England), of Bangladeshi origin, studied the classical Indian dance style known as Kathak under the famous dancer and teacher Sri Pratap Pawar, eventually merging that training with contemporary dance through his work for Anne Teresa de Keersmaeker's Belgian company X-Group project (http://www.rosas.be/), among others. Truly multicultural, Khan founded his own company in 2000 (http://www.akramkhancompany.net/) and was recently one of the ten international Associate Artists at the Sadler's Wells in London.

Typical of his far-reaching collaborations, the 2008 *Bahok* involves dancers who move and speak in diverse styles and languages while performing to a work by Khan's frequent composer-producer, famed Indian-British Nitin Sawhney (b. 1964). Originally set on dancers from the National Ballet of China (www.youtube.com, search "Bahok—Akram Khan & National Ballet of China"), the work was eventually performed by his own company's lithe, whippet-like Chinese, Korean, Indian, South African, and Spanish dancers. An excerpt of his 2006 *Sacred Monsters*, with the choreographer himself in a duet with the ubiquitous Sylvie Guillem, can be seen at www.youtube.com, search "Sacred Monsters–Akram Khan and Sylvie Guillem." A fascinating mix of Kathak and classical ballet and gesture, Khan and Guillem bring a characteristically striking juxtaposition to the audience's mind.

Hofesh Shechter

The popular Hofesh Shechter Company (f. 2003, http://www.hofesh.co.uk/), is centered in London but led by its Israeli-born, Batsheva Dance Company-trained dancer-choreographer Hofesh Shechter (b. 1975 Jerusalem). Shechter is also his own composer for his dances, in part because he was a former drummer in a rock band. As a choreographer, he loves floor work; actually, he *really* loves floor work—crawls, rolls, "monkey" runs, knee "scurries," flops, and more. *In Your Rooms* (2007, excerpt at www.youtube.com, search "Hofesh Shechter In Your Rooms") is typical, as he "…shows that physical invention as part of a fiercely contemporary universe: pounding soundscapes, brilliantly moody lightscapes, changes of scene as abrupt as flickering television channels…And the dancing itself…wildly, roughly physical and large scale, it is also manically precise and detailed…The fragmented, rich, disordered world they show is the one we live in now."[19]

Shechter's 2006 *Uprising* is equally hyperkinetic at ground level (excerpt at www.youtube.com, search "Hofesh Shechter 'Uprising'"). His work for the British TV Channel 4's second season of *Skins* in *Maxxie's Dance*, a stripped down dance for its trailer (www.youtube.com, search "Skins/Maxxie's Dance/ E4"), again includes his singularly aggressive floor slides.

Sidi Larbi Cherkaoui/Cedar Lake Contemporary Ballet

It helps to have money. Cedar Lake Contemporary Ballet (CLCB, f. 2003, www.cedarlakedance.com), centered on West 26th Street in the art-rich Chelsea area of Manhattan, is a company of the world, in large part due to its astounding dancer and choreographer diversity. Its seventeen company members, including their current Artistic Director, Benoit-Swan Pouffer, hail from places as far ranging as Paris, South Africa, Romania, Switzerland, Germany, Korea, Spain, Puerto Rico, Japan, and The Netherlands. They are primarily funded by Walmart heiress Nancy Walton Laurie, thereby allowing the ensemble to remain together and learn not only Pouffer's work, but also those by a host of "associate" resident creators and many of the latest cutting-edge choreographers from mostly outside the United States. For a short idea of the varied choreographies that pass through its doors, have a look at www.youtube.com, search "Cedar Lake 2009 Demo."

As an example of multiple cross-cultural experimentations, CLCB commissioned a 2009 Jacob's Pillow Dance Festival premiere by the popular Moroccan and Flemish choreographer Sidi Larbi Cherkaoui (b. March 10, 1976, Antwerp) for its company members. The in-demand Cherkaoui has collaborated around the globe with Akram Khan (2005) in *Zero Degrees*; and with the Chinese Shaolin Monks in the 2008 *Sutra* (www.youtube.com, search "Sutra—Sidi Larbi and Antony Gormley with the Shaolin Monks"). This was set to the Polish composer Szymon Brzóska's atmospheric score and danced within, around, and on top of twenty of Antony Gormley's mobile, human-sized pine boxes. Are they coffins, or doors-to-other-worlds metaphors? Regardless, viewers are drawn into a unique, multiple cross-cultures, and contemporary experiment.

One of CLCB's recent projects is called project52, a year-long documen-tary in 52 one-minute segments. Featuring the dancers and collaborators at Cedar Lake Contemporary Ballet, project52 creates intimate vignettes of the lives of performers and artists. The documentary focuses on human stories and the intersection of life and dance (http://www.facebook.com/video/video.php?v=758134250773).

One of the one-minute sections (Chapter 28: "Books") is a recording of an installation dance in the Salt Lake City Public Library (http://vimeo.com/channels/project52#3122956) with dancers moving around the stacks, performing inside the glass-sided elevator as it traveled from floor to floor with and without everyday library visitors, and alongside folks reading or perusing or just standing around fascinated.[20]

Such site-specific dance remains an important rule-breaker of the moderns and contemporaries, literally forcing audiences to re-evaluate their assumptions about where performances should occur. Cedar Lake's own roomy space in Manhattan is large enough to allow the audience to stroll about during certain dances permitting multiple viewing angles. (Cunningham had done this for years—and more and more choreographers are doing it.)

Certainly as Sokolow, Limón, Primus, and Helen Tamiris (1905–1966) before them, some of the postmoderns may be given credit for making dances and events that make us think deeply about our society's condition, as they hold the mirror up to our own faces and ask us to consider who that person is and where does she or he fit into that society.

Sonya Tayeh

In season four of *So You Think You Can Dance* (SYTYCD), 2008 newcomer choreographer Sonya Tayeh (b. 1977, Brooklyn, New York) knocked out both judges and American television viewers when Courtney Galiano and Mark Kanemura brought Tayeh's comic-book characters to life in their *Jazz* routine set to musician Mirah's (Mirah Yom Tov Zeitlyn, b. 1974) "The Garden" (www.youtube.com, search "Courtney & Mark ★ Jazz - The Garden").

Self-proclaimed as a "contemporary funk and progressive contact" choreographer,[21] inspirations such as Jiří Kylián, Twyla Tharp, and the Mexican artist Frida Kahlo began to show as early as July 2008 with her aggressive, angst ridden "combat jazz" style. Teaching at the EDGE Performing Arts Center (f. 1988; http://edgepac.com/) in Hollywood, Tayeh's super-fast yet precise routines remain hot-hot-hot among contemporary choreographers of the 21st century's second decade.

Was it serendipity, an essential arts stimulant, that auditions for a 2011 SYTYCD show were held at the Mark Morris Dance Center in Brooklyn, Tayeh's hometown? Time will tell if Tayeh, who has already been successful in the commercial world, can take her work into the broader concert stage world. The summer of 2010 found her choreographing to *The Last Goodbye*, a musical adaptation of *Romeo and Juliet* at the Williamstown Theater Festival in Massachusetts, a springboard for many nationally-known stars. Now in Los Angeles, will she move on to Broadway like Garth Fagan or Bill T. Jones before her?

Kyle Abraham

Hyperkinetic like Tayeh, Kyle Abraham's (b. 1977 Pittsburgh, Pennsylvania) fast-twitch fibers happily contrast with tai chi-like serenity in his company, the Brooklyn-based Abraham.in.Motion (f. 2005, www.abrahaminmotion.org). Trained in cello, piano, and the visual arts, the choreographer starts with his own "mixtape" of often melodic but high-energy hip hop, classical, and eclectic contemporary compositions and then erupts from there. The 2008 *Brick* (excerpt at www.youtube.com, search "Lil Wayne A Milli Kyle Abraham/ Abraham.In.Motion Excerpt of Brick"), one of several earlier pieces expanded and adapted into the full-length *The Radio Show* two years later, exemplifies Abraham's amalgamation of influences and interests. The latter addresses Alzheimer's disease, gender and sexuality issues, and the black community in Abraham's home town of Pittsburgh, all set to The Shirelles, the scratchy sounds of changing radio stations, Aretha Franklin, and call-in voices.

Hubbard Street Dance Chicago

Founded in 1977 by Lou Conte (b. 1943), Hubbard Street Dance Chicago (HSDC) helped establish the Windy City as perhaps the most important dance city in the Midwest. Possibly because Conte's experience on Broadway and in summer stock at first made Hubbard Street seem more like a jazz company, their website reflects a broadening of its mission by claiming to have "always been a repertory company representing numerous choreographers and styles."[22] Works performed by HSDC reflect that global vision with choreographers hailing from Sweden (Johan Inger), Israel (Ohad Naharin), The Netherlands (Jiří Kylián), Finland (Jorma Elo), Spain (Nacho Duato and Alejandro Cerrudo), and the United States (Susan Marshall), among others.

In the second decade of the 21st century, HSDC had entered into several energizing collaborations with conventionally nondance focused institutions: live music performances (since 2004) with the venerable Chicago Symphony Orchestra and public space performances as the dance component of the "500 Ways of Looking at Modern" program in the new Modern Wing of the Art

Institute of Chicago are just two examples of the company's explorations with other art forms.

The duet *Kiss* (1987) by Susan Marshall (b. 1958) explores air-time longer and more poetically than Streb's dangerous dives into walls and near-misses with concrete slabs for her company. Hung at the hip with suspended ropes, a man and woman gently embrace each other as the arc of their pendulum swings rise and fall with their touching, pushing, and pulling (www.youtube.com, search "Kiss by Susan Marshall–Hubbard Street Dance Chicago").

The Finnish choreographer Jorma Elo (b. 1962), trained with the great Russian Kirov Ballet, Birgit Cullberg, and Nederlands Dance Theatre, and resident choreographer at the Boston Ballet (BB, f. 1963) since 2005, had his inscrutable 2009 *Bitter Suite* commissioned for Hubbard Street (www.youtube. com, search "Hubbard Street Dance Chicago at Jacob's Pillow"). Hard to read at first if not familiar with his style, Elo's work demands repeat viewings. Heads bob for seemingly no reason, extended stillnesses by the *corps* are held while prone on the floor, juxtaposed with a rapid-fire and quirky *pas de deux*. Elo's choreography is exhausting work (Boston Ballet dancer Sabi Varga said "it's sort of like running 15 times around the block lifting two mail bags in your hands"),[23] typically idiosyncratic, and, as with *Bitter Suite*, sometimes set incongruously to the classicists Mendelssohn and Monteverdi.

By the beginning of our century, hyperkinetic dance had become a staple in many contemporary ballet companies.

Dance Umbrella

Ever increasing diversity within choreography remains a major goal of England's Dance Umbrella, bringing new dance to London since its founding in 1978 (www.danceumbrella.co.uk). They keep count, too: 665 contemporary dance artists/companies from over 28 countries, 1770 performances at 48 different venues.[24] Their annual festivals occur each October and a recent version was typically eclectic: familiar names like Stephen Petronio, Trisha Brown (a 40-year retrospective), and Merce Cunningham, but mostly less well-known choreographers like the eccentric, high-energy Portuguese German Rui Horta (b. 1957; www.youtube.com, search "Scope–Rui Horta"), the serious Algerian French Nacera Belaza, and the justice-driven Congolese Faustin Linyekula (b. 1974).

Since its inception in 2007, their free Dance Umbrella Outdoors project has been especially successful, intriguing over 21,000 audience members in unusual venues around the city—such as inside the Clifford Chance law firm building and on and around a five-ton mechanical digger in a construction site! *Bodies in Urban Spaces* (2009) involved 20 dancers leading its audience around to everyday spaces between street signs and walls, doorways and passageways where they constructed momentary "body sculptures" for fleeting viewings (www.youtube.com, search "Theater Heilbronn: Willi Dorner–bodies in urban spaces"). The contemporary dance world not only traverses the planet now but the planet itself has become its venue.

River North Chicago Dance Company

Another "big" Chicago dance group, River North Chicago Dance Company (RNCDC, f. 1979, www.rivernorthchicago.com), regularly presents that wonderful 21st century mix of virtuoso contemporary, ballet, and jazz dance. In Artistic Director Frank Chaves's 2009 *Forbidden Boundaries*, for example, all thirteen company members push, pull, and tug on each other's brilliantly lighted, all-white stretch-fabric vests in soaring, high-octane duets, trios, quartets, and other myriad groupings (see a rehearsal excerpt at www.youtube. com, search "Forbidden Boundaries"). Lizzie MacKenzie is flung aloft much of the time in the second section of the dance "Hidden Truth" by fabric holders Michael Gross and Ricky Ruiz (the pulling back on the reins of the three muses in Balanchine's 1928 *Apollo* seems an obvious reference). Her marvelously tender solo reminds us of Graham's sorrowful, stretch-suited character in *Lamentation* (1930).

> The shirts are stretchy, twisting easily into ropes that suggest straitjackets or leashes as the caught dancers strain to get away. Telling and crucial as these props are, they also add a wacky, difficult variable to the partnering equation, as one dancer holds another at a precipitously leaning angle or pulls his partner into an unwanted embrace. The most alarming and passionate of the dance's four sections —the trio "Hidden Truth," for two men holding a woman by her sleeves—heightens these challenges.[25]

As noted with several other contemporary companies, RNCDC boasts double-digit numbers of resident and guest choreographers, a guarantee of versatility that consistently challenges dancers and audiences alike. Their vision statement notes that the company is "dedicated to the creative advancement, presentation and preservation of jazz-based contemporary dance" (http://www.rivernorthchicago.com/about.asp). That mélange of styles has been borne out in MacKenzie's master classes—ostensibly in jazz—when she clarifies the company's assertion by saying her style was not only contemporary jazz but "contemporary-modern."

In fact, her class incorporates the attacked accents and syncopations normally associated with jazz, as well as near-split floor work walks (a healthy stretch that she borrowed from "numerous therapy bouts," in her own words), but there are also many Graham-like contractions and releases and a clear use of internalized energy projected outwards—modern plus jazz, perhaps.

As dancer MacKenzie said,

> [D]on't be afraid of or intimidated by the unusual [because] the "unusual" is where [the dance world] is going! Pick up the styles but within that there's a lot of room for individualization and personal uniqueness and intention…Everyone has something important to say and, while I love beautiful and incredible technique, to dance is human and we all have an innate ability, so I'm more interested in seeing a clear intention.[26]

As the reader can see, many of the choreographers and companies born in the 1970s currently hold the reins of the future of dance in our 21st century. Honoring those who came before while pushing the envelope of what can be done today, the contemporary dance world is becoming more and more versatile—and rich with cross-currents of styles and global influences—with each passing month.

Selected Videos/DVDs/Films

Cloud Gate Dance Theatre
Bamboo Dream (2002), Dance Horizons.
Cursive II (2006), Dance Horizons.
Moon Water (2004), Dance Horizons.

Khan, Akram
Sacred Monsters (2009), Amazon.com.
Zero Degrees (2008), Amazon.com.

McGregor, Wayne
Three Ballets by Wayne McGregor (2011), Dance Horizons.

Pilobolus
Last Dance (2002), Dance Horizons.
Pilobolus (1997), Insight Media.

Pilobolus Dance Theatre (1998), Amazon.com.

Smith, Santee

Freedom (2009), Amazon.com.

Notes

1 Gia Kourlas, "Endless Motion, Sharply Defined: From Gawky to Sleek and Back Again," *The New York Times*, February 13, 2010, http://www.nytimes.com/2010/02/13/arts/dance/13entity.html?ref=dance.

2 Alastair Macaulay, "Unconventional Approaches and Grand Designs in a City Ballet Premiere," *The New York Times*, May 16, 2010, http://www.nytimes.com/2010/05/17/arts/dance/17serenade.html.

3 Roslyn Sulcas, "3 Modern Collaborators Add a Victorian Shadow," *The New York Times*, December 10, 2011, http://www.nytimes.com/2011/12/06/arts/dance/undance-by-wayne-mcgregor-and-friends-in-london-review.html.

4 Alastair Macaulay, "Veering from the Standard, Returning to the Spirit," *The New York Times*, July 10, 2008, http://www.nytimes.com/2008/07/10/arts/dance/10pilo.html?_r=1&scp=1&sq=veering%20from%20the%20standard,%20returning%20to%20the%20spirit&st=cse.

5 TED (f. 1984) stands for Technology, Entertainment and Design. All talks are limited to less than 18 minutes and can be found at www.ted.com.

6 Rose Eichenbaum, *Masters of Movement: Portraits of America's Great Choreographers* (Washington, D. C.: Smithsonian Books, 2004), p. 58.

7 Allen Robertson and Donald Hutera, *The Dance Handbook* (Boston: G. K. Hall, 1988), p. 235.

8 Ibid., p. 234.

9 Phoebe Hoban, "That Seventies Sensibility," *ARTnews*, November 2011, p. 96.

10 The German television *Deutsche Welle* program arts.21 (http://www.dw-world.de/dw/0,,7885,00.html) can be easily confused with the similarly-focused PBS television program art:21, begun in 2002 (www.pbs.org/art21).

11 Author unknown, "Arts.21: Straddling East & West," *Deutsche Welle*, http://www.youtube.com/watch?v=RHMhjpGpmDU.

12 Eichenbaum, *Masters of Movement*, 2004, p. 186.

13 Alastair Macaulay, "A First Turn for Wheeldon and Company," *The New York Times*, August 13, 2007, http://www.nytimes.com/2007/08/13/arts/dance/13morp.html?ref=christopher_wheeldon.

14 Alastair Macaulay, "Wheeldon's 'Ghosts,' Haunted by Dead Choreographers Society," *The New York Times*, February 14, 2010, http://www.nytimes.com/2010/02/12/arts/dance/12opus.html?ref=dance.

15 Raymond Stults, "New World Ballet," *The Moscow Times*, March 2, 2007, http://www.themoscowtimes.com/arts_n_ideas/article/new-world-ballet/363582.html.

16 Marc Strauss interview with Robert Battle, October, 2008, Cape Girardeau, Missouri.

17 Two years after hearing this list of influences, it was no surprise to read in the *New York Times* about that very lineage, for not only Carolyn Adams but David Parsons and Paul Taylor were in the Gala Night audience for Ailey's annual season at City Center in New York; Brian Seibert, "Starting a New Era with Graciousness, Taste and Tradition, http://www.nytimes.com/2011/12/02/arts/dance/alvin-ailey-american-dance-theater-at-city-center-review.html.

18 Harkarvy had a long and storied career training at the School of American Ballet, cofounded the Nederlands Dance Theatre in 1959, worked at the Harkness Ballet in 1969, and taught at Juilliard from 1990 until his death in 2002.

19 Roslyn Sulcas, "A Fragmented World, Not Far From This One," *The New York Times*, July 11, 2008, http://www.nytimes.com/2008/07/11/arts/dance/11shec.html?ref=roslyn_sulcas.

20 Facebook, a free-access, social-networking website, and Vimeo, a video-sharing network, were founded in 2004 and rival YouTube for up-to-the-minute videos.

21 http://www.facebook.com/pages/Sonya-Tayeh/23277784637?ref=ts.

22 http://www.hubbardstreetdance.com/index.php?option=com_content&view=article&id=99&Itemid=92.

23 Essdras M. Suarez, "On the Move with Jorma Elo," *The Boston Globe*, February 25, 2007, http://www.boston.com/ae/theater_arts/articles/2007/02/25/on_the_move_with_jorma_elo/.

24 The city of Boston had its own similarly envisioned Dance Umbrella from 1980 to 2001, but had to close due to financial troubles.

25   Laura Molzahn, "River North Chicago Dance Company," *Chicago Dance*, November 9, 2009, http://seechicagodance.com/performance/68.

26   Author's notes, Jazz Dance Master Class, Southeast Missouri State University, March 1, 2010.

Chapter Ten
The 1980s and 1990s

Contemporary Technique II, Brooklyn Academy of Music, The Joyce Theater, Alonzo King LINES Ballet, Lyon Dance Biennale, Joanna Haigood's Zaccho Dance Theatre, Monica Bill Barnes & Company, DanceNOW NYC, Chunky Move, Older Dancers, Venice Biennale

The dance boom of the 1960s and 1970s was like the Big Bang to the universe; companies kept evolving and crossing geographical and artistic boundaries and subject matter at an astronomical rate. By the 1980s, the evolution of technique, artistry, and experimentation that had developed over the 350 years of ballet history and more than 60 years of modern dance became the foundational roots that influenced the next four decades and beyond.

Contemporary Technique II

The rejection of (or, equally, just plain noninterest in) classical ballet technique by modern dancers—and then the subsequent development of choreographer-specific techniques such as Humphrey, Graham, Limón and their next-generation descendants that became no less rigorous than the canon of the *danse d'école*—may have come full circle by the latter part of the 20th century and the beginning of the 21st: it has become clear that more and more contemporary ballet companies (and some classical and neoclassical ones) have come to fruition borrowing and commissioning modern dance ideas, themes, steps, and choreographers themselves.

The list keeps growing larger with each year, due to the essential usefulness of the classical ballet technique as a foundation upon which increasingly more difficult physical demands are placed on contemporary dancers in all styles. One need only look at many of the works of Matthew Bourne, Mats Ek, William Forsythe, Nacho Duato, James Kudelka, Jiří Kylián, Lar Lubovitch, or dozens of other contemporary choreographers often initially trained (if not remaining rooted) in the classical world to know that the line between ballet and modern dance has become increasingly blurred, if not eradicated.

Among the multitude of trailblazing approaches, the use of multimedia in works of dance, theater, film, spoken text, has become ubiquitous in the last couple of decades. Big Dance Theatre (BDT, www.bigdancetheater.org), founded in 1991 in Brooklyn by Paul Lazar and Annie-B Parson, is one of those using that approach. Neither dance nor theater yet both and more, BDT calls on its audience's multitasking skills by layering the onstage contents in loosely narrative synchronous and asynchronous ways as in their 2007 full-length work *The Other Here*,

> Okinawan music, dance, and stories, with motivational talk drawn from transcripts of an annual gathering of top insurance salesmen. While this isn't a dance performance per se, there is dancing within it, which mostly appears and disappears organically as part of the "plot," such as it is. But in a greater sense, the entire piece, which takes place on multiple levels and in layers of innovative movable staging, is strictly choreographed as a movement piece, such that even when people are ostensibly walking, talking, or gesturing as actors, they do so with clear, dance-like intention.[1]

Brooklyn Academy of Music

Even though the Brooklyn Academy of Music (www.bam.org) was founded during the Civil War in 1861, its title reads as if the organization presented only music performances, but the acronym, BAM, is perfect for its often explosive interdisciplinary mission. BAM is "America's oldest performing arts center and proudly remains a place for progressive and avant-garde performance" for all the performing arts—dance, music, theater, and film.[2] Since 1977 it has been home to the annual DanceAfrica Memorial Day weekend festival, celebrating African traditional and diaspora contemporary dance, and since 1981

> the (Next Wave Festival) has (been) comprised of exploratory, provocative work, providing New York audiences access to now-renowned artists such as Trisha Brown, Robert Wilson, Meredith Monk, Philip Glass, Lucinda Childs, and Laurie Anderson. The Next Wave Festival has nurtured the careers of many other artists such as Mark Morris, Eiko & Koma, Bill T. Jones, Susan Marshall, Robert Lepage, and John Jasperse. While familiar names now, many were just beginning their careers when they made their Next Wave debuts.[3]

For example, BAM's spring 2009 season was no exception to its commitment to present contemporary dance work, comprised as it was with concerts by the socially conscious Ohad Naharin's Batsheva Dance Company (f. 1964 by Martha Graham and Baroness Batsheva de Rothschild, Tel Aviv, Israel), a celebration of Merce Cunningham's 90th birthday for a three-day run in April, the Alvin Ailey American Dance Theater, Trisha Brown Dance Company, and, of course, DanceAfrica in May—a typical dance season.

And in 2010, the BAM-produced dance project, DanceMotion USA, was launched by the Bureau of Educational and Cultural Affairs section of the Department of State. Its goal was to showcase three companies touring to "three countries in one region [where] each tour [took] place over a month-long period, with the companies in residence for a week in each country."[4] Two of Brooklyn's own—Urban Bush Women (www.urbanbushwomen.org) and Evidence, A Dance Company (www.evidencedance.com)—and San Francisco's ODC/Dance (www.odcdance.org) initiated the program, spending quality dance time in Indonesia-Myanmar-Thailand, Brazil-Colombia-Venezuela, and Senegal-Nigeria-South Africa respectively.

The end of 2011 saw its 150th-year anniversary celebrated with the publication of *BAM: The Complete Works* (Brooklyn Academy of Music/The Quantuck Lane Press), a compendium of the highlights of this still provocative institution—historian Elsa Dixler reminded us it is called "New York City's Left Bank."[5] In 2012, Mark Morris chose BAM for the world premiere of his newest work, Beethoven's *Fantasia in C minor for Piano, Chorus and Orchestra Opus 80*. The Royal Ballet and the Bolshoi were there, too, as well as Dance Africa 2012 (under the artistic direction of Chuck Davis, b. 1937) and Dance Africa master classes.

The Joyce Theater

Founded in 1982 on Manhattan's 8th Avenue, the year after BAM's Next Wave Festival, the Joyce's mission (www.joyce.org) is to

> serve and support the art of dance and choreography, promote the richness and variety of the art form in its fullest expression, and enhance the public interest in, and appreciation of, dance and the allied arts of music, design, and theater.[6]

Residency initiatives, international and States-based company performances, and the downtown Joyce SoHo (f. 1996 in an old firehouse) and DANY (Dance Art New York) studio spaces, the Joyce—since it was once a cinema, all of its 472 seats have great sight lines—remains one of the premier spaces wholly dedicated to dance in New York City. As an example of its typical lineup, in 2012 performances by Dance Brazil, Sylvie Guillem, Ballet Hispanico, Alonzo King LINES Ballet, Cedar Lake, Keigwin + Company, Limón Dance Company, Ronald K. Brown/Evidence, and Pilobolus were presented.

Alonzo King LINES Ballet

Among the many dance companies hosted by BAM, Alonzo King LINES Ballet (http://www.linesballet.org/), founded by King in 1982, continues to be one of the models for contemporary ballet technique and virtuosity in the 21st century. As with many other similar ensembles, it keeps reaching out across the world far beyond its home in San Francisco. For example, *Rasa*, from 2007, parades the company's nine sculpted dancers in glorious undulations set to the hypnotically rhythmic tunes of Northern Indian tabla music (excerpt at www.youtube.com, search "2010 Rasa—Alonzo King Lines Ballet"). The clarity of the dancers' hyper-extended lines properly describes the company's name.

In *Long River High Sky* (also in 2007) King collaborated with the Shaolin Monks of China (developed in the sixth century) in a piece that allowed two distinct cultures to mash up against each other in a jarring yet respectfully conversational way (excerpt at www.youtube.com, search "LINES Ballet in Collaboration with the Shaolin Monks 2007"). "When you see great dancing," says King, "it really is an example of how life can be lived, because you're observing people who have the ability to get lost in an idea. It's like the best of human character in movement."[7] Certainly the choreographer, using Chinese ideas rooted 1600 years ago or music from India, embodies the integration of world dance and the globalization of dance, as well as the diversity of dance in North America.

A half-hour film, *Alonzo King Goes to Venice* (www.youtube.com, search "Alonzo King Goes to Venice"), closely follows the company's dancers perform five of its pieces all around the Italian water city in site-specific works and onstage during the 2011 Venice Biennale (f. 1895 for art, 1999 for dance; www.labiennale.org).

Lyon Dance Biennale

The 1980s and 1990s saw an increasing number of dance companies and festivals spring up out of the postmodern revolution of the 1960s and ballet boom of the 1970s—sometimes explosively bringing together more and more distinct styles into more and more *mélanges*. Founded in 1984, the Lyon Dance Biennale (LDB) in Lyon, France, celebrated its 25th anniversary in 2009 with its 13th edition, *Retour en Avant* (Past Forward). In a 2008 interview with dance critic Isabelle Danto, LBD's Artistic Director since its inception Guy Darmet (b. 1947) neatly summarized their global, multidimensional mission with a description of that year's event:

> Our commitment hasn't wavered since 1984. Remember that the first three editions were devoted to the history of German expressionism, to four centuries of dancing in France, and to modern American dance. Issues to do with history and tradition are constantly evolving, and are today informing the work of many choreographers: Olga de Soto [b. 1970] with *Le jeune homme et la mort*; Wen Hui [b. 1960], who on the eve of the Olympics Games is boldly questioning China's cultural revolution; Singaporean Ong Keng Sen [b. 1963], who refuses to forget that the Khmer Rouge wanted to destroy Cambodia's Royal Ballet; Angelin Preljocaj [b. 1957], who is revisiting the fairy-tale genre and the realm of wonder with Blanche Neige; and Matteo Levaggi, searching for new forms rooted in the grammar of ballet.[8]

Joanna Haigood's Zaccho Dance Theatre

Since 1993, Joanna Haigood (birth date unknown; San Francisco Bay Area) has annually directed Breaking Ground: A Dance Charrette,[9] an organization that alerts five choreographers (and the public, free) five days in advance to create and then simultaneously perform five five-minute works at a previously undisclosed New York location. It's like a mini-marathon of five Cunningham pieces juxtaposed together at the same time for one two-day run! In 2008, performances took place in October at the airplane Hangar B of Floyd Bennett Field in Brooklyn in and around historic fighter planes; others have taken place at a skateboard park, an old tobacco warehouse, and Wall Street's Federal Hall National Memorial. In 2012 she explored the rise of contemporary racism in a three-day continuously running dance/theater performance (*The Monkey and the Devil*). [www.youtube.com, search "Joanna Haigood The Monkey and the Devil (promo reel)"]

Haigood's own company, Zaccho Dance Theatre (f. 1980, www.zaccho. org), centered in San Francisco, has its own mission of social awareness that is perfectly in keeping with the contemporary exploration of place and space:

Zaccho Dance Theatre (ZDT) creates and presents performance work that investigates dance as it relates to place. Artistic Director Joanna Haigood's creative work focuses on making dances that use natural, architectural and cultural environments as points of departure for movement exploration and narrative. Haigood's innovative work involves in-depth research into the history and the character of sites, often involving local communities in the creative process, and typically integrates aerial flight and suspension as ways of expanding performers' spatial and dynamic range. In addition, Zaccho provides performances in San Francisco, nationally and internationally as well as an arts education program for the local community.[10]

Several of the unique sites for ZDT's performances include dances on San Francisco trolleys (*Trolley Dances*, 2004), hanging around (literally) the famous clock tower of the Ferry Building (*Noon*, 1995, www.youtube.com, search "Zaccho Dance Theatre NOON"), in the Berkshire Mountain woods surrounding Jacob's Pillow [*Invisible Wings*, 1998; www.youtube.com, search "Invisible Wings excerpts (Jacob's Pillow Dance Festival 2007)"], and throughout the Oliver Ranch in Geyserville, California (*Into the Well of Dreams*, 2011—on the ground *and* in the air).

Monica Bill Barnes & Company

Monica Bill Barnes & Company (www.monicabillbarnes.com), founded by Barnes in New York City in 1995, brings humor, talent, and poignancy to the contemporary dance world, a (sadly) all-too-infrequent combination. A Californian moved east, Barnes (birth date unknown) is a dynamo as both performer and choreographer. "[A]s always with Barnes, comedy and tragedy interweave [*Suddenly Summer Somewhere* (2007); www.youtube.com, search "Suddenly Summer Somewhere"] like human sine and cosine waves, with a frill of pathos all around the edges."[11]

Barnes's *Game Face* (2008) was performed outdoors at the Robert Wagner, Jr. Park as part of the Lower Manhattan Cultural Council's (f. 1973, www.lmcc.net) annual Sitelines (f. 2004) site-specific dance series. Set to Elvis Presley tunes, the dancers and tourists mingled together in ways that were carefully choreographed and included karaoke-type sing-a-longs coexisting in the same space. As Barnes herself says, "I have a real interest in having dance be something that's very popular…in that it exists more immediately in people's lives. And one way to physically do that is to bring the dance into a public space and make it part of that day's events."[12]

Her full-length *Another Parade* (excerpt at www.youtube.com, search "Monica Bill Barnes & Company, Another Parade"), commissioned for the 92Y Harkness Dance Festival in 2009, was charmingly rickety, beautifully tawdry, and profoundly good-hearted. Performer Deborah Lohse, in particular, provides a lot of sustained stage charisma, self-reflexive tics and quirky facial expressions for the quartet, but it is worth the price of admission just to see the power in these sinewy dancers. Rhythmically and musically sensitive, Barnes's choreography is full of alternating stillness and propulsion, rounding out the ensemble's engaging performances.

DanceNOW NYC

Also founded in 1995, DanceNOW NYC (www.dancenownyc.org) presents annual autumn festivals that stress the "less is more" concept. Their artistic challenge remains limiting dances to seven minutes or less—"speed-dating for dancegoers,"[13] notes the online *Dance View Times*. Such a "short takes" framework helps novice audiences get turned on to the contemporary art form via concise and diverse dance bites in buffet-style samplings that are easy on the palate. DanceNOW provides that rare opportunity for young choreographers to develop their chops in a nurturing space. It collaborates with New York Live Arts, Joe's Pub (f. 1998), a showcase for live music and performance, DeSales University in Pennsylvania, and many other organizations around the New York area. Young up-and-coming companies such as Tami Stronach Dance (f. 2000; www.tamistronach.com) and Yin Yue Dance Company (f. 2009; http://www.yinyuedance.moonfruit.com/), along with dozens of others, are provided support and venues through DanceNOW.

Chunky Move

Australia's Chunky Move (f. 1995; www.chunkymove.com), cofounded by choreographer Gideon Obarzanek (b. 1966), takes William Forsythe's multimedia productions one step further with its sophisticated technological-movement "mash ups." *Mortal Engine* (2008) is a perfect example, with *The Australian* calling it "something of a bodysnatcher. It physically invades the viewer."[14]

> *Mortal Engine* is a new dance-video-music-laser performance using movement and sound responsive projections to portray an ever-shifting, shimmering world in which the limits of the human body are an illusion. Crackling light and staining shadows represent the most perfect or sinister of souls. Kinetic energy fluidly metamorphoses from the human figure into light image, into sound and back again.[15]

Dancers slowly crawling, twisting, and touching on a tilted platform present an "intensely physical, sensual, and visually daring work [that] uses movement- and sound-responsive projections that morph human figures into light and sound and back again... [I]nteractive systems allow light, video, sound, and performers to respond to each other in real time."[16]

A six-minute excerpt, available at www.youtube.com, search "Mortal Engine by Chunky Move," may make you want to watch it again and again to see how it is done and relive its images and impressions. One can only imagine where such "real-time interactions" between light, sound, and movement will take performers and viewers in the years to come.

Older Dancers

Choreography for "older" persons—the performance of dance has traditionally been for "younger" people (hence the difficulty, particularly by the 1980s and 1990s, of finding accurate birth dates)—has seen a strong growth over the last several decades. There is something compelling for all ages in watching more mature dancers perform. The jumps may not be as high or the turns as fast but the movements often reveal a richer wellspring of thought and feeling. See Mikhail Baryshnikov and Ana Laguna in excerpts from *Place*, choreographed by Mats Ek (www.youtube.com, search "Place – Mikhail Baryshnikov").

The year 1998 saw the founding of the PARADIGM: Dance Legends in Concert (http://www.paradigm-nyc.org/) by Gus Solomons, Jr. (b. 1940), Carmen de Lavallade (b. 1931), and Dudley Williams (b. 1938), a trio of self-professed "mature artists" who perform contemporary work well into their seventies and eighties. Legends indeed: among countless other projects, these three alternately and together performed for years with Graham, Cunningham, Horton, McKayle, and Ailey—all legends themselves.

> PARADIGM's long-term goals are to promote and celebrate the talents of mature artists on stage, illustrating the eloquence that years of experience bring to the stage, as well as create a dance repertory specifically for seasoned mature, professional dancers. This repertory is being commissioned from a number of choreographers of different ages and styles. Of special interest to the ensemble is to work with young and emerging choreographers.[17]

Many countries throughout the world have celebrated veteran performers older in age than the typical teens, twenties, and thirties. To name just two: Nederlands Dance Theatre's NDT3 employed dancers 40 years and older during its 15-year existence (1991–2006), performing contemporary works by noted world choreographers. Liz Lerman's "cross-generational" Dance Exchange (f. 1976, www.danceexchange.org), centered in Maryland, involves "dancers whose ages span six decades."

Venice Biennale

Like its neighbor in France, the Lyon Dance Biennale, another important European festival is the Venice Biennale. It has been in existence for over a century, since 1895, but the Dance Section was not initiated until 1999. The year 2010 saw the 7th International Festival of Contemporary Dance brought to fruition (entitled "Capturing Emotions"), the dance world catching up to the other arts in Venice. William Forsythe won their Golden Lion for Lifetime Achievement award. Some of the extraordinary range of works included contemporary pieces from Germany, Brazil, China, and Canada, listed here as an example of the festival's depth and breadth:

- The breathless premier of *Oxygen* created by the sculpturally vigorous, Germany-based and Brazilian-born choreographer Ismael Ivo (b. 1955 São Paulo, Brazil) excerpt at www.youtube.com, search "Oxygen by Ismael Ivo");

- Highly theatrical 2009 shadow-dance inflected *Dark Matters* (*à la* Kabuki) set on the Vancouver company Kidd Pivot Frankfurt RM (f. 2001, www.kiddpivot.org) by artistic director Crystal Pite (b. 1970 Canada; excerpt at www.youtube.com, search "Dark Matters, Kidd Pivot Frankfurt RM");

- Wen Wei's (b. 1965) 2006 *Unbound* (excerpt at www.youtube.com, search "Wen Wei Dance Company—Biennale Danza 2010"), a dance exploration of gender roles involved with the tortuous disfiguring tradition of foot-binding, set on his Quebec-based Wen Wei Dance Company (f. 2003; www.wenweidance.ca).

By the turn of the millennium, the globalization of dance companies and performers and choreographers had become the norm.

Selected Videos/DVDs/Films

Alonso King LINES Ballet

Alonzo King LINES Ballet (2012), Dance Horizons.

Chunky Move

Chunky Move: I Want to Dance Better at Parties (2010), Insight Media.
Chunky Move: Two Faced Bastard (2008), Artfilms.

Older Dancers

Place with Mikhail Baryshnikov and Ana Laguna (2012), Dance Horizons.

Notes

1 Seth Rogovoy, "Big Dance Theater at Jacob's Pillow," *The Rogovoy Report*, July 13, 2007, http://rogovoy.com/news1482.html.

2 "Brooklyn Academy of Music," Wikipedia, http://en.wikipedia.org/wiki/Brooklyn_Academy_of_Music.

3 BAM website, http://www.bam.org/view.aspx?pid=395.

4 http://www.dancemotionusa.org/about.aspx.

5 Elsa Dixler, "The Joys of BAM," *The New York Times*, December 6, 2011.

6 http://www.joyce.org/about/mission.php.

7 http://www.youtube.com/watch?v=2bf77Lcj_wE.

8 "Interview with Guy Darmet, Artistic Director," http://www.biennale-de-lyon.org/danse2008/angl/projet.html.

9 http://www.dancinginthestreets.org/programs/breaking-ground/.

10 http://www.zaccho.org/about.html.

11 Brian McCormick, "Monica Bill Barnes Re-Interprets Las Vegas Classics," *downtown express*, November 16–22, 2007, http://www.downtownexpress.com/de_236/monicabarnes.html.

12 Michelle Vellucci, "Exclusive: Monica Bill Barnes is Not Just Another Nut on the Street," *flavorwire*, March 6, 2009, http://flavorwire.com/13059/exclusive-monica-bill-barnes-is-not-just-another-nut-on-the-street.

13 http://dancenownyc.org/storage/presskit/Festival%20Press.pdf.

14 http://www.chunkymove.com/Media-Room/Mortal-Engine.aspx.

15 http://www.chunkymove.com/Our-Works/Current-Productions/Mortal-Engine.aspx.

16 Philadelphia Live Arts Festival: Philly Fringe; http://www.livearts-fringe.org/details.cfm?id=6845.

17 www.paradigm-nyc.org.

Chapter Eleven

2000 and Beyond: The New Century

**Sadler's Wells, Baryshnikov Arts Center, AscenDance Project,
La MaMa Moves! Dance Festival, Dancing on the Edge Festival,
Center for Performance Research (CPR), Ballet Across America,
Jacoby and Pronk**

The beginnings of the new century and beyond augur well for continuing the groundbreaking work of modern dance begun more than a century ago. So many ballet companies today have embraced the modern world that their very names include the word "contemporary"—Complexions Contemporary Ballet (f. 1994, New York City, www.complexionsdance.org), Cedar Lake Contemporary Ballet (f. 2003, New York City; http://cedarlakedance.com/), and Company C Contemporary Ballet (f. 2002, San Francisco, www.companycballet.org), are just three.

Equally important, the more traditional classical ballet companies now include their own "feeder" programs that commission or encourage contemporary input. San Francisco Ballet's (www.sfballet.org) New Works Festival (presented during their 75th anniversary in 2008), for example, premiered ten works by the world's most diverse choreographers, young through veteran: Julia Adam, Val Caniparoli, Jorma Elo, Margaret Jenkins, James Kudelka, Mark Morris, Yuri Possokhov, Paul Taylor, Stanton Welch, and Christopher Wheeldon. Even the venerable New York City Ballet (f. 1948) created its New York Choreographic Institute (NYCI) in 2000 to develop talented choreographers and a chamber company, NYCB MOVES, which performs and tours smaller-scale repertory. It premiered in 2011 at the Vail (Colorado) International Dance Festival (f. 1994, www.vaildance.org).

Sadler's Wells

The Sadler's Wells London Dance House (originally named after actual water wells discovered underground; www.sadlerswells.com), even though it came into existence in 1683, embodies many of our 21st century contemporary concepts that were initiated by the "moderns" of the early 20th century:

> Sadler's Wells is the United Kingdom's leading dance house, uniquely dedicated to bringing the very best international and UK dance to London audiences. We are committed to producing, commissioning and presenting works of the highest standards, crossing the boundaries between different art forms. We believe dance is the art form of the moment. No other form has the potential to reach so many people, crossing cultural boundaries and appealing to diverse audiences. From contemporary dance to tango, hip hop to flamenco, tap to kathak, choreographers are reinventing dance and undertaking bold collaborations with visual artists and musicians. Sadler's Wells is playing a leading role in making this happen through the commissioning of new work. Since 2005, we have commissioned or produced 39 new dance works by leading artists.[1]

Like Holland's Nederlands Dans Theater (NDT; f. 1959; www.ndt.org), with its sixteen Resident Choreographers (as of January 2010), Sadler's Wells represents a full baker's dozen choreographers and companies, called Associate Artists and Resident/Guest Artist Companies. Their list is a Who's Who of cutting-edge artists presenting their own bold visions (many of whom are discussed in this book): companies include Ballet Boyz, Matthew Bourne, New Adventures (Bourne's Company), Sidi Larbi Cherkaoui, Jonzi D, Sylvie Guillem, Akram Khan, Russell Maliphant, Hofesh Shechter, Jasmin Vardimon, Christopher Wheeldon, Wayne McGregor/Random Dance and Morphoses.

Contemporary Dance Presenters

Baryshnikov Arts Center (BAC)

Founded by famed Kirov-trained classical ballet-turned-modern dancer Mikhail Baryshnikov (b. 1948) in 2005 in the Hell's Kitchen neighborhood of New York City, the Baryshnikov Arts Center (BAC) boasts a mission "emphasizing multidisciplinary work, emerging talent, and international artists who might not otherwise have the opportunity to perform in the United States,"[2] an obvious continuation of Baryshnikov's own story after defecting from the Soviet Union in 1974. For example, in June 2010 the French Cambodian dancer-choreographer Emmanuèle Phuon (b. November 11,

1966 Paris) performed her *Khmeropédies I & II* (slideshow gallery at http://www.bacnyc.org/gallery-phuon/), a piece that explored the relationships between traditional Cambodian Khmer dance and Western traditions.

Earlier that month, the New York City-based Donna Uchizono Company (f. 1990; www.donnauchizono.org) presented *Longing Two* in two sections—the first at BAC and the second, after a bus ride to the downtown dance space The Kitchen (on West 19th Street), exploring the same piece at a different time and space. Donna Uchizono (birth date unknown), known for her close collaborations with resident composers and her work as an Artist Advisor and founding member of Danspace Project, allows her ideas and themes to develop in their own time—the works have an unmistakable Asian aesthetic of unfurling—as in her deliberate and juicy 2002 duet *Low* [www.youtube.com, search "Donna Uchizono Low (2002)"], or the understated multimedia *Thin Air*, from 2007 [www.youtube.com, search "Donna Uchizono Thin Air (2007) Clip 2"].

BAC premiered its 300-seat Jerome Robbins Theater in February 2010 just before the radical, envelope-pushing Wooster Group (f. 1975) became its resident theater-dance-video-audio-tech company. The spring 2012 performance season included the Kidd Pivot Frankfurt RM (Canadian Crystal Pite's company; www.kiddpivot.org), Robert Wilson's re-staging of five parts of his famous 1976 opera *Einstein on the Beach*, a dance theater piece by a Barcelona collective called *por instantes*, and its first collaboration with Performance Space 122 (f. 1979; www.ps122.org). With its pedigree, the state-of-the-art Baryshnikov Arts Center should prove fruitful for years to come.

AscenDance Project

Another intriguing contemporary dance presenter, AscenDance Project (www.ascendanceproject.com), a Berkeley, California-based company that has its performers moving vertically on climbing walls to choreographed rhythms in music and silence, was founded in 2006. Artistic Director and founder Isabel von Rittberg (b. September 4, 1980, Haan, Germany) was driving through Utah's Virgin River Gorge during sunset and was stunned by

> ...the red sandstone cliffs surrounding [her and] enjoying imaginary bodies dancing on the immense vertical terrain....When rock climbing, it was the continuous flow of vertical movements that generated a strong mental focus and a powerfully physical strength that allowed [her] to gracefully overcome [her] body weight. [Her] vision of

climbers executing technical and powerful movements to music was clear and strong.[3]

As with Elizabeth Streb, Cirque du Soleil, and Momix before her, von Rittberg discovered a new and unique venue for "dance" performance.

La MaMa Moves! Dance Festival

Even though La MaMa Experimental Theatre Club (www.lamama.org) was founded in 1961 in Manhattan's East Village by Ellen Stewart (1919–2011), the La MaMa Moves! Dance Festival began its annual showcases in 2007. Over three weeks every spring, the festival groups special evening events by themes such as American Hybrids, Dancing Divas Night, Group Dynamics (large group works), Mavericks in Motion, Higher-Ups (aerial dances), and Rossobastardo (Italian-based choreographers), among a slew of other topical and quirky titles.

"Experimental" is the operative word with La MaMa, dance or otherwise (see also The Chocolate Factory; www.chocolatefactorytheater.org), as much of the work involves all sorts of intense meditations on innumerable varieties of ideas, exercises, and explorations by up-and-coming choreographers as well as established artists. In 2010, La MaMa presented works by more than 75 performers, including young choreographers aged 8 to 17, mid-career creators such as Saar Harari and Lee Sher (artistic directors of LeeSaar The Company, founded in Israel in 2000), veteran multimedia artists like Meredith Monk (she has performed at La MaMa since the 1960s), and speakers including esteemed dance critics Deborah Jowitt and Marcia Siegel.

Dancing on the Edge Festival

Multicultural contemporary organizations supporting more and more far-reaching ethnicities in dance keep springing up around the globe. Also founded in 2007, the Dancing on the Edge Festival (DOTEF, www.dancingontheedge.nl) has showcased contemporary Egyptian, Palestinian, Moroccan, Iranian, Iraqi, Lebanese, Israeli, Syrian, and Jordanian dancers (with more countries entering each year) from the Middle East. The festival's organizers prefer their own term of geography, "Eastern Mediterranean."

More than half of the performers are female, "a remarkable feat considering the restrictions placed on women in some of these countries."[4] Mia Habis, dancer for the Lebanon-based Maqamat Theatre Dance (www.maqamat.org; www.youtube.com, search "On the lips, snow–A dance performance by Ali Chahrour"), accurately captures the DOTEF spirit in a

YouTube interview: "What's good about [the] dancing is that it goes beyond language, culture…it's about feelings, it's about sensing so no matter the country…it's the body language so everybody can understand it and that's why anyone can connect."[5]

Many of DOTEF's pieces address highly charged personal and political issues such as women's rights, oppression, war, and social mores. Of the fifteen works in the 2009 festival, held in five cities throughout the Netherlands, several were provocative in true modern-contemporary custom, especially *aataba* (Arabic for "threshold"), performed by the Moroccan Compagnie Anania (f. 2003), with choreography by Taoufiq Izzediou (www.youtube.com, search "'Aataba' de Taoufiq Izeddiou"). The piece

> …examines the contradictions of the individual and the society in Moroccan society. The duality of life there—what behavior is expected and what actually happens, is shown by revealing the teeming sensuality which breaks loose in the night clubs and bars and discos— hidden from view but not illegal. According to the choreographer, "On the streets the exhibition of professional status or religion prevails, and the bodies cease being themselves. In the basements, though, they do not hide any more: they dare, they live, they enjoy. This freedom, even the perfume of it, is what we seek in such hidden places." As for the structure and movement material of the piece Izzediou explains: "We, who have studied in France, in Europe, and elsewhere, do not want to appear as Moroccans imitating Western prototypes, but neither do we want to present traditional dances in an Oriental exoticism that does not take into account our research abroad. It is thus necessary to create new work that combines our own gestures, our own steps, and our heritage with our understanding of the dance of today."[6]

Likewise, a dance called *Waiting Forbidden*, a collaboration among three companies—the Dutch Le Grand Cru, the Jordanian Al Balad Theater, and the Palestinian El Funoun—is about

> …a sense of displacement, fear and resistance—a production about being Palestinian and being of Palestinian descent. These are people connecting and struggling with their own relationship to oppression and statelessness—a mental labyrinth of sixty years of violence in a place where nothing seems innocent any more, and where time is moving forward. At least time moves forward…. The performance is inspired by the stories of the dancers and the work of Mona Hatoum, a

well-known visual artist of Palestinian descent. In her work, home is a mythical location—a place charged with loss and violence.[7]

Overlapping ethnic concerns and influences from around the globe will no doubt continue to occur with greater frequency in our ever-smaller 21st century planet.

Center for Performance Research (CPR)

The Williamsburg (a section of Brooklyn, New York) based Center for Performance Research (CPR, f. 2008, www.cprnyc.org) is still another arts facility that strives to provide reasonably priced studio space for performing arts professionals to explore their medium, often focusing on social issues. Important purposes of CPR are "pedagogical engagement" and community building, as noted on their website. Contemporary dancer-choreographers Jonah Bokaer (b. 1981) and John Jasperse (b. 1963) cofounded CPR, but the organization supports events other than dance, including theater pieces, workshops, performance art, gay-focused projects (the "Queer Conscience" series), installations, and music.

Ballet Across America

Even the biennial Ballet Across America, begun in 2008 at the Kennedy Center in Washington, D.C., with no "contemporary" in any of the companies' titles, nevertheless has an up-to-the-minute feel. The 2010 version included performances by the Houston Ballet (f. 1955, www.houstonballet.org), Suzanne Farrell Ballet (f. 2000, www.suzannefarrell.org), Ballet Memphis (f. 1986, www.balletmemphis.org), Ballet Arizona (f. 1986, www.balletaz.org), Pacific Northwest Ballet (f. 1972, www.pnb.org), Aspen Santa Fe Ballet (f. 1990, www.aspensantafeballet.com), Tulsa Ballet (f. 1957, www.tulsaballet.org), and Joffrey Ballet (f. 1956, www.joffrey.org), presenting works by Stanton Welch (b. 1969), George Balanchine, Jean-Pierre Bonnefoux (b. 1943), Trey McIntyre, Ib Andersen (b. 1954), Benjamin Millepied (b. 1977), Jorma Elo (b. 1951), and Edwaard Liang (b. 1975) respectively—all neoclassical or contemporary ballet choreographers.

Jacoby and Pronk

Where is contemporary dance going today? Better, how might one explain its character development by the second decade of the 21st century? The team of Drew Jacoby (b. September 2, 1984, Boise, Idaho) and Rubinald (Rubi) Pronk (b. July 17, 1979, The Hague, Netherlands) may very well embody the newest of the new, mixing technical virtuosity with artistic determination—both woman and man respectively are equally strong, lithe, and musically sensitive. They founded their partnership Jacoby & Pronk Contemporary Dance Artists (www.jacobypronk.com) in 2008 and have been showcased around the world together and separately in works choreographed by a Who's Who of notables.

Side by side their body types are so similar—ectomorphs with extremely fast twitch fibers—one wonders whether audiences lose the sense of gender identity through such androgyny. Yes, no, perhaps. "Jacoby's steely strength and Pronk's fluid hyper-flexibility defy the normal gender norms of a ballet partnership," says Kina Poon in the August 2009 *Dance Magazine*.[8]

In a *pas de deux* from their 2009 *B Sonata*, choreographed by Serbian Leo Mujic (birth date unknown), Jacoby oozed female sexuality while exploding through nonstop torturous steps and phrases; Pronk projected both animus *and* delicacy (excerpt at www.youtube.com, search "Drew Jacoby and Rubinald Pronk in B Sonata"). It seems that second-decade 21st century dancers like these two are working hard to get beyond trading off artistry for showiness, tricks over integrity.

As with *B Sonata*, *One* (2008), choreographed on the couple by Belgian-Columbian Annabelle Lopez Ochoa (b. 1973), occurs at breakneck speed for a solid eight minutes [entire piece at www.youtube.com, search "Drew Jacoby & Rubinald Pronk–Performance of ONE (2008)"], and there is not a breath or hair out of place by its end.

Perhaps the economic struggles at the turn of the decade have forced dance to become more conveyable; that is, fewer dancers—two, three, four, six, in companies that can travel quickly and easily—rather like the young Joffrey, Taylor, and Cunningham companies of the 1950s. For example, Jacoby and Pronk invited dancers David Hallberg from ABT (at the time, December 2011, he was with Russia's Bolshoi Ballet!), Shirley Esseboom, formerly with NDT, Victor Mateos Arellano from Dresden's Semperoper Ballett, and dancer-choreographer Leo Mujic to join them for their 2010 Jacob's Pillow performances. Likewise, freelance dancer Taylor Gordon, just 21, races between jobs at Radio City Music Hall and the Ailey center—a typical bohemian lifestyle in the dance world.[9]

Is everything old, new again? Not really. But the contemporary borrows from history shamelessly, or honorably—or rejects it indiscriminately, or on purpose. Contemporary dance is always in the moment, now; that's the nature of a performing art. May the reader keep looking at dance—forward, and backward.

Notes

1   http://www.sadlerswells.com/page/aboutus.

2   http://www.bacnyc.org/about.

3   http://www.ascendanceproject.com/about.html.

4   "Vital Signs: These Women's Works," *Dance Magazine*, December 2009, http://www.dancemagazine.com/issues/December-2009/Vital-Signs.

5   http://www.dancingontheedge.nl/2009/?page_id=15&lang=en.

6   Ibid.

7   Ibid.

8   Kina Poon, "Otherworldly," *Dance Magazine*, August 2009, http://www.dancemagazine.com/issues/August-2009/Otherworldly.

9   Claudia La Rocco, "Ballet for Hire: Will Run Nonstop for a Chance," *The New York Times*, July 13, 2010, http://www.nytimes.com/2010/07/18/arts/dance/18dancer.html?ref=dance.

Bibliography

Books

Acocella, Joan. 1993. *Mark Morris*. New York: Farrar Straus Giroux.

Anderson, Jack. 1992. *Ballet and modern dance: A concise history*, 2nd ed. Hightstown, NJ: Princeton Book Company.

Bremser, Martha, ed. 1999. *Fifty contemporary choreographers*. London: Routledge.

Brown, Jean Morrison, Naomi Mindlin and Charles H. Woodford, eds. 1998. *The vision of modern dance*, 2nd ed. Hightstown, NJ: Princeton Book Company.

Chujoy, Anatole, and P. W. Manchester, eds. 1967. *The dance encyclopedia*, rev. and enlarged ed.. New York: Simon and Schuster.

Coe, Robert. 1985. *Dance in America*. New York: E. P. Dutton.

Cohen, Selma Jeanne. 1966. *The Modern Dance: Seven Statements of Belief*. Middletown, CT: Wesleyan University Press.

Conrad, Christine. 2000. *Jerome Robbins: That Broadway man*. London: Booth-Clibborn Editions.

Craine, Debra and Judith Mackrell. 2010. *Oxford dictionary of dance*, paperback and 2nd ed. London: Oxford University Press.

Cunningham, Merce. 1985. *The dancer and the dance*. New York: Marion Boyars.

Dils, Ann, and Ann Cooper Albright, eds. 2001. *Moving history/dancing cultures: A dance history reader*. Middletown, CT: Wesleyan University Press.

Dunning, Jennifer, Joseph McLellan and Steven Winn. 1997. *Great performances: A celebration*. San Francisco: Bay Books.

Eichenbaum, Rose. 2004. *Masters of movement: Portraits of America's great choreographers*. Washington, DC: Smithsonian Books.

Garafola, Lynn, ed. 1999. *Dance for a city: Fifty years of The New York City Ballet*. New York: Columbia University Press.

Garafola, Lynn. 1989. *Diaghilev's Ballets Russes*. New York: Oxford University Press.

Garis, Robert. 1995. *Following Balanchine*. New Haven, CT: Yale University Press.

Graham, Martha. 1991. *Blood memory*. New York: Doubleday.

Greskovic, Robert. 1998. *Ballet 101: A complete guide to learning and loving the ballet*. New York: Hyperion.

Harris, Melissa, ed. 1997. *Merce Cunningham: Fifty years*. Denville, NJ: Aperture.

Jonas, Gerald. 1992. *Dancing: The pleasure, power, and art of movement*. New York: Harry N. Abrams.

Jones, Bill T. 1995. *Last night on earth*. New York: Pantheon Books.

Kirstein, Lincoln. 1978. *Thirty years: Lincoln Kirstein's The New York City Ballet*. New York: Alfred A. Knopf.

Lawrence, Greg. 2001. *Dance with demons: The life of Jerome Robbins*. New York: Berkley Books.

Louis, Murray. 1980. *Inside dance*. New York: St. Martin's Press.

Martin, John. 1965. *The modern dance*. Brooklyn, NY: Dance Horizons. First published 1933.

———. 1952. *World book of modern ballet*. Cleveland, OH: The World Publishing Company.

Mason, Francis. 1991. *I remember Balanchine: Recollections of the ballet master by those who knew him*. New York: Doubleday.

McDonagh, Don. 1990. *The rise and fall and rise of modern dance*. Pennington, NJ: A Cappella Books.

Mitoma, Judy, ed. 2002. *Envisioning dance on film and video*. New York: Routledge.

Nadel, Myron Howard, and Marc Raymond Strauss. 2003. *The dance experience: Insights into history, culture and creativity*. Hightstown, NJ: Princeton Book Company.

Reynolds, Nancy, and Malcolm McCormick. 2003. *No fixed points: Dance in the twentieth century*. New Haven, CT: Yale University Press.

Robertson, Allen, and Donald Hutera. 1988. *The dance handbook*. Boston: G. K. Hall.

Taylor, Paul. 1987. *Private domain*. New York: Alfred A. Knopf.

Tharp, Twyla. 1992. *Push comes to shove*. New York: Bantam Book.

Tracy, Robert. 2004. *Ailey spirit: The journey of an American dance company*. New York: Stewart, Tabori and Chang.

Selected Websites

www.adfvideo.com/adfv.html

www.amazon.com

www.art-books.com

www.artslynx.org/dance/video.htm

www.dancefilmsassn.org

www.dancehorizons.com

www.danceonvideo.com

www.dancer.com/dance-links/misc.htm

www.facets.org

www.insight-media.com

www.kulturvideo.com

www.multiculturalmedia.com

www.PBS.com

www.vimeo.com

www.youtube.com

Selected DVDs/Films/Videos

It is possible to view the works discussed in this book in their entirety on DVD Listed at the end of each chapter). DVDs include extra benefits like interviews with the choreographer, dancers, and composers or conductors, and synopses of the stories, in several languages. Filming from different angles and close-ups give the viewer a different perspective of stage patterns, gestures and facial expressions, not clearly seen from the audience in a concert space.

Index

Note: Bolded page numbers indicate primary discussions.

About the Authors

Marc Raymond Strauss is a professor of Theatre and Dance at Southeast Missouri State University in Cape Girardeau, Missouri. Dr. Strauss received a B.A. in Education at Hobart College, an MFA in Dance Teaching and Choreography at Smith College, and a Ph.D. in Dance and the Related Arts at Texas Woman's University. He is the author of *The Dance Criticism of Arlene Croce: Articulating a Vision of Artistry* and *Hitchcock Nonetheless: The Master's Touch in His Least Celebrated Films*, among others. He is co-editor with Myron Nadel of *The Dance Experience: Insights into History, Culture and Creativity, 2nd Edition* (Princeton Book Company, Publishers) and the upcoming third edition.

Dr. Strauss's research and teaching interests include dance history, the aesthetics of movement, the history of the musical, dance on film, and ballet and ballroom dance. He lives in Cape Girardeau with his wife, Sarah Riley.

Myron Howard Nadel is a Professor of Dance at the University of Texas at El Paso where he has also served as Associate Dean of the College of Liberal Arts. A graduate of the Juilliard School and Columbia Teachers College, Nadel wrote the first edition of *The Dance Experience* in 1969 with Constance Miller. He is co-author and co-editor with Marc Strauss of *The Dance Experience, 2nd Edition*, with whom he is working on the third edition.

His major teachers were José Limón, Betty Jones, Antony Tudor, Louis Horst, Lulu Sweigard and Martha Hill. His choreography has appeared with the Milwaukee and Maryland Ballets, CBS Repertory Workshop, and companies in Australia and Norway. He has performed professionally as a dancer and actor since his youth. He was founding Chair of the Dance Department at the University of Wisconsin/Milwaukee, the Coordinator for Music Theatre at Carnegie Mellon University, and Chair of Performing Arts at Buffalo State College. He has been a member of Actors Equity Association, The Society of Stage Directors and Choreographers, and served as Vice President of the Texas Council of the Arts in Education, as well as a member of the Board of the National Dance Education Organization.

He lives in El Paso with his wife, Jane Poss.